PRAISE FOR *High School*

"This may prove controversial, but I strongly believe that every book should be a nineties lesbian high school memoir cowritten by twins. A tender and nostalgic read that seemed to send powers of protection and courage far back into my own adolescence, to those times and places where they were needed most." —PATRICIA LOCKWOOD

"*High School* embodies the singular gift of words leaping off the page and becoming feelings, rattling around in the hearts and minds of a reader. The truth of nostalgia is that it must have multiple lenses to operate in its most flourishing form. Much like in their music, in this book, the voices of Tegan and Sara are two distinct bodies of water flowing into the same harmonious river, spilling through the echoing hallways of old high schools, through the bedrooms of first heartbreaks, through the old haunts that remind you of your own. This book is a triumph of memory, affection, and engaging writing." —HANIF ABDURRAQIB

"It should come as no surprise to anyone who has ever listened to a song by Tegan and Sara that not only are they able to convey the raw and complex emotions of the high school experience, the aimlessness of suburban life, and the exhilaration of finding your way out, they also speak universal truths about intimacy between families and sisters, friends and lovers. They've captured a time and a place so perfectly, I can't exactly be sure that I wasn't there." —BUSY PHILIPPS

"With their music, Tegan and Sara offer listeners a glimpse at a specific time and place. In *High School*, they throw the door open and allow readers the opportunity to become fully immersed in their world. Tegan's and Sara's stories of first loves, self-discovery, and the insights into their relationship with each other are deeply moving and relatable. They never hold back from the absolute authenticity they are known for. I never wanted it to end." —CLEA DUVALL

"This book is the LSD-fueled, wallet-chained, Kurt Cobain–inspired handbook for how to become young, queer rock stars, written by chapter-swapping twins whom I wish I had read when I was in high school. This book would have changed everything. I recommend reading it under the covers with a flashlight, and hiding it from your mother."

—IVAN COYOTE

"*High School* highlights the indisputable fact that Tegan and Sara were never just musicians—they are also master storytellers. In reflecting on that torturous span of time spent agonizing over one's body, friendships, parents, and desires, this book highlights how high school is less of a place or memory but rather a metaphor for uncertainty, and underlines the salvation that can be found only in music. *High School* foreshadows the beginning of a rich and riveting literary career."

—VIVEK SHRAYA

"This book is one of the most interesting and brave coming-of-age stories I have read in many years. Tegan and Sara reveal the confusion, the unraveling of personal truths, the fear, the excitement, the shame, and the seclusion that many of us endure as we make our way through the world. This is also a book about how music saves people, how music gives us a voice and a reason to keep going."

—JANN ARDEN

"Tegan and Sara have pulled back the curtain on a formative chapter in their lives and offer a gloriously dizzying, richly observed account of how they became who they are today and what inspired the music we've come to know and love. Funny, frank, and so very cool, *High School* is basically the teenage best friend I always wanted growing up."

—DAN LEVY

HIGH SCHOOL

SARA QUIN & TEGAN QUIN

HIGH SCHOOL

MCD FARRAR, STRAUS AND GIROUX NEW YORK

MCD
Farrar, Straus and Giroux
120 Broadway, New York 10271

Library of Congress Cataloging-in-Publication Data
Names: Quin, Tegan, 1980– author. | Quin, Sara, 1980– author.
Title: High school / Tegan and Sara.
Description: First edition. | New York : Farrar, Straus and Giroux, 2019.
Identifiers: LCCN 2019014934 | ISBN 9780374169947 (hardcover)
Subjects: LCSH: Tegan and Sara. | Quin, Tegan, 1980– | Quin, Sara, 1980– |
    Singers—Canada—Biography. | Musicians—Canadá—Biography. |
    LCGFT: Biographies.
Classification: LCC ML421.T408 Q56 2019 | DDC 782.42166092/2
    [B]—dc23
LC record available at https://lccn.loc.gov/2019014934

Designed by Abby Kagan

Our books may be purchased in bulk for promotional, educational, or
business use. Please contact your local bookseller or the Macmillan
Corporate and Premium Sales Department at 1-800-221-7945,
extension 5442, or by e-mail at MacmillanSpecialMarkets@macmillan.com.

www.mcdbooks.com • www.fsgbooks.com
Follow us on Twitter, Facebook, and Instagram at @mcdbooks

10   9   8   7   6   5   4   3   2   1

The names and certain other details of many characters appearing in
High School have been changed.

FOR OUR FRIENDS IN THE HALLWAY,
MOM, DAD, AND BRUCE.
WE CAN ALWAYS GO BACK.

—SARA AND TEGAN

CONTENTS

HiGH SCHOOL

I have no visual memory of Tegan before we were four years old. There is proof of her existence: scores of photographs of us posed together on couches, sitting on laps, or standing side by side in our cribs. But the snapshots in my mind contain no trace of her. What I can summon is the *feeling* of her. As if she existed everywhere, and in everything.

In preschool, a lump was found in her left arm that required surgery. We were separated for the first time since birth. On the first day of her hospital stay, I was left in the care of another woman with a set of twins, the same age as Tegan and me. While her children played together, I sat on the floor of their bedroom, stunned by my sister's absence. On the second day, I lay on our grandmother's living room couch with a fever. Opposite me, I registered the empty space.

Without Tegan I had become *me*. And it was awful.

When we were three years old, Sara suffered from a
bout of night terrors. I have a vivid memory during that
time of her flat out on her back, in the hallway outside
her bedroom, her pajamaed limbs flailing, and my
parents on either side of her trying to calm her down.
In the memory, I am reassured by my mom and dad
that Sara is okay, that everything is fine. But I am left
uneasy, unsettled.

When I shared this memory years later, my mom
and dad were quick to correct me: it was me who
suffered from the terrible dreams all those years ago,
and Sara who watched from her bedroom at the end of
the hall. I have it backward, they insist.

I wonder frequently how many of the memories
I carry of Sara are actually my own. How much of
my early life have I confused with hers? Our tangled
nature makes even *me* feel interchangeable with Sara—
indistinguishable, bound, and suffocated. There is often
a violent urge in me to tear those early memories of us
apart, even if just in my own head. But I admit, there
is also great comfort that comes from traveling through
life with a witness, an identical twin to corroborate your
version of things.

INTRODUCTION

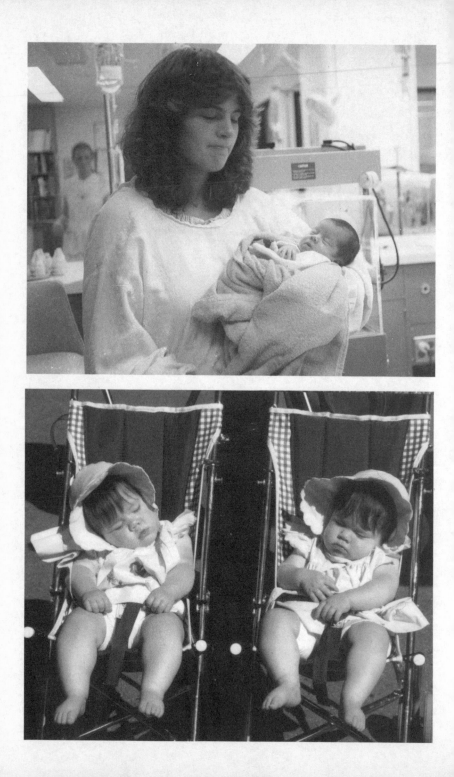

Imagine the map of Canada. If you placed your finger on the Pacific Ocean just north of the U.S. border and dragged it east across the Rocky Mountains until the topography flattened out and the states of Idaho and Montana were stacked below, you'd find the city of Calgary sprouting between the foothills and prairie of Alberta. In the 1970s an oil boom doubled the city's population and sent skyscrapers shooting up along the bank of the Bow River. The cold mountain water sliced the wealthy western quadrants into north and south before it converged with the Elbow River, vertically splitting the city's southeast side in two. Beyond the suburban sprawl was a sea of mustard yellow farmland thick with barley, and in every direction a sky blue as the ocean. From September to early June, temperatures dipped as low as minus thirty degrees Celsius and snowstorms buried entire streets of cars under snowbanks frozen like waves in midcurl. When the chinook winds from the west raised normally frigid temperatures above freezing, people swarmed the streets in short sleeves. The summers came and went quickly, and the long, desert-dry days were broken up by storms that rolled in from the south and the east in cinematic scope. Hailstorms of golf ball–size ice exploded windshields, split foreheads, and dented cars. The sun didn't set until 10:00 p.m.

My twin sister, Tegan, and I were born at Calgary General Hospital on September 19, 1980. Our parents had met six years earlier at Saint Mary's High School. Both arrived in Calgary under duress as teenagers: my father an orphan from Vancouver, and my mother fresh from Catholic boarding school in Saskatchewan. Our mother briefly dated our father's brother, and our father dated our mother's best friend. After graduation, our father took a job working at a lumberyard, and our mother attended community college, where she earned a diploma in youth and child development. They began dating in the autumn of 1977 and married in June of 1978. With money for the down payment from our grandfather, they bought a house, and our mother became pregnant with twins. Thirty-two weeks later, we were prematurely born into the world eight minutes apart. Baby number one, born at 5:56 a.m., was my sister, Tegan Rain Quin. Baby number two was me, born at 6:04 a.m. and given—according to my mother's retelling—her second-favorite name, Sara Keirsten Quin. When Tegan and I finally left the hospital a month later, we were still so tiny that our mother dressed us in doll's clothing.

By all accounts we were extremely easy babies, soothed by the sight of each other, delighting in hand-to-hand combat for hours on a blanket spread out on the living room floor. Our parents' marriage, however, was difficult. Our father often seemed depressed and prone to long silences that stretched for weeks; our mother was explosive and at her wit's end. They separated in 1984, and our dad took off for Mexico. When he returned a few months later, he slept in one of a set of wooden bunk beds in the unfinished basement of our house, his alarm clock casting a hellish red glow. The summer before Tegan and I started grade one, he moved out for good and the divorce was finalized. In 1987 our mom started dating Bruce, a handsome man who worked at a steel mill and drove a Camaro. He moved in with us in 1990, and though he and our mother were not married, we referred to him as our stepdad.

In the early 1990s, after Calgary's economy bounced back from a recession, Bruce and our father worked for competing construction companies that built large houses in the subdivisions multiplying at the edges of the sprawling city limits. Tegan and I spent Saturdays with our father, who moved annually between sparsely furnished apartments and newly built homes. We lived with our mother and Bruce in half a dozen neighborhoods before we finished junior high. Mom hated the suburbs and the identical houses that duplicated and tessellated like cells, so she and Bruce bought a plot of land in the inner-city neighborhood of Renfrew and began to draft a blueprint for a new home.

Our relationship with our mother had grown difficult during our adolescence, but on this one fact the three of us could agree: the move would bring us near to the heart of the city. For our mother, it was a signal that we were moving up in the world. For Tegan and me, Renfrew's proximity to the record stores, skate shops, and fast-food restaurants downtown meant freedom. In the spring of 1995, a land title for the house was submitted to the school board, proving our intention to relocate to Renfrew the following year. Though we would continue to live in the suburbs while the new house was being built, an exception was made and Tegan and I were officially enrolled at Crescent Heights High School. After Labor Day we started our first day of grade ten. This is where our story begins.

GRADE TEN

1. TEGAN WELCOME TO HIGH SCHOOL

"Tell her to get out. Tell her to leave us the fuck alone," Sara screamed as we brawled and Mom tried to separate us. "Naomi's *my* best friend. Tell her to get one of her own."

It took all the air from inside me when Sara said it, like a bad fall.

The summer before we started high school, Sara and I were virtually estranged. During the day you could find me moping in the basement of our baby blue two-story house, deep in the suburbs of northeast Calgary, watching TV alone. If I wasn't there, I was in my room with the door locked, playing music so loud my ears rang. While my mom and stepdad, Bruce, were at work, Sara and I either aggressively ignored each other or were at each other's throats. We fought, mercilessly, for time alone, but I still felt a primal fear of being apart from her, especially as high school loomed. I was plagued with anxiety dreams all summer, in which I wandered the halls of our school searching for her. The dreams stoked the dread I already felt, adding layers of questions I avoided in the light of day like I avoided Sara. We hadn't always been like this.

Naomi had complicated things. We met her in grade nine, our final year of junior high, when the French immersion program she was enrolled in moved to our school. Naomi was small, blond, with lively, sparkling green eyes.

You couldn't miss her in the halls. She dressed in brightly colored clothes and said hi to everyone. She oozed friendliness and kindness. Around her, a tight-knit pack of equally cool-looking girls we'd nicknamed the Frenchies was always with her. Sara and I became fast friends with all of them, but Naomi drew Sara and me in closest. For a time, we were both Naomi's best friends. This was nothing new; Sara and I had always shared a best friend growing up. Our shared best friends acted as a conduit between us: we confessed to them what we couldn't tell each other, and knew they'd pass along the message. We seemed to prefer it this way. But at the end of grade nine, Naomi and Sara forced an abrupt unraveling of this friendship after Naomi told us she and some of the other Frenchies planned to attend Aberhart High School, instead of Crescent Heights, like us, that fall. After that, Naomi and Sara acted as if Naomi were being shipped overseas, rather than across town. They isolated themselves as summer started, hid behind the locked door of Sara's room, and left me out of their plans for sleepovers. I felt confused, injured, abandoned. I instigated violent clashes with Sara in front of Naomi when they left me out, further damaging whatever bond remained between the three of us. It was war.

After the fight, Mom followed me back to my room, where she watched as I sobbed on top of my bed, gulping back lungfuls of air, trying to calm down. Mom was an intake worker on a mental health line, working long shifts that meant Sara and I were free to kick the shit out of each other without a referee in earshot all summer. Throughout most of our lives, she balanced school and work, getting first a bachelor's and then a master's in social work while holding down a job. She was also a cool mom, someone our friends could confide in when they had problems at home or school. "Your mom's so easy to talk to," my friends constantly told me. But as she watched me cry, I felt her analyzing the situation, and me, and I felt resentful; I just wanted to be left alone.

"I don't know why you two aren't getting along anymore. You used to be so close. I mean, my god, you used to cry the first day of school, every single year, because you weren't allowed to be in the same class together."

It was true. When Sara's name was called and she reluctantly walked away from me toward her own class, my eyes would fill with tears every time, despite my attempts to will them away. When Sara turned back, she'd look stricken when she saw the tears racing down my cheeks. Growing up it had hurt to be without her, but somehow by the end of junior high, she had turned into someone it hurt to be around.

"She's . . . mean . . . I . . . don't . . . know . . . why . . . they . . . leave . . . me . . . out . . ." As I tried to get out an explanation through hiccups and near hyperventilation, Mom just nodded sympathetically, which made me want to throw myself out the window.

"You might like having your own best friend," she suggested. "You've always had to share with her, Tegan. It could be nice for you to have someone of your own. Don't you think?"

I didn't bother answering. She couldn't possibly understand what Sara had taken from me that night. It wasn't just the loss of Naomi; it was that no one could replace Sara.

The morning of our first day of grade ten, while Sara and I waited for Bruce to drive us to the bus stop, I suggested we steal a few loonies from his ashtray so we could buy Slur-pees. Sara egged me on and kept a lookout as I pocketed the change. I felt united with her in our entitlement to his money. We blamed him for moving us to the suburbs, where no direct buses to school went and none of our friends lived. An hour later I grabbed Sara's arm as we pushed through the towering wooden doors at Crescent Heights into the two-story student center. "Come on. Let's go find our friends." Around us, arriving students permeated the space with the smell of fresh clothes and new rubber-bottomed sneakers. I sensed nervousness in the faces of everyone we passed, even Sara's. Somehow, I felt calm. Junior high had been an end-less shitshow, an exhausting hellscape that lasted the entire three years we were there, never letting up or letting go. High school couldn't possibly be worse.

"There," I said, grabbing Sara's arm. "There she is."

"Kayla," Sara yelled, waving her arms wildly to get her attention.

Before we shared Naomi, we shared Kayla. I guess that made her our ex–best friend.

I had spotted her in the gymnasium on the first day of grade seven. She was lean and tan and had curly brown hair, and her eyes were every shade of blue. Those first few weeks of grade seven everyone vied for her attention: her friends, boys, me, and Sara. She moved with the confidence of a cheerleader, even though she had braces. We were impossibly uncool, clinging to the bottom rung of the social complex, but Kayla and Sara shared a homeroom and became friends, leapfrogging Sara from obscurity to notable best friend over-night. By proxy, I leapt, too. For a time, the three of us were always together in the halls at school. At sleepovers on week-ends, Kayla always insisted our sleeping bags go on either side of hers. But the friendship was tumultuous, complicated by the shrapnel of adolescence, and by the end of grade eight Sara and I had emancipated ourselves from the larger group we shared with Kayla. Now that Sara was officially calling Naomi *her* best friend, I was secretly hoping to reconcile with Kayla to make her mine. *All* mine this time.

"Hi," Kayla gasped happily when she reached us, throwing her arms around Sara and me. Kayla's older sister was two years ahead of us in grade twelve, and the kind of popular that made you consider throwing yourself down a set of stairs to make room for her if you were in her way. Kayla gave off the kind of confidence endowed by a popular older sibling, and I basked in her embrace, hoping it might bolster me for later, when I would face the halls and my classes alone. At a minimum, I hoped that knowing Kayla meant anyone who might bother me would think twice about messing with me, a friend of Kayla's sister.

An announcement over the P.A. ordered us grade tens toward the gymnasium. We joined a line of kids who were already making their way there. Inside, we left Kayla to find the table with the letter of our last name to get our locker assignments and student agendas.

"You're next to each other," the grade twelve said, checking off Sara's name and mine from the list in front of her as she handed us our locker combinations. "Twins?"

"Yes," we answered together.

"Cool."

We reunited with Kayla in the wooden bleachers and compared class schedules. I squealed when I saw we shared a class in sixth period called Broadcasting and Communications.

"What is it?" Kayla scrunched her face and laughed, locking her wide eyes on me waiting for an explanation.

"I can't remember." I shrugged. "Something about making movies? Who cares, we're together, that's what matters."

When a balding man in a tan suit with a wide striped tie took the stage, the gym quieted quickly. In a booming voice that didn't match his small frame, he welcomed us to our first day of high school and introduced himself as our principal. Then he explained the first day was a half day. This inspired a round of cheers. After that he recited the school rules, finishing with the rule he considered most important, in a stern tone of warning: "Crescent Heights has a zero-tolerance policy when it comes to drugs. If you are caught with any illegal substance on school property, or under the influence at any time, you *will* be expelled. *No exceptions.*" At this, the gymnasium exploded into hooting, jeering, and whistles that went on for a full minute. A group of guys from our junior high who'd been mixed up in a gang whistled and stood, high-fiving one another. I marveled at their disregard for authority, even if they were jerks. Kayla, Sara, and I rolled our eyes at one another as the principal shushed the block of students in front of him. "This is *not* a joke, folks. I don't encourage you to test me on this policy, because I assure you we are quite serious here at Crescent Heights about drugs."

Kayla, Sara, and I had dropped acid a few times that past summer, and it had unexpectedly mended the broken parts of our friendship with Kayla. But I also noticed that while we were high, Sara and I got along. We even had fun together. It had been so long since that had felt possible that I'd forgotten Sara could be fun. The two of us talked almost constantly, when Mom and Bruce weren't around, about where we could find acid again and when we could do it next. After nearly an entire summer of *not* talking, we had

found a way to connect with each other again. Acid provided a small square of neutral territory, relief from the war
that had been raging between us since Sara and Naomi had
bounced me from their union. But the LSD also provided a
bridge. And it seemed that in order to get past where we'd
been stuck for so long, Sara and I needed one. For all intents
and purposes that bridge was drugs, specifically acid, which
we couldn't have been more thrilled about.

"I'm serious about drugs, too," I whispered to Sara and
Kayla, who chuckled conspiratorially.

"Shhh," Kayla said, looking around guiltily as the principal continued his speech. "If my sister finds out I did acid,
no—check that, if she finds out *any of us* tried acid, she'll
fucking kill us."

"Well, don't tell her," Sara said.

"Yeah, don't ruin it for us," I added.

"Then keep your fucking voices down."

"Alright, chill." I laughed and threw my arm around her.
"No one will find out," I whispered.

Just then the bell rang and six hundred grade tens stood
in unison, forcing the three of us to our feet. As we made
our way down the bleachers, I clutched the back of Kayla's
jean jacket; behind me, Sara clutched mine. We slowly made
our way toward the doors that would lead us to the hallways
I'd been anxiously dreaming about all summer.

Before we got there, the principal took to his mic one
more time: "Welcome to high school," he boomed. "Good
luck."

At school, I took the hit of acid in my mouth and flushed the foil down the toilet. Through the seams of the bathroom stall, I watched the girls standing guard at the sinks. They brought hair dryers, curling irons, and pouches loaded with makeup, like they were going to a club and not first-period English. At lunch, in the student center, I watched them stroke their boyfriends' faces and sit in their laps, while our teachers watched from the perimeter. In the halls between classes, my eyes locked on these girls' chests, on the delicate jewelry disappearing into their cleavage, on the track jackets they draped off their bare shoulders. The clothes I wore to school every day in grade ten were two or three sizes too large for my shoulders and hips. I hid my breasts under layers—a T-shirt, a hoodie, and a heavy coat. My long wallet chain, cut from a spool of heavy metal at the hardware store, bounced off my side and left soft blue bruises on my thigh. Sometimes I noticed students shaking their heads at me in disbelief, even disgust. I tried not to look into mirrors when I was on acid. In those distorted reflections my armor sagged to reveal the body I hated underneath. With my jacket sleeves pulled beyond my fingertips and the torn hems of my pants dragging behind my heels, I looked rotten.

Sitting on the bus after school, those same girls from the bathroom noticed Tegan and me in the crowded seats near the back.

"What are you looking at?" one of them asked us. I stared out the window.

"What the fuck are they looking at?" she asked her friends. I kept my eyes pinned to the glass.

"She better not be looking at me." I didn't dare.

Those girls' eyes were drawn to our bodies, too, tracking us with searing disapproval wherever we went. In those first few months of high school, I learned to avert my eyes, to show them submission, to be a ghost.

I was in sixth grade when the first suggestion of change occurred to my body. I stood in a hallway mirror that hung between the three bedrooms in our house, staring at my bare chest. I was afraid someone would catch me inspecting myself, but as with any gruesome discovery, I couldn't stop looking. The permanence of the change upon me altered how I felt about my bathing suit. That summer, on vacation in Georgia and Florida, I started to wear a T-shirt over my one-piece. When asked why, I claimed I was cold. I devised ways to get in and out of pools and the ocean quickly and then plant myself belly down on the towel stretched next to my younger cousins. I hated how exposed I felt on the crowded beach while my mom rubbed sunscreen onto my back. My vulnerability and shame made me curl my shoulders.

That same summer I found myself unable to turn away from the older girls who lay out confidently in their bikinis near our family's cluster of deck chairs. I was nervous that one of them might catch me looking in their direction, so I squinted and played dead when their eyes occasionally met mine. These roots of attraction didn't yet register as sexual. Instead, I became obsessed with trying to look like them.

I stopped wearing my hair up in a ponytail and let my curled ends fall past my chin. I stood for long periods at the bathroom mirror and wondered if I was pretty. It was clear to me that neither Tegan nor I looked or acted like those girls from the beach, but at night on the pullout couch that we shared, I never dared to ask if Tegan was scrutinizing them as carefully as I was. The physical intimacy between our aunt and her daughters that summer seemed like a language I'd forgotten between childhood and adolescence. Longing to be comforted, I watched Tegan and Mom embrace on the beach at dusk and found I could no longer close the gap between us. My body had become a stranger, and so had my mind.

During those early adolescent years, Mom's bathroom was littered with makeup and electronics. Before classes at the college where she was earning her bachelor's degree in social work, she doubled the size of her perm with a flat iron and rollers. Tegan and I perched on the closed toilet lid and watched as she painted her face brilliant pinks and reds and blues. She was the target of male attention everywhere we went. Horns honked, men whistled, boys from school blushed. Calling her "Mom" in public was shocking to strangers. Men and women alike insisted, "You look like sisters!" I was at ease with her beauty and adored watching my stepdad take pictures of her on the front lawn. Those black-and-white photographs were framed and placed with pride all through the house: Mom in profile, Bruce's leather jacket pulled down off her shoulders as she cast sultry looks into his lens.

When my body began to betray me, it should have been

her I turned to for guidance, but instead I disguised the change occurring beneath my clothes. I looted the vanity in her bathroom for deodorant, perfume, and cover-up that I applied ineptly over my pimples. Although she offered her closet full of trendy clothes, fashionable overalls, and black Doc Martens, Tegan and I opted for Disney Epcot T-shirts and our gramma's hand-me-downs.

"Get your noses pierced!" Mom screamed excitedly at me and Tegan on a back-to-school shopping trip before grade seven. We stood paralyzed near the glass case of piercing jewelry, unable to accept her help.

In junior high physical education class, I developed a method that involved wearing multiple shirts in order to avoid removing my clothes entirely in the locker room. Running laps slowly only encouraged the leering from boys, so I began to fake injuries like a pulled muscle or a twisted knee and sat slumped on the lacquered floors beneath the basketball hoops, watching my flat-chested friends sprint across the court. Jumping jacks were out; so were push-ups. I stopped wearing my backpack on both shoulders, preferring to hang it off my right side and folding my left shoulder inward.

"Lily said you guys have floppy tits," a friend told Tegan and me at a sleepover. I broke down into sobs, choked by shame. This cruel teasing forced us to finally suggest to Mom that we might need sports bras for gym class. At a department store downtown, we rode the escalator behind her in embarrassed silence. A measuring tape was tightly cinched across our breasts by a sales clerk in the lingerie section. I selected the first bra I found in my size, tugging it down quickly and then off again behind the locked dressing room door. "This one" was all I said as I handed it back to Mom. Later, in the privacy of my bedroom, I checked to see if the bra would restore me to my original flatness as I pulled my T-shirts and sweatshirts on and then off.

Among the popular grade-eight girls, our large breasts had been considered a joke, and their malicious gossip was the final humiliation that compelled us to address the situation. But when we returned to school our bras seemed only to inspire further contempt, and their punishment scaled with our cup size. We became the enemies they kept close, rejecting us and then returning when it suited them. When a much-desired senior, Matthew, asked for my phone number, these girls banished us once again from their circle. My crime, scribbled on foolscap, was folded and left for me to find on the corner of my desk the following morning: "You knew that Lily liked him."

In exile, Matthew told me about his favorite band, Smashing Pumpkins, and loaned me his well-worn copy of *Siamese Dream* so I could dub it to a cassette tape. Matthew had assured me "Today" was the best song on the album. After school in the basement at home, I placed the CD in the tray and selected the third track. Tegan sat on the couch, and I remained crouched near the stereo. I turned up the volume.

"Today is the greatest day I've ever known," Billy Corgan sang from the black foam of Bruce's speakers. Goosebumps spread across my ribs as the bass sucked air in and out of the subwoofer. Each lyric provoked a desperate reply in me. I couldn't wait for tomorrow either; I wanted to burn my eyes out, too; I wanted to turn someone on.

"Amazing, right?" Matthew asked me the next day in the library.

"Yeah," I said, passing the CD to him.

"I'm going to bring you the Pumpkins' first album, *Gish*. It's gonna blow your mind," he said.

"Cool."

Matthew was the first boy who shared something with me that I didn't want to reject, but I had nothing to offer him in return. Over the holidays he stopped calling me, and by January he was flanked in the hallways by a girl who could have been his twin. In their arms, they were cradling skateboards, and their baggy pants were pulled low by the chains of their wallets.

"Hello, Sara," he said, dipping his chin at me as they passed by.

"Hi." I nodded back, avoiding his girlfriend's eyes. Her indifference suggested that I posed no threat. She was exactly what I wasn't. I shrank from Matthew's greeting, ashamed I'd ever thought he was into me.

When the bus pulled up to the stop near our house, Tegan and I hurried past the girls who'd threatened us, grabbing our wallet chains in our fists, just in case we had to run. At home I went up to my bedroom and slipped headphones over my ears. They were Bruce's, borrowed after much begging and a promise to handle them with care. The soft black leather ear pads and headband pressed against my head. I hit Play on a fuzzy recording of "Bullet with Butterfly Wings" that I'd dubbed from the radio. I pretended my hands were wrapped around a microphone, and I howled Billy's words as if they were my own. The imaginary crowd watching me was filled with my friends, but also with my bullies from junior high and the intimidating girls from the bus. In my mind's eye, I stretched myself thin and tall, erasing my breasts from my silhouette onstage. A single spotlight burned white on my face. When the song ended, I sat up and leaned across the mattress to press Rewind, then Play. I listened until my ears rang.

In the morning when my alarm went off, my hair was tangled in the headphones. Taya, the oldest of our three cats, was curled by my hip under the blanket. I let the dread of the day ahead foam up in my chest. In the bathroom I jerked a brush roughly through the knots in my hair before dropping it on the counter with a sigh. I grabbed my backpack and coat from my bedroom.

"Let's go," Bruce shouted up the stairwell.

"I'm coming!"

Downstairs Tegan was rushing around in the same disorganized panic as I was. Her feet were wedged halfway into her purple sneakers, the sleeve of her jacket dragged behind her on the floor.

"Feed the cats!" Mom yelled down the stairs.

"We're late!" Tegan shouted.

"Whose fault is that?" she answered, annoyed.

I grabbed my shoes and swung the interior garage door open, jumping down the stairs onto the cement in my stocking feet. Bruce had already pulled his pickup truck out onto the parking pad, and I could hear U2 blasting from the stereo. He leaned across the seat and swung open the passenger door. I slid to the middle—the worst spot, because you had to keep his leather briefcase between your knees—and balanced my backpack and shoes on my lap. The silver wrappers from the Wendy's burgers he ate daily were balled up near the pedals on the floor. The dashboard and seats were dusted with grit from the construction sites he managed, and the whole car smelled of onions and his musky cologne. Tegan swung her backpack onto the seat and climbed in next to me. Before she'd even closed the door, Bruce backed into the street and joined the trail of red taillights headed for the highway. It was a ten-minute drive to the bus stop, just enough time to hear three songs from Bruce's mixtape. The three of us sang the chorus of "Where the Streets Have No Name" in full voice as Bruce hammered his large hands on the steering wheel to the beat of the snare. His work clothes mostly consisted of Springsteen and U2 T-shirts that he hacked into muscle tees with scissors. His biceps were the size of my thighs and his skin carried a deep tan from working outside. When we'd first met him as kids, we'd been impressed by the long scar that ran between his shoulder and elbow. Drawing his fingers across the gash, he'd told us that the doctor who delivered him at birth was drunk and had nearly cut his arm off.

Bruce took a squealing left turn into the neighborhood of Abbeydale, where we caught the charter bus to Crescent Heights every morning. The small bungalows and split-levels were interchangeable with the houses we'd grown up in; I knew each floor plan like the back of my hand. The patch of yard outside our house in Monterey Park was laid with fresh strips of sod. Every driveway had a basketball hoop planted in it like a flag. The kids who lived in Abbeydale thought that living in Monterey Park made you rich.

Bruce pulled a U-turn across the intersection, stomping hard on the brake pedal in front of the bus shelter, where a group of kids was smoking and kicking at a pile of glass.

"Have a good day, girls." He pulled a ten-dollar bill from his wallet.

I took it from him and smiled. "Thanks."

The money Bruce gave us wasn't enough for the new Smashing Pumpkins album, *Mellon Collie and the Infinite Sadness*, but Tegan and I agreed that we'd go downtown after school anyway just to get a look at it. In the months leading up to the album's release, I had carefully cut any mention of the band from the pages of *Rolling Stone* and *Spin* magazine and pasted them to the wall of my bedroom. I suffered a hunger to consume every new song in one giant helping. This would be *my* album, dislocated from the trauma of junior high and the disappointment of being ditched by Matthew. When the bus arrived at the stop, I pulled Bruce's headphones from my bag and disappeared into my own world.

When Tegan and I got home after school, Mom's Jeep was parked in front of the house. Her shift at the Distress Centre started after her university classes in the late afternoon. Most days we didn't see her until after midnight, if we saw her at all.

"Shit," said Tegan. "Why is she home so early?"

"Maybe she's downstairs working in the office," I said as Tegan punched in the security code beside the garage door.

We slipped under the garage door and into the house. The water was running in the kitchen: busted.

"Hi," we both said.

"Where were you?" she asked as she stood by the sink, loading the dishwasher.

"Downtown at A&B Sound. The album was already sold out. I told you it would be," I said, opening the refrigerator.

"What a shame," Mom said.

"Sara . . ." Tegan stammered. I turned. Sitting on top of the kitchen table was *Mellon Collie and the Infinite Sadness*.

"Oh my god!" I rushed to grab it, holding it against my chest, laughing, nearly crying. "Thank you, thank you, thank you."

"You're going to pay me back," Mom said, smiling. "And clean the goddamn litter box before you listen to a single note of that!"

Upstairs I unwrapped the package in my lap. The case squeaked open to reveal a bubble-gum pink disc inside. It was epic. I pulled it out, placing it carefully into the tray of my stereo. I pressed Play. A simple piano progression started. I removed the lyrics booklet and opened it across my lap. My face was wet with tears. Nothing had ever sounded more important to me. Billy's words spoke directly to the places inside of me that were hurt. His suffering reflected my own, and briefly, I felt less alone.

3. TEGAN EVERY BUS RIDE'S A GAMBLE

A cluster of guys pushed in front of Sara and me, knocking us into each other as we waited in line to board the last charter bus in front of the school to go home. I recognized two of them, Felix and Joseph, preps from my science class, who slicked back their short hair and wore ironed polo shirts and boot-cut jeans.

"Fuckers," Sara said under her breath.

"Great," I moaned quietly. Felix and Joseph were the kinds of guys who were offended by girls like Sara and me: girls who wore baggy, secondhand clothes from Value Village and paid little or no notice to guys like them. The girls I saw them with at school wouldn't be caught dead in Value Village. Though Sara and I were content to ignore their existence, they seemed obsessed with ours. In the science lab, Felix liked to edge his desk forward ever so slowly, trapping my long hair between the back of my chair and the front of his desk so that when I stood at the bell, I was yanked back down into my seat. He'd laugh every time it happened, and I'd have to pretend not to care. Outside the lab I did everything I could to avoid him. But he lived in Abbeydale, and there were six buses that went between Abbeydale and school. Our odds each morning were one in six that we'd have to see him. That day we'd bet on the wrong one.

"Do you know you have gum in your hair?" Sara asked as we took seats as far from Felix and his friends as we could.

"What? No. Where?"

"At the back."

"Shit."

"And it's pink."

"It's *pink*?" I whispered. My fingers searched frantically in the mess of my long, thick brown hair.

"Can you help me get it out?"

"It isn't coming out right now, trust me. Ask Mom when we get home."

Sara was annoyed, but I could also see she was embarrassed. Had she been the one with gum in her hair, I'd have reacted the same way. We carried each other's wins and losses, fair or not. Even a month into school, we were still impossible to tell apart to anyone who didn't know us well. The gum in my hair might as well have been in hers. The subtext to Sara's embarrassment was *What did you do for us to deserve this?*

I sank deeper into my seat, and my eyes welled up. "Fuck."

Earlier that day, I'd scoffed at Felix for snickering when I got an answer wrong in science class. I'd spun around to shoot him a dirty look, to stand up for myself, and he'd lurched forward and snapped, "Loser." As he laughed with Joseph after, I'd seen a pink blob of gum spinning in his mouth like clothes inside a dryer. Now, on the bus, I watched as Felix flicked his lighter near the hair of some girls in front of him and knew definitively the gum in my hair was his.

"Prick," Sara said.

"Douche," I agreed as I picked at the gum self-consciously.

The flame of Felix's black Bic lighter got closer to the girl's hair as the bus banked around a turn. The girl squealed, but in a way that made it clear she liked the attention he was paying her. My empathy diminished with every giggle. Finally, another girl standing nearby, small and blond, dressed like Sara and me, lashed out and knocked the lighter out of Felix's hand. She was from a crew of kids who waited at the same bus stop as us every morning, a group I was curious to know, though I'd yet to work up the courage to say hi. They were always laughing and making jokes, and I'd seen them share a joint a few times as they walked toward the bus stop. I had no classes with them, rarely saw them unless I cut through the smoking area outside the student center, which I rarely did. But in the mornings and on the bus, I watched them from afar wishing they'd become friends with us. Felix snarled at her after his lighter hit the floor. He slapped his hands together, trying to make her flinch; she and her friends only laughed. Inside, I cheered.

"Fuck you, bitch."

"Fuck you, asshole."

"Fucking trash."

"Fuck *you*. You're the trash. You prep piece of shit."

Using their backpacks as shields, the girl and her friends created a circle, locking themselves together. I wanted nothing more than to fuse to their protective shell. I slid deeper into my seat and tried not to think about the gum.

Mom managed to get the gum out, freezing it with ice cubes. The following morning, I stalled outside the wide door to science class to steady myself. I took a few deep breaths before I stepped across the threshold of the sterile science lab toward my bullies. Immediately I saw Kayla was sitting in my seat under the burn of fluorescents above her. She exploded in laughter in response to something Felix said, and my heart sank as I trudged toward them. But when I reached my desk, Kayla stood up and threw her arms around me. "Hi!" she practically screamed. "It's my best friend. I missed you." She introduced me to Felix and Joseph, and as she did it was as if she were drawing an invisible line in the small space between our desks. Joseph and Felix swung their chins out in greeting, mumbling hello sheepishly. They seemed diminished in the presence of Kayla, who actually held some power in the school. I nodded and mumbled back a similar greeting, keeping my eyes mostly trained on Kayla. She bid us farewell and raced off as the second bell rang, driving us all into our seats—my back to Felix and Joseph once again. I wasn't so naive to think that would be the end of the teasing I took daily. Felix was just one prep in a school with hundreds of them, one bully of many. I wasn't about to change how I dressed or looked, and he didn't seem on the precipice of a change either. But I was grateful, and something had shifted slightly that day in the lab, I could feel it.

I found Kayla by her navy-blue locker at lunch. "How did you know about Felix?" I asked. "And thank you."

"Sara came and found me this morning before first period," she answered. "She was worried. Said she thought I might know him."

I swelled with appreciation for Sara. She'd protected me, and in doing so, herself also.

"With guys like that, you just need to tell them to fuck off and they will," Kayla said as we walked toward the student center. "They bug you because you let them. You have to stand up to them. And if they bug you again, tell me. Seriously, I'll come fuck them up."

We both laughed. But I honestly wouldn't have put it past her. She was slowly integrating into a tougher crew of older kids who probably *would* fuck someone up for her if she asked. She was my secret weapon, but I hoped never to need her again.

After school, Sara and I got in line to board the bus. We were next to the girl who'd knocked the lighter out of Felix's hand the afternoon before.

"You're our hero," Sara told her.

She laughed. "That fucking piece of shit? *Please*, Felix doesn't scare me. He went to my junior high. He's a fucking pussy."

I immediately liked her. Felix was no pussy, and her lack of fear meant she wasn't either.

The next morning when she and the Abbeydale crew strolled up to the bus stop, I waved.

"Hey," she called out. They flanked the bench where we were waiting, shivering. "I'm Veronica." She introduced us to her friends: Emma, Jasmine, Corrine, and Spencer. As we followed them up the back stairs of the bus, I recited their names in my head again and again so I wouldn't forget or mess them up. Every morning I'd watched them, every morning I'd waited for this moment. I hesitated at the top of the stairs, unsure if we should follow our new friends or not. I saw Felix and his crew in the back corner. I stalled. "Come stand with us," Veronica called out.

Sara pushed me toward them as the bus lurched away from the curb. I grabbed hold of the pole; Felix caught me looking toward him as I did, but he just nodded and turned to his friends. I relaxed and let myself laugh at the jokes that Jasmine and Veronica, the chattiest in the group, told as we headed toward school. It was the first enjoyable bus ride I'd taken all year. Even Sara seemed happier.

A few mornings later, someone yelled our names as we waited in the cold at the Abbeydale bus stop. We both spun around.

"Come hang out," Veronica yelled from across the street, where she stood on the steps of the house where her crew waited for the bus.

"Is this your house?" I asked as we approached.

"It's Emma's," she answered. "I live next door. Come on."

Emma's kitchen was small and cramped. Around the kitchen table, Spencer and Corrine were smoking and sipping black coffee. Spencer's hair was dyed black and cut bluntly. He had a square jaw, and a low voice that didn't match his baby face. Corrine was sweet, almost silly, but biting, too; she had the posture of an athlete but she was no jock. None of them were. Slinking around us in their off-white tube socks, Veronica and Jasmine argued over a TV show they'd watched together the night before; they opened and closed drawers as if they lived there. I wondered where Emma's parents were. Everyone spoke over one another constantly, tossing four-letter curse words as they riffed and moved around us.

"Two minutes," Emma announced, her head cocked with the tan receiver of the wall phone pressed into her shoulder. I watched her brush her blond hair back from her face and stare out at us all with protective amusement. This was her crew; that much had become evident in the ten minutes we'd been there. And if we wanted into this group, and I did, it was Emma I'd have to get to know, Emma who'd grant me entry. I fell in next to her as we walked the fifty yards to the bus stop and gushed my thanks for welcoming us into her kitchen.

"Sure," she said. "Anytime."

I smiled and felt myself blush. I looked down at my shoes as we boarded the bus with our new friends. Ahead of me Veronica and Spencer cheered; at the top of the stairs I saw why—the bus was empty. We claimed the back bench and sprawled along its length, crisscrossing our limbs, expanding into our good fortune.

4. SARA ACID

"It's freezing out!" I protested.

Tegan just shrugged. "I'm still too high to sleep." She pulled herself through the window in my bedroom and out onto the roof of the garage. She was sneaking out to go smoke a joint with a new friend crush, Emma, who lived a forty-minute walk away. I went to the window and watched as she crab-walked across the shingles. At the edge of the house, she sat on her butt and swung her legs over the gutter. She pushed off and I watched her drop out of view. I heard her feet on the shed below and then the slap of her shoes hitting the sidewalk a few seconds after that. I kept my eyes focused on the street, waiting for her to reappear, and when she did, she turned and waved up to the window where I was standing. I imagined the headline: *A fifteen-year-old girl on acid was last seen walking alone at midnight along the highway.* The cold air from outside felt like an intruder. I turned the crank on the window slowly, leaving a space for Tegan to pull it open when she got home. I climbed back in bed to wait. What if she died? What if she got lost and froze somewhere in the dark next to the highway? I should have gone with her. If something happened to her it would be my fault. I brokered with the universe: *If Tegan makes it home alive, I'll never get high again.*

———

Tori Manis sold me my first tab at an amusement park on the outskirts of the city six months earlier. I remember the drug taking effect from beyond my periphery, closing in on me from all sides. I spent the long days of summer in the blacked-out basement watching films with story lines heavily influenced by drugs: *Kids*, *Dazed and Confused*, *Rush*, *The Doors*. Some part of me wanted to be scared by these stories, but what they inspired in me was entirely the opposite. Tori had warned me that I'd end up with a "spine full of the shit" if I did acid too often, but I couldn't stop plotting the next time. *You have to try it*, I told Tegan dozens of times over the summer, but she remained adamant that she had no interest, retelling our mom's story about a friend who'd done the drug only once and had a schizophrenic break. I wouldn't let up, and when Tegan finally gave in, we agreed that I would stay sober to ensure nothing went wrong while she took her first hit.

I watched Tegan put the paper square on her tongue in Naomi's kitchen. A flush spread across her cheeks and neck. The moaning and chewing of her hands started quickly after that. *Don't bite*, we kept telling her, pulling her knuckles from her mouth. I felt like a villain in an after-school special, guilty of peer pressuring my innocent sister. After she peaked, she stretched out on the carpet, so captivated by the sound of her own voice that she recited to us for hours the plot of *The Clan of the Cave Bear*.

On our next acid trip, I dropped first, and when the world around me turned to rubber, so did my defenses.

"Teegy." My childhood nickname for her bubbled out of my mouth between giggles. "We should play Nintendo!"

She returned from the garage with the dusted box as if it were a treasure. She stuffed a game cartridge into the slot, and the familiar twinkle of the *Super Mario Bros.*'s theme song began to play. Tegan studied the screen, jerking her hands and the controller through the air. I was mesmerized.

"Isn't it weird that he's collecting *mushrooms*?" Tegan said, turning toward me. "Mario is stoned, *too*."

I met her eyes, reveling in her genius. There was no one cooler; the rest of the world and everyone in it ceased to exist. Everything she said made me laugh as if she were tickling my actual brain. I felt tears spill from my eyes, letting out groans of laughter. When the trip went sideways, and the thoughts cycling through my brain turned dark, she steered me back toward the light.

When the grip of my high relaxed, Tegan placed a hit of acid in her mouth and my focus shifted. It was her turn and I wouldn't let anything bad happen to her. The drug felt like an antidote, a magnet that pulled us back together.

When we started breaking out of the house to smoke cigarettes in grade nine, we'd stayed in the yard, or walked to the park a few blocks away. Eventually we discovered that the perimeter fence had a break in it, and the farmer's field on the other side became our primary destination after dark. Away from the houses, we were less afraid of being spotted by neighbors, and our voices got louder and misdeeds more daring. Chasing the burn of weed smoke with stolen alcohol, we'd lie back in the field looking at the stars, spooking each other with unreliable sightings of coyotes in the distance. It didn't feel dangerous, because we were together.

I considered all of this as I lay in bed, waiting for Tegan to return from hanging out with Emma. I thought about waking my parents up, imagining the three of us in Mom's

Jeep, searching for her in the ditch. I didn't have to admit she was high, just stupid. A paralyzing fear scratched at the back of my skull. I wished I was telepathic, that I could feel her pain. *Send me a twin signal, for fuck's sakes.* As the minutes stretched by, I prayed, an act totally foreign to me. *Please let her be okay*, I chanted over and over.

Just after 2:00 a.m., I heard her climb onto the roof. Then I saw a purple shoe and fingers on the window frame. Landing in a crouch on my carpet, she smiled at me and said, "Hi, I saw horses!" I was relieved that she was safe, but heavy with guilt. Seeing my own recklessness reflected back to me in Tegan's behavior was truly terrifying, as if only when she was in danger could I realize that I was, too.

5. TEGAN WE'RE HOLDING IT FOR A GUY

Christina was upset that Sara and I bought two tabs at lunch to take after school before her Halloween party. She was even more furious when we got to her house and Sara realized she had somehow lost her wallet, with her tab of acid inside, and suggested the dealer come by to sell her a replacement.

"Sorry you lost your fuckin' drugs, Sara, but you can't have your drug dealer come to my house," Christina argued.

I was sprawled on the carpet of Christina's bedroom floor, stifling a laugh as I watched her, dressed as a ladybug for her Halloween party, desperately trying to pry the phone out of Sara's hands.

We met Christina in grade nine. She was a part of the Frenchies crew but decided to come to Crescent Heights with Sara and me rather than go to Aberhart with Naomi. Christina and Naomi had been best friends since they were kids; like me, Christina was adjusting to having lost her best friend to Sara. From time to time, in moments like this one, an edginess would appear in Christina toward Sara, revealing the hurt she still harbored.

"It's fine, Christina."

"It's *not* fine, Sara. My dad is in his room."

"Relax," Sara screeched, prying Christina's fingers off the receiver. "I promise your dad won't find out."

Christina sighed heavily and turned around. Her blue eyes warmed slightly as she crouched down in front of me where I was lying. I stuck out my tongue, where my square of acid was still seeping into my bloodstream.

"I'll literally kill you two if my dad finds out you're on acid tonight."

"Don't worry," I purred. "You know he won't."

"He better not."

Jasmine offered to drive Sara on her scooter to meet Garrett, the dealer, a compromise that eased Christina's anxieties. Sufficiently fucked up, Sara and I spent a lot of the night in the front entryway, welcoming kids, reminding them to take off their shoes, and instructing them not to pick up the family dog, who'd just had surgery—all as penance to win back Christina's love. When other kids who'd taken acid frothed and flailed, I discreetly moved them outside, buoyed by my ability to behave normally even though I was high. To me the best part of acid was bottling up how out of control it made me feel and forcing myself to not let on what was happening inside me. Watching Sara do the same felt exhilarating. Half the motivation was doing it when the threat of getting caught was around every corner.

Around eleven Mom picked us up and I made effortless small talk in the front seat, while Sara and Kayla giggled in the back.

"Did you guys smoke pot?"

"No." We all laughed.

"You can tell me, and I won't care."

"Mom, gross." I smiled back at Sara and Kayla.

As we walked up the front steps, the front door flew open. "What's this?" In Bruce's hand was Sara's wallet.

"Whoa." Sara sighed into the cold air.

"Where did you find it?" Kayla chirped. "She left it on the bus."

All I could think about was the tab of acid in the wallet and if Bruce had seen it. Considering how Sara looked, I was pretty sure that was all she was worried about, too.

"You know how much that bus pass costs?"

"Yes." Sara grabbed for the black wallet. Bruce pulled it back out of her reach.

"You didn't think to mention that you'd lost your wallet? Did you even care that if someone hadn't brought it here and dropped it off, it would have cost your mom and me seventy bucks?"

"I . . ."

"Isn't that why you wear that chain, to make sure something like this doesn't happen?"

"Yes. I'm sorry, Bruce. I'll take better care of it."

Bruce handed the wallet to Sara and disappeared up the hall toward the living room with Mom close behind.

I mouthed "Fuckkkkkk" to Sara and Kayla as I closed the door behind us.

Sara unsnapped the leather and tugged the tinfoil wrapping the acid out from behind the bus pass.

"Holy fucking shit," she mouthed toward me. "It's still in there. What should I do?"

"Flush it," I mouthed back.

Between us, Kayla's head ping-ponged watching our silent conversation.

"I'm going to take it," Sara mouthed.

"No, don't."

"I'm gonna do it." She unwrapped the tinfoil fast and popped the paper in her mouth. Smiling at me like a crazy person, she grabbed Kayla and pulled her into the kitchen.

I abandoned them to the bright glare of the kitchen lights. *Idiot*, I thought.

An hour later, Mom busted into my room and demanded to know why I was on the phone after curfew. I glanced at the clock and swallowed hard. It was almost midnight. Bruce was over her shoulder, the two of them back in detective mode. Ripping me out of the dark of my bedroom, she pinned me to the wall and raced through an accusation that left me dizzy.

"Explain this: Your *sister* just spent the last hour in the garage with Kayla—*Rollerblading*. She lost her wallet tonight. You've all been giggling and acting strangely. Now *your* pupils are huge, and you're flushed, and you've been in your room, in your shoes and jacket, talking after curfew when you have a friend over. So, you tell me right now, or I'm calling Christina's dad: Did you guys get high tonight?"

I smiled casually at her as adrenaline flooded my insides, making me feel even higher. "Mom. *Relax*. Emma is home alone. I was just keeping her company until her parents got in. And I have my jacket on because it's cold in my room. Go check?" I pointed for effect. *God, I'm good.* "And how the hell do I know why Sara and Kayla were Rollerblading? Ask them. I've been up here the whole time."

She leaned in. The acid was making her face look melty. I tried not to cringe or turn away. "Go get your sister right now and come downstairs."

"Sure," I said, shrugging my shoulders coolly. I walked away very carefully. "First, fuck you both," I said to Sara and Kayla when I was safely inside Sara's room. "Why were you guys Rollerblading in the fucking garage?"

They both looked stricken with fear.

Sara said, "I don't know . . . I guess—"

"Forget it. We have to go downstairs right now. So you

better figure out how *not* to seem like you're on two fucking hits of acid, because you look really fucking high right now."

"I am really fucking high right now," Sara said.

"Wait, why are you wearing only long underwear?"

Kayla giggled.

"Should I change?"

"There's no time, Sara. Fuck," I gasped. "Jesus. Come on."

Downstairs, Kayla and I flopped onto the couch next to Mom and Bruce as Sara folded herself into the chair across from us.

"Did you guys get high at Christina's?" Mom asked, muting the movie she and Bruce were watching.

"Didn't you already ask us that in the Jeep?"

"If you guys smoked pot, we won't be mad. Experimenting is normal."

I tried to shake my head at Sara. *Don't fall for it*, I thought. *Stick to the plan.* Mom was always reassuring us she wouldn't be upset if she found out we tried drugs. Neither of us bought it.

"No, we did not smoke drugs. Are my eyes red? No. Do I look high? No."

She did.

"The first thing you did when you got home was make food. There wasn't food at Christina's? You sure you don't have the munchies?"

I died.

Sara burst out laughing. "No."

"Something just seems off with both of you tonight."

"You're being very paranoid, Mom," Sara said. "Did you and Bruce get high?" Both of them scoffed at this.

"Can we go now?" I asked.

Mom looked between us and finally said, "Go."

Upstairs the three of us lay in Sara's bed giggling. I felt invincible. We were getting so good at pretending we weren't high.

The next Friday we smoked up with Kayla while Bruce was at hockey and Mom was at work. An hour later I nearly fainted when she walked into the kitchen, surprising me.

"Hi," she said flipping through a pile of mail.

"Hey. You're home early."

"Is that allowed?"

"Of course. Duh."

I turned back to the toaster and tried to steady my knees. *Did I smell like weed?* All I smelled was the toast I was buttering. *How long had I been buttering it?* I picked up the plates and slowly turned around, but to my relief she wasn't there. I quickly descended the steps to the basement. I felt suddenly aware it was much too quiet inside the office where I'd left Sara and Kayla. Rounding the corner, I swallowed hard. Mom was already in there. Sara and Kayla were frozen together on the couch. I smiled. They did not smile back.

As if in a horror film, Mom spun slowly around in her office chair, the plastic bag of weed we'd bought earlier suspended between her hands. "Hi. Is this yours? I asked those two, but they aren't sure whose it is. We've been waiting for you, hoping you could help us figure it out."

My mouth opened, but nothing came out. I thought for a second. "Um, we're holding on to it for a guy at school."

Sara and Kayla turned to look at me.

"You're 'holding on to it'? 'For a guy'? Really?" Mom said, letting out a chirp of laughter.

Sara and Kayla laughed, too.

"Yes," I repeated confidently. "We're holding it for a guy."

"What guy?"

"I don't want to say."

"We can't rat, Mom."

"Excuse me? You can't '*rat*'?"

"Yeah. Sara's right, we can't rat."

"Do you even know where this 'guy' got this? It could be full of poison, or PCP. Did you know that? They sell you idiots shake and soak it in PCP if you're *lucky*. But this is probably just stewed in Lysol. Do you guys want brain damage? Would you guys like that? Would that be a cool Friday night if Kayla got brain damage?"

I giggled, and Sara did, too.

"It's not funny."

I put down the toast and sat on the carpet with a sigh. "That seems extreme, Mom."

"Really? Does it? I spend every night going to collect people who smoked or took something and then had a psychotic break. That's my job. So, I think I know a lot more than you do."

"We didn't smoke it yet," Sara said.

I pumped my fist internally when she said it. Genius.

"Oh, you didn't smoke it? Hmm? You've just been sitting down here watching TV with it?"

"It's not ours," I said. "We're hold—"

"You're holding it for a guy. I heard you."

"We can just give it back to the guy," Sara said.

"You're telling me you didn't smoke any of this before I got home."

"No," the three of us said.

"We weren't even trying to hide it from you. We know it was stupid and we're sorry."

Mom gave us what can only be described as a look of total disbelief. *We are screwed*, I thought.

"Okay, well, let's smoke some now, together. Since it's someone you know, it should be totally fine."

"Mom, come on."

"No, seriously. It will be great, Tegan. Let's all get high together. I haven't smoked since New Year's Eve."

"Mom, gross. Knock it off," Sara warned.

"Why? Weed's cool. It's so cool to get high."

"Mom," I said. "You can't smoke pot with your teenagers and their friend."

"I'll smoke with you, Sonia," Kayla said.

"Kayla!" Sara and I shouted. "She's joking."

"Oh," Kayla replied, giggling.

Mom stood up, the weed still in her hand. "You'll have to tell the guy you were holding it for that your mom smoked it all. I'm not giving this back; Bruce and I are going to get stoned while you're at your dad's tomorrow." There was no universe where that would happen.

"Whatever." I laughed. I felt relieved; somehow, though we'd been caught, we'd gotten a pass from her. Then she dropped down between Sara and Kayla on the couch and said, "What are we watching?"

Mom smiled to herself through the entire movie as each of us slowly burned out next to her. She was quite content to let us suffer, exacting the best punishment she could have handed down. Next time we'd be more careful; we'd think twice about taking such a significant risk at home.

The next morning when Dad arrived to pick us up, Mom told him she'd caught us with weed.

"Well, if I remember correctly, you used to smoke a lot of weed when you were their age, Sonia," he joked.

"Oh, is that right? And you didn't?"

He chuckled. "Never."

"I seem to remember you and your brother picking me up and getting me high on the way to school in grade twelve, hot boxing that little Bug he had."

"Let's go, babes. Your mom's memory can't be trusted."

"Tell them about the Supertramp concert, Steve, and the time you made me take acid," she shouted as Dad closed the front door. Though they'd been divorced most of our lives, they remained good friends. This kind of back and forth wasn't uncommon.

Sara and I laughed on our way to his truck. "You and Mom took acid?"

"All lies," he said, smiling.

It was minus twenty degrees Celsius, and I wasn't wearing long johns under my ripped jeans. The exposed skin on my knees had turned purple, and the wind burned my cheeks and the tips of my ears. Burying our hands in the shallow pockets of our winter coats, Tegan and I didn't speak as we made our way from the bus stop on the highway across the subdivision's shortcut to our house. At home, we hovered near the back deck. We smoked a pinch of weed I spilled into a crushed Coke can punctured with pinholes.

"Hurry" is all Tegan mustered as I flicked the lighter with my frozen thumb, forcing sparks but no flame. "Give it to me; we'll die out here."

Sucking deeply, she passed the can back and I inhaled the smoke lacing out of the hole. When we got inside, I should have done homework, but I went straight to the basement, where I used Mom's computer to write secret letters about the girl I liked. It was still a shock to feel desire for girls, addictive thoughts that stole hours of my time at school and in bed before I fell asleep.

Girls had always been interested in Tegan and me. They sometimes followed us home from school or watched us at choir practice. As a twin, I was used to being stared at by people, but this was different. I started imagining them observing me, even when I was alone. I wanted these girls to look at me; I wanted to be seen.

Tegan came into the office and flipped on the television. "What are you writing?"

"Nothing."

I always told lies to protect her from what scared me, but this one I told only to protect myself. I printed what I was working on and walked upstairs to my bedroom, where I stashed the pages deep inside the torn-out gut of a stuffed animal. A few months earlier, Mom had come into my room and read a few lines of a letter I'd accidentally left in the printer tray downstairs. It was addressed to my best friend, Naomi.

"Do you like Naomi as more than a friend?" she asked, saying each word carefully.

My arms and cheeks went numb. "I just wrote the words to see what it would feel like."

Her face softened, and she placed the paper next to me on the bed. "You know, when I was fifteen—"

"Mom, I don't want to hear again about how you kissed a girl at boarding school!"

She flinched. "Well, in the future, if you don't want people to read your thoughts, then don't leave them where everyone can find them."

A few weeks later, Tegan found my stash of letters, pulled them straight from the gut of my hiding place. "Stay out of my shit!" I hollered at her, ripping the papers from her hands, then slamming both our bedroom doors so hard the windows rattled. I cut each page into strips and threw them in the garbage. Then I called Naomi and told her what I'd done.

"I wish you hadn't thrown them away. They were so beautiful."

"No one in this house respects me or my privacy!"

I knew both Mom and Tegan were trying to figure out what was going on with me. But the harder they looked, the more I wanted to retreat. I was afraid of being caught in a trap.

I wasn't just kissing girls.

I was in love with my best friend.

When I met Naomi on the first day of grade nine, I had never seen a girl quite like her. The short skirts and tall, striped socks she wore in a rainbow of colors became my obsession. Because she was sequestered with her French peers in private classrooms, I caught only glimpses of her and her best friend, Christina, in the hallway between bells. Her walk was more of a march, and her heavy backpack was like a turtle's shell, always pulled up high on her back. When she smiled at me, my reflex was to place my hands out in defense. I met her gaze and later searched those moments endlessly for meaning as I succumbed to the intricate fantasies unfolding in a constant loop in my mind. My grades plummeted.

Basketball tryouts gave Tegan and me an excuse to finally meet her. She bounced over to us with her hand out: "Hi! I'm Naomi!"

She seemed so confident. I felt off-balance, giddy. We were the same height, and when I spoke, she leaned in close to my face. Her entire head snapped back on her neck when she laughed.

Our team was awful, but tournaments on the weekend meant sleepovers and sleepless nights eating cookie dough and lying together in her brother's waterbed. Eventually, the sexual tension between Naomi and me was increasingly hard to mask, and I began to leave Tegan out of our sleepovers. We watched *Reservoir Dogs* and *Pulp Fiction* with our legs draped across each other and found reasons to hold hands or stay locked in eye contact. We exploited the intimacy acceptable between girls of our age with sleepovers every weekend and marathon phone calls that stretched into hours each night after school. Our handwritten notes became so numerous that we grew bolder and began to collect them in colorful folders. But despite the pleasure of it all, my feelings were far from simple.

One night, alone in my bed with Naomi, I admitted how guilty I felt about excluding Tegan from our hanging out. "I feel so bad for her."

"I get it," she said. "Christina says she feels like she never sees me anymore."

It was during one of those conversations that Naomi slowly drew me across a line I'd never dared to cross before with a girl. After months of unbearable tension between us, she suddenly reached out in the dark and ran her thumb along my lips and my ear.

"Is this okay? I've wanted to kiss you for a very long time."

After the kiss, I wordlessly disappeared into the bathroom. I sat on the edge of the bathtub waiting to throw up, and eventually did. Splashing water and a glob of toothpaste into my mouth, I quietly climbed back into the bed and under the covers.

Later, in the dark, she said, "I still like boys."

"I do, too," I said. Only after the words left my mouth did I realize this was a lie.

In the following weeks, I didn't want to do more. "I just like kissing you." I'd repeat it like a warning.

"But *I* want to do more," she replied one night. And, so,

like with our first kiss, she led me exactly where I wanted to go.

There was no school on Friday, so on Thursday night Tegan and I went to Christina's for a sleepover. I had never discussed with Christina the fact that she'd been Naomi's sole best friend before meeting me, but it was a source of tension nonetheless.

"Is it okay if I call Naomi?" I asked nervously.

"Why?"

"We're hanging out tomorrow."

"She told me she had too much homework to hang out," Christina said. I shrugged.

"Whatever," she said, turning up the TV.

I went into Christina's bedroom and dialed Naomi's number.

"Hi!" I said, smiling when I heard her voice.

"I wish I was there," she said. "What are you getting up to?"

"We might do something that you hate."

"You won't get any sleep if you do that tonight." She sounded angry.

We'd fought about drugs in the past, and I didn't want to let her down. I carefully copied the instructions for the bus I needed to take to her school the next day and reassured her one last time that I'd be there on time. After I hung up, I joined Tegan and Christina in the living room, where they were calling around to find acid. Christina's mom was working the midnight shift, so we knew we'd be unchaperoned till the morning. Tegan called our friend Garrett, who offered to drop the drugs off at the apartment.

"Let's just do it," Tegan said, and cupped the phone. "Right?"

We gave her the thumbs up. When Garrett got to Christina's, he kept passing his Snapple around for people to take sips, and after we were high he told us he'd poisoned the bottle.

"You're ruining our trip!" Christina said, pushing him out the door.

Christina turned the television to MuchMusic. We sat dazed on the futon, twisting the couch cushions between our hands. I stood and walked down the dark hallway to the bathroom. Sitting on the tiled floor with my toes stuck under the gap and my knees pressed to the wood grain, I placed my forehead against the door. I was too high; the panic expanded in my chest. I dug my nails into my jeans and the skin of my calf.

"We need fresh air!" Christina screamed through the door.

Yes, fresh air.

We were in the snow outside the apartment complex, running our hands along the banks of ice, when Heather, Christina's older sister, appeared on the balcony.

"Get inside, someone will see you!" she screamed through a clenched jaw. Rolling in the snow, we laughed and laughed. "Someone will see us!" we chanted to one another.

We were awake past sunrise; we slipped in and out of waking dreams. When I finally crawled from the mattress and into the bathroom, I stared at my stoned reflection and then quietly shut the door of the apartment behind me.

There was a fresh dusting of snow on the sidewalk, and I left deep shoe prints up the street to the bus stop. I stood shivering next to the bench inside the shelter, too cold to sit down on the frosted planks of wood. Unsure of how much time had passed, I walked across the street to a pay phone and plugged a frozen quarter in the slot. I dialed the bus directory, pressing the cold plastic earpiece to my head. The bus was thirteen minutes away. I'd miss the connection to my second bus downtown for sure. I was going to be late.

"I'm so sorry," I whispered through numb lips when I walked through the door of Naomi's house hours later. Her cheeks were pink, warm. Her hair was done up in Princess Leia buns, my favorite of her intricate hairdos. I knew she'd done it special for me.

"You must be hungry," she said. We went to the kitchen where she made me a sandwich. I picked at the food, not yet ready to put anything into my stomach. I looked pathetic, and she led me upstairs to her bedroom where we lay on her single bed and talked.

I told her the story of our night over and over again, my eyes spilling tears onto her pillow. She was laughing, catching my tears with her thumbs. Sliding her leg between mine, her green eyes watched me as I drifted off to sleep.

It was the sound of the door that woke me up. Naomi's mom's face appeared and then disappeared back into the hall. Naomi woke up, too.

"Your mom was just in here. She saw us."

Naomi said nothing, but she flipped over and opened the door.

"Mom?" she called down the stairs.

"Just seeing if you girls were home safe!"

"It's fine," Naomi said and rolled back over to face me.

When Naomi called the next day, she was crying. "After

you left, Mom asked me what we were doing sleeping like that. She saw us on the bed holding each other. She said girls aren't supposed to do that."

I felt dizzy. "What did you say?"

"I told her we're just best friends, and sometimes we cuddle."

"And . . ."

"She said you couldn't sleep here anymore." Naomi broke down in sobs.

Tears sprang from my eyes. I wrapped the telephone cord around my wrist until the veins on my hand swelled with blood. "I'll talk to my mom. Maybe she can talk to yours?"

"Okay."

Downstairs in the living room, I sat on the couch next to Mom. Her lap, as always, was guarded by our male cat, Taz. I reached out and pet his back, and he began to purr softly. I didn't quite know what to say. "Can I talk to you?" I asked.

She pointed the remote to pause a recording of *Days of Our Lives*. "What's up?"

"Yeah, so, Naomi's mom saw us, sleeping. On Naomi's bed together. Her single bed, like close together."

The conversation jerked and started. It felt honest when I repeated, "We are just friends. We weren't doing anything!" because we hadn't been doing anything—on *that* day. I didn't consider it a lie when I promised her that if I were gay, I'd tell her. Because I didn't think I was gay.

She sighed. "I'll call her mother."

"Thank you!"

I went upstairs and quickly called Naomi with the good news.

"I think it's going to be okay," I said.

The words she spoke next sounded flat in my ears: "I think we need to go back to just being friends."

When Dad grabbed Tegan and me Saturday morning from Mom's, the first thing that he asked when we climbed into the car was, "No Naomi?"

He enjoyed having her around almost as much as I did. I didn't tell him that Naomi and I hadn't spoken in a week, the longest period of time we'd been out of touch since we'd met. Instead, I made up a lie, telling him that maybe she'd come over on her own later that day. Dad was in a good mood; his blue eyes flicked up to the rearview mirror as I spoke. He had the rock station blasting out the speakers. His hand gestures, and the way he laughed and then drew his face into a dark pout, reminded me of me. And Tegan. He was half Bruce's size, lean and short. On the weekend he wore sweatpants, nearly disintegrated at the knees, and T-shirts that he pulled at relentlessly until he'd stretched the necks low and wide around his throat. We rarely saw him out of this uniform. He wore the same gray hooded sweatshirt under his bulky letterman jacket branded with the logo of the housing company he worked for, no matter how low the temperature plunged in winter. He hated socks and didn't wear them. That he wasn't suffering from one of his migraines meant that we would spend the day running his errands.

When we got to his house in the late afternoon, I couldn't stand it any longer. I dialed Naomi's number and pleaded my case. "I need to see you. Nothing has to happen between us, I promise."

"I'd have to see if my brother can drive me," she replied.

"Please, please, you know how much better it is when you're here."

She agreed.

When Naomi arrived, Dad drove the three of us to Blockbuster, and we walked up and down the aisles arguing over movies just like we used to in grade nine. When we were young, Dad never checked the advisory on the back of the cases, and we often ended up awkwardly sitting with him through sexually mature or violent films that we knew not to tell Mom about. He also didn't mind our penchant for repeat viewings of classics like *Goonies*, *Ferris Bueller's Day Off*, and *Labyrinth*.

"Should we rent *Bound* again?" I winked at Naomi.

"I didn't really like that one." She moved down the shelf, picking up boxes and reading quietly to herself. There weren't very many movies that featured two girls kissing or having sex, but if they existed, I knew about them. Maybe tonight wasn't the right occasion; I wished I'd kept my mouth shut.

Back at the house, I stretched out in front of the gas fireplace, while Naomi and Tegan shared the couch with Dad. I replayed every possible scenario in my head about what might happen when we went upstairs to bed. When Naomi started sleeping over, Dad had suggested that we might be more comfortable in his bedroom and offered to crash on the couch. Tonight, there didn't seem to be a way to address a different sleeping arrangement without making things really weird. Still, I selfishly wanted to be alone with her.

When the movie finished, I charged up the stairs ahead of Tegan and Naomi, and instead of turning down the hall to Dad's room, I went into the bedroom that Tegan and I shared. It was empty except for a set of bunk beds, and a *My Girl* movie poster that we hung up as a joke. I rolled onto the lower bunk bed, and Tegan climbed up to the top. Naomi joined me on the bottom and rested her leg casually against mine.

"That movie was fucking awesome," Tegan said.

"You two always pick bad movies," Naomi teased.

As we joked back and forth, I felt my body go slack. The fist in my stomach unclenched.

"I'm going to get ready for bed," Tegan said, and dropped down from above onto the carpet.

"Me, too!" Naomi said, rolling off the mattress.

"Me three." My heart skipped a beat. I waited for what would happen next.

"Goodnight, Tegan!" Naomi said, turning down the hall to Dad's bedroom.

"Night," Tegan said, closing the door to the bathroom.

When Naomi and I finished brushing our teeth in Dad's bathroom, I twisted the lock on the door to his bedroom as silently as I could, hoping Naomi didn't hear me do it.

"Are you wheezing?" Naomi asked me as I climbed into the waterbed.

"I guess a little." I had asthma attacks every now and then.

She rolled over and placed her hand on my chest, watching me in the dark. My heart thundered in my ears, and my shallow breaths made the asthma attack worse. I sat up.

"I hate this," I said. "I feel so bad."

"I know. I really missed you this week. I just needed some time apart."

"I don't want that. We're already at different schools. I never see you!"

We went in circles like that for an hour. I was pleading with her, but for what? Reassurance? Sex? How did I become the only one who wanted this?

"What are we?" I asked.

For a long time, she didn't answer. Then she said, "I like boys. But sometimes I like you, too."

The part of me that trusted her disappeared with a violent swoosh. Her body became her mother's, a stranger.

"Well, I just like you," I said.

We lay still for so long that I was afraid that she'd fallen asleep. I couldn't bear to look over at her, but eventually, she turned and rolled on top of me.

"I want to," she whispered.

In the morning we ignored what happened the night before. In the car on the way to her house, she was back to normal. Before she closed the door outside her home, she leaned into the car and said, "I'm seeing you on Friday, right?"

7. TEGAN YOU CAN'T SAY "FAG"

"Open the door, now."

I paused the CD I was listening to in my room, Nirvana's *In Utero*, and shouted, "What?"

"Open the door."

I sighed and stood up. Flinging open my door I said, *"What,"* a second time.

"Excuse me?" Bruce was in his workout clothes, a pair of black weight-lifters' pants and a Gold's Gym tank top from a visit to Atlanta we'd made a few years earlier. His face was red, but it was clear he hadn't just worked out—he was just pissed off.

"Can I help you?"

"Yes, you can turn that off."

"Why? It's Nirvana."

"Because I said so."

"Can't I just turn it down?"

"No. Turn it *off.* I'm tired of hearing that song."

"What song?" I had been blasting the song "Rape Me" when he banged on my door.

"I'm not going to say the name of it, Tegan. Just turn it off." He went to go back down the stairs.

"Have you even listened to the lyrics?" I called after him. "It's actually an anti-rape song, Bruce. Kurt was showing support for *women.* If you *listened* to the lyrics instead of just judging it because you don't like the word 'rape' and how it makes you feel, you *might* understand that."

Stopping halfway down the stairs, Bruce turned and glowered at me through the banister spindles. "This is not a debate. I'm not arguing with you. I'm the parent, you're the child, and I said to *turn it off*. So, do it."

"Why are you telling me what music I can listen to?"

I could see his jaw clench, the muscle on either side was pushing through the skin as he pressed his teeth together. He was fuming, but so was I.

"I'm not telling you what music you can listen to. What I said was for you to turn off that song. *Now*."

"No, you said to turn off the whole CD actually—"

"You're pushing me right now, Tegan. In two seconds, I'm going to take your stereo and *all* your CDs, and you're not going to have any music to listen to for the rest of the week. Don't play them again."

"You said the other day you like 'Teen Spirit'—"

"No, I didn't."

"That's a lie. You absolutely did. We were in the truck—"

"I don't know what you're talking about; I think Nirvana sucks."

Back and forth like brother and sister, rather than parent and child, we interrupted each other until Sara's door flew open. "What the hell is going on out here?"

"Bruce hates Nirvana now," I said childishly.

"Why?"

I shrugged. "Ask him. Apparently, he thinks they're terrible, and now we have to destroy all the records in the house. So, if you have any Nirvana CDs you better hide them before the police show up."

"Tegan, you're getting really close to losing your phone privileges for the night—"

"*You* said I couldn't play Nirvana—"

"I said I was tired of hearing that song. I don't know why your mother lets you listen to it," Bruce said. "And that guy was *weird*, he wore makeup."

"Kurt? Do you mean Kurt?" I was taken aback. "How was he *weird*? What does that even mean?"

Smirking, Bruce turned around and under his breath said, "I mean he was a *fag*."

It was like a punch to the gut.

The first time I heard the word "fag" was in elementary school. Back then it was a playground insult, like idiot or loser. I don't think anyone had a clue at that age what it actually meant, or how derogatory and hurtful the word was. Coworkers of our dad had used it in front of Sara and me around that time, too. "Did you know your dad's a fag?" They'd laugh as we awkwardly stood next to him at work events or on the floor of the warehouse he worked at.

We'd shrug and scamper away as he laughed and said, "Oh, that's a nice thing to say in front of my kids."

By the time we hit high school, we'd learned the word's real meaning, and it had become passé to say, at least in our group of friends, who were growing increasingly political and protective over those experimenting with their sexuality.

I had not heard it in so long that it took me a minute to recover from hearing it from Bruce's mouth. I looked at Sara, whose eyebrows were arched in shock. She took a step back into her room, closing the door gently, shooting me a *you're on your own with this one* kind of look as she did.

"Oh my god," I yelled at Bruce's back as he disappeared

into the kitchen. "You didn't just fucking call Kurt Cobain a fag."

I caught up to him in the basement, as he sank heavily onto the desk chair in his office.

He looked at me, exasperated. "*What?*"

"You can't say the word 'fag.'"

"Why not?"

"You know you can't say that word. I can't believe you're homophobic."

"I'm not," he said. His arms, thick as tires, were crossed defensively across his barrel chest. Bruce had a tough exterior; he worked construction and played hockey, but under his armor he was a softie. He'd been nothing but gentle and playful with Sara and me since he'd come into our lives when we were little kids. When Grampa teased about our oversize pants or men's work shirts, Bruce was quick to point out he'd given them to us. At the mall when people stared at us, he glared back at them. When I wanted to spray-paint my metal chain different colors, it was he who hung it up in the garage and provided me with a mask and the spray. I couldn't reconcile the two very different men Bruce apparently had inside him.

"Why did you call him a fag then? I don't understand. Who even says 'fag' anymore? Is that how you talk when we're not around when you're with your hockey buddies?"

"No."

"So?"

"I just think it's weird that he wore makeup."

"He didn't wear makeup all the time. He's wearing it in like, one poster in my room. And so what? He was alternative. Like Sara and me. Do you think we're *weird*?"

He sat silently after that, refusing to speak.

"You know people call us weird every single day. We get made fun of for being different all the time. When we were little, people called us boys and made fun of us for having short hair. Would you like it if someone were calling us dykes? Because they already call us freaks and fuckups because of how we look."

He smirked. "That's not the same thing."

"Actually, it is," I said, tearing up. "People like you see people like us and don't even try to understand us."

"These aren't the same things."

"Just say sorry for calling him a fag. For saying he was weird. Say sorry and promise you won't use that word. Then it can be over."

"No."

I let out a long cry of frustration and then burst into tears, my midsection crumpling as I started to heave into my legs.

Eventually, he got up and sat down next to me, dropping a box of Kleenex on the coffee table. "I'm sorry, Tegan. I should never have used that word. He wasn't a fag. I was an asshole."

"But what if he were?" I said between sobs.

"Even if he were gay, that's . . . okay."

"You can't say 'fag.'"

"I won't, but you need to remember where I come from, how people talk on the job sites, at the mill, on the ice . . . I'm better than most, and I'm learning. Your mom has taught me a lot. But I still make mistakes. I'm not perfect. Sometimes I say stuff, and I don't think. I'm a man after all," he said, laughing. "I'm sorry. I really am."

It was far from a perfect apology. But I was far from being articulate about a topic I was just starting to understand myself. My own language was still developing, my own comfort around the concept was still forming. But I believed Bruce was sorry. And I didn't imagine that many other dads of kids I knew could have that kind of conversation. I knew Bruce was different, the way my mom was different from most of the other kids' parents we knew and hung around. They prided themselves on being the kinds of parents we'd come to if we were in trouble. They wanted to ensure there was always a bridge between us, no matter how far away we felt; they provided us a way back. I knew he was trying to close the gap between us.

After we made up, I played him the *MTV Unplugged* album Nirvana had recorded before Kurt's death. Bruce loved David Bowie, and when "The Man Who Sold the World" played, he palmed the disc case and nodded along. "You're right, they are good." When it finished and I went to go upstairs, he said, "Leave that CD here, I'm going to make a copy to play in my truck."

"Is Tegan depressed?" Mom asked me, point blank, one day after school. She stood against the closed door in my bedroom, her arms folded across her chest like a TV mom.

"Um." I looked down at the open binder on my bed, turning the page away from the poetry about death and suffering that I was writing. "No, I don't think she's depressed."

"Depression runs in your dad's family."

"Mom, it runs in everyone's family."

"You'd tell me if something was going on?"

Would I?

I didn't tell her that when I was fourteen I spent the summer writing suicide notes to the girls who'd bullied me for two years. She was more than qualified to deal with the situation—she'd worked at a suicide prevention center since the mideighties. I didn't tell her in grade nine when a friend threatened to take a handful of Tylenol at a sleepover, or about the time Naomi's boyfriend had a knife pressed to his wrist. I'd become dangerously latched to the idea that I could determine which of those threats required parental intervention and which did not. In my own case, I knew that I didn't want to die. I took for granted that Tegan felt the same way as me.

"Tegan's fine," I said.

Mom nodded. "And you? Are you depressed?"

"Mom!" I laughed. "No!"

"Suicidal?" She stood there, unmoved.

I closed my binder, swung my legs off the bed. "I'm not depressed or suicidal. I'm not anything!"

She blinked. "Are you on drugs?"

"Are you?"

"I know you and your sister are doing drugs."

"Mom, get out of my room. I have to do my homework."

"If you're doing drugs, tell me. I'd rather buy you weed myself, so I know what's in it."

"I don't want you buying weed. We're not doing drugs."

"I'd rather you smoke weed than drink. If I ever find out you're in a car with someone who's drunk driving, I swear to god—"

"Mom, we're not idiots!"

Mom's questions about Tegan lingered in my mind. I didn't think Tegan was suicidal, but the way her face went slack, sometimes for days at a time, did remind me of Dad. His moods were similarly hard to predict, and when he was depressed, he wore that face like a mask.

"Do you think Tegan seems sad?" I asked Naomi when she called later that night.

"Like, more than normal?"

"Mom asked me if she was depressed."

"I worried about you, last year. You were sad a lot."

"Yeah, but that was different."

"Remember when you were obsessed with calling the Teen Line?"

I'd started calling the help line *because* of Naomi and the shame I experienced for the feelings I had for her. They became too difficult for me to contain, especially after a night of drinking. With the room and my head spinning, I found gravity in the voice of a stranger. "When I turn sixteen, I'm going to volunteer at that helpline," I said.

"You should!"

"I like hearing other people's problems because it makes me feel less lonely."

"Lucky that you found me, because you'll never feel lonely." She laughed. "Do you think that maybe Tegan is sad because we kind of ditched her?"

A familiar knot tightened in my gut. "We didn't ditch her!"

"Maybe she feels lonely, like you did last year, before you and I became close."

"Why is it my responsibility to figure this out?" I said, far too loudly.

"It's not your responsibility. But, if you're worried—"

"Mom's not asking *Tegan* if *I'm* depressed! She loves Tegan more than me."

"I don't think that's true." She paused. "She trusts you and confides in you. And maybe she thinks Tegan will tell you if something is wrong because you're her twin sister and not her mom."

I sighed. "What do I say to her?"

"Just ask her if she's okay."

"Fine."

I stood outside Tegan's door and knocked.

"What?"

I let my eyes adjust to the darkness as I stepped in her room. I could make out her body under the blankets, the telephone cord disappearing under the covers. Even the remnants of childhood in her room—a few stuffed animals banished to a top shelf over her desk—seemed sad. The shrine she'd built to Kurt Cobain had grown substantially in the two years since his suicide, and every inch of her walls was covered with his face.

Kurt and our step-grandfather, Ed, committed suicide two days apart when we were fourteen. On the morning of Ed's funeral service, spread across the front page of the local newspaper was news of Kurt Cobain's suicide. Dead at twenty-seven from a self-inflicted gunshot wound. It was a gut punch in all the ways the news about Ed wasn't. Tegan's face crumpled; he was her hero.

"Take that paper upstairs," Mom whispered. Sitting in silence in Tegan's bedroom, we read the details of his death on the pages of the newspaper between us. The space had been a sanctuary, a place to shut ourselves inside and worship Kurt's lyrics; but at that moment, it felt like a grave. Bruce knocked on the door, telling us it was time to leave for the church. On the way down the stairs, resting his hands on both our shoulders, he offered his condolences, as if we were in black clothes for Kurt Cobain's funeral, not Ed's.

After the service, when our house was finally cleared of guests, Tegan and I disappeared into the basement to watch the Nirvana marathon on MuchMusic. We admitted to each other how much worse we felt about Kurt's death than about our step-grandfather's.

"We didn't really know Ed," Tegan said. Did we know Kurt? It felt like we did. After his death, it seemed that everywhere we went we heard his voice on loop, saw his face draped across every chest and stuck to every wall. His omnipresence was like a resurrection.

That night, Tegan took a safety pin and scratched the

Nirvana logo into her left ankle, promising to rip the scab off and recut it until it was a scar.

"Can I talk to you?" I asked her now, gesturing for her to hang up the phone.

"I'll call you back," she said into the receiver. She hung up and rolled the duvet down past her chin. "What do you want?"

"Mom thinks you're depressed."

"What? I am not."

I studied her reaction. "Well, your room looks like a suicidal teenager's room."

"Fuck off."

We both laughed, and she got off the bed and turned her stereo on. Green Day spilled from the speakers. She spun open the dark blinds in her window, pulled the covers on her bed straight. I sat down on the carpet.

"Do you think Kurt liked Green Day?" Tegan asked me.

"I don't think he liked anyone."

"He liked gay people!"

"And hated mean people!"

"Turn this one up!" Tegan stood up and headbanged, flopping her hair forward and back, her face scrunched up and serious.

"You're such a banger." I laughed.

When the song finished, I stood up to leave.

"Want to walk to 7-Eleven with me?" I asked her.

Tegan bounced herself off her mattress like it was a trampoline, a blush spreading across her cheeks.

"Sure!" she said. She grabbed her coat from the floor and together we headed downstairs.

Broadcasting and Communications was my favorite class. A few months in we still hadn't been allowed to touch a camera or use the recording equipment, but the assignments were easy, and the class was helping my overall grade point average, which needed all the help it could get. It was also the only class I had with Kayla that semester, and our teacher, Mr. Kim, a small, nervous, absentminded man, basically let the two of us get away with murder while we were under his supervision. When we showed up late, he never got mad. If we left early, he didn't report us. Friends would skip class to hang out on the orange velvet couch in the back corner of the adjoining room, where the equipment was kept, and Mr. Kim didn't seem to notice the extra bodies.

But my absolute favorite part of the class was getting to hang out with Spencer, from the Abbeydale crew. After Emma invited us to come wait at her house in the mornings, he started sitting with me and Kayla in Broadcasting class. He had the longest lashes I'd ever seen on a boy. When we talked in class, I tried not to stare at them when he spoke, but it was hard; he was beautiful. My room was covered in Green Day posters and I started to think of Spencer as my real-life Billie Joe.

"Did you dye your hair black to look like him?" I asked Spencer one afternoon as the two of us sat in the back of

Mr. Kim's class and flipped through a *Rolling Stone* with Green Day on the cover.

"No, he dyed his hair to look like me."

He was a boy of few words, but when he did talk it was often to spit short, witty, sarcastic quips under his breath. I strained to never miss one.

Kayla and Spencer fell into a comfortable rapport during this time, too. It was obvious to everyone, including me, that they were crazy about each other, and when she asked him out before Halloween, he said yes. I was happy for Kayla, and in no rush to get a boyfriend, so it didn't bother me she snagged him first. Nothing changed between the three of us when they started going out anyway. We joined ski club and skipped Mr. Kim's class to smoke weed. After school we'd crowd together on the couch in Kayla's basement to watch MuchMusic. Mr. Kim called us the Three Musketeers.

"Oh my fucking god you guys," I shouted, racing into Mr. Kim's Broadcasting class just before the final bell.

"Language." He sighed from next to the chalkboard.

"Sorry, Mr. Kim."

I tossed my backpack off and leaned into Kayla and Spencer. She was sitting on his lap at our usual table at the back of the class. "Green Day announced a show here," I squealed in their faces. "They're coming to the Saddledome, so we have to get tickets. And Bruce told me and Sara this morning that we can skip Friday to go line up for tickets. And my mom will come get us after. You guys have to come with."

"YES!" they yelled at the same time.

"Tegan, please, can you sit so I can start?" Mr. Kim whined from the front. "And Kayla, how many times do I have to say no food in class?"

"It's not food, Mr. Kim. It's a Slurpee."

He sighed heavily, and the three of us laughed.

"Why do we have to line up?" Spencer whispered as Kayla slipped off his lap into her own seat and Mr. Kim started his lesson.

"We *have* to get floor seats," I whispered back. "So we can mosh."

"Duh," Kayla added.

Spencer cringed. He was a worrier. He was risk averse to an extreme level. He refused to try acid with us even though all his friends dropped almost every weekend. "I don't want to have a psychotic break," he claimed when I pressed him to do it. "What if mental illness runs in my family?"

"Trust me," I said quietly, before turning my attention to the front of the class and Mr. Kim's lecture. "You'll love being up close. Moshing is so cool. Maybe we can even crowd-surf?"

"Oh my god, no way," Spencer said, shaking his head. "What if someone drops me and I break my neck?"

Friday afternoon Sara and I went downtown with Kayla and Spencer to get tickets, and that night I pinned my ticket up next to my bed under a Green Day poster and thought about Spencer as I drifted off to sleep.

A few weeks later Sara, me, Kayla, and Spencer met at Sunridge train station to head to the arena for the show.

"I hope we don't get crushed when the train comes." Spencer swiveled his head, frantically scanning the growing crowd gathering on the platform around us. "Or knocked onto the tracks. Maybe we should step back."

"No one is going to push us." Sara laughed. "Relax."

When we boarded, the train was crammed with people wearing Green Day shirts. Spencer, Sara, and I squeezed into a row together, and Kayla sat on our laps.

"What if one of us falls and gets trampled by people moshing?"

I shook my head. "Spencer! Oh my god, stop worrying! You're going to be fine."

"I think we should all link arms the whole time. Promise you guys won't let go of me."

"We won't," Kayla and I both said at the same time.

Against the black metal barricade near the stage, Kayla and Spencer and I linked arms as a deafening roar spread from the back of the venue and the overhead lights started to flicker. As Green Day sauntered onstage, a surge of bodies from behind pressed us into the metal, pushing the air out of my lungs. I felt scared for a second, but when the tide went out, and air gushed back into me, I screamed, "THIS IS FUCKING AMAZING!" in Spencer's face.

He just opened his mouth into a terrified O shape and then closed it.

Billie Joe barked something into the mic, and the crowd roared even louder. After that, I didn't hear any other voice but his. The speakers in front of us came alive with the first notes of "Basket Case." When the front light hit Billie Joe in the chorus, I gasped. It was strange to see someone famous, right there, so close.

We'd seen New Kids on the Block in that exact room when we were nine. But Sara and I had been in a box seat with Dad's boss, so far away we had watched the show mostly on the screens on either side of the stage; it was more like watching TV than being at a live show. Bruce had taken us to see Bruce Springsteen when we were twelve. Again, we'd been in the second tier, a hockey rink's distance from the Boss, mostly watching him on the screens. Now, standing just a few feet from where Billie Joe was snarling and tearing at the strings of his guitar, a guitar hanging so low it forced him forward into a nearly ninety-degree angle, I felt starstruck, overwhelmed, consumed.

At the end of the show, we were all breathless. I rubbed the tender parts of my arm where Spencer had clung to me through the lightning-fast sixty-minute set. Lingering at the front of the stage, kicking empty plastic beer cups and lost shoes from crowd-surfers, the four of us reluctantly made our way out of the arena to where Mom was waiting outside to drive us home.

"How was it?" she asked when we climbed into the Jeep. The overhead light of the car illuminated a smile that stretched across her face as she took in the damage. My pants were ripped to my knees. Sara's hair was a hive of knots from the pit. Spencer and Kayla looked windblown, and all of us were red-faced and shaking with adrenaline. Our ears were ringing, and as we answered her questions about the concert, I could tell we were yelling as if still in the arena, trying to be heard over the music.

"Amazing," I shouted. "We were at the front the whole time. I could literally see the pupils of Billie's eyes."

"And we moshed, and people were crowd-surfing, and Billie kept swearing at the audience to get crazy," Sara yelled from behind me.

"And some of Billie's spit got on us," Kayla said seriously.

"He spit on you?" Mom looked amused.

"Yes," we all shouted happily.

"It was so cool," I said, and sighed.

"Spencer, what did you think? You're being awful quiet about it. Not a fan?"

"No, I love them. But we almost died," Spencer answered flatly from the back. "It was terrifying. I had to watch out for them the whole time."

"As if," I said.

"That's a little twisted," Kayla said. "I think it was *us* looking out for you."

"Well, I'm glad it was so fun," Mom said, putting the Jeep into drive. "Alright, who am I dropping off first?"

I slouched against a row of wooden cabinets. I was studying the short script that the drama teacher had handed to
me at the theater door. Rail thin, wearing fitted light denim
pants, white socks, and sandals, Mr. Russel had a crooked,
toothy grin stained with black coffee and cigarettes. If he was
aware of the rumors that swirled about his sexuality, he
made no attempt to dispel them. I'd already begun to doubt
my chances of being cast in the school play, when Tegan and
Stephanie joined me. Stephanie was tall and striking, and
she folded herself down to the floor next to me in a dramatic
swoop. Her hair was a washed-out ketchup color, and her
blue eyes locked onto mine. She asked if we wanted to drop
acid after school and go on an adventure with her and her
best friend, Zoe. We accepted her invitation and began dis-
cussing blowing off the rest of the tryout.

"Grade tens don't get cast," she told us. "And you have to
be at every rehearsal and have your locker downstairs, so *they*
can keep their eye on you."

They were the Drama Society kids, who huddled around
Mr. Russel at all times before and after school. The Pit, a
space cluttered with rundown couches and a wardrobe stuffed
with moth-bitten clothes, was their clubhouse behind the
stage. "I just want to act, not be part of some cult," Stephanie
said, landing one final punch. We stood up and made our
way to the exit.

After class, Stephanie and Zoe met us at the front of the school, twinned in corduroy bell-bottoms and buttoned-up paisley shirts. Stephanie carried a notebook crammed with receipts and drawings, yarn, and sketches of swirls and melting faces. They called it their "adventure book" and inside they recorded details about each of their acid trips. Zoe wore a faux-fur coat that dropped below her knees, and my instinct as soon as we were high was to bury my face in its depths. Her eyes were wolfish and sad, and up close her skin was unblemished, nearly opaque. With perfect posture, they both seemed to tower over Tegan and me. They'd slipped a tab of acid inside a folded note for each of us, our names scribbled in bubble cursive on the outside. In the bathroom stall, my heart pounded as I carefully untucked the paper, afraid to drop the tab in the toilet. A burning sensation boiled up from inside my chest as I threw the foil in the garbage can on the way back out the door. The four of us crossed the block to Centre Street and caught the bus downtown. Zoe's boyfriend, Jonathan, was waiting for us when we arrived at the CTrain station.

The drugs twisted my self-esteem into self-loathing. Jonathan and Zoe soared above me. The ooze of the acid trip made them look utterly matched, and I couldn't stop staring down in disgust at my lumpy hoodie and baggy pants. On the train, Stephanie bounced from bench to bench, blurting every thought out loud.

"I love your hat!" she said to an elderly woman, who appeared spooked by us. Gregarious and rubbery, Stephanie was our uninhibited adventure guide and seemed to command the doors of the compartment open as we sailed out in a gush of air onto the platform. Tegan and I had permanent grins, and I peaked in the parking lot below the train station on our walk.

"I love it here," Tegan said as we stepped into the blast of heat from the grates in the entryway of Marlborough Mall. We stamped our feet in circles on the pale beige tiles slick with melted snow. Coins, buzzers, and gunfire trilled from the arcade, and we stood, mesmerized, as we watched a preteen playing *Street Fighter*.

"This way," Stephanie said, twirling her hand above her head.

We orbited a table in the food court next to an A&W. Jonathan bought a single carton of fries that no one ate, but the orange tray on our table ensured that the mall security guard ignored us for a while. I said zero words before the group wandered off, leaving Tegan and me to ponder our existence in silence. Intrusive thoughts pulsed my mind: *What if Gramma is here at the mall and sees us? What if I'm high forever? What if I come down, but Tegan is high forever?* Tegan nervously dug through her backpack, and I realized I'd said all those thoughts out loud. She retrieved a brush snarled with hair and wordlessly set it down between us. We marveled at its grotesqueness.

When our friends returned, we dumped our tray in a trash can and disappeared into the Sears department store. Zoe and I ran our hands along the washing machines and kitchen appliances, and the smells from the restaurant sent happy shivers through my limbs. Back outside in the brutal cold, we crossed the parking lot and then crowded together on the platform waiting for our train. Jonathan stood behind

Zoe with his arms wrapped around her chest, his face resting on top of her head. They were silent, but I imagined they were communicating through the drapes of their hair.

When the train arrived, we squeezed in between the rush-hour commuters, greedily tilting our frozen faces and fingers up to the heat vents. Outside the window, red cardiac lines shot from the taillights of cars, and my mood shifted to something darker. Tegan and I disembarked first, and we called out muffled goodbyes from inside the scarves we'd wrapped around our faces.

The following week, Stephanie asked Tegan and me if we wanted to come with her to Zoe's house after school. "We're doing tie-dye," she told us.

On the train to Zoe's house, Tegan and Zoe did most of the talking. They were in the same English class and traded stories about getting caught skipping. Stephanie and I gossiped about our drama teacher and the casting for the school play.

I stole looks at Zoe. She didn't look like anyone else I'd ever seen, and I felt a pang of guilt thinking about Naomi. They were different in every way; Naomi was outgoing and studious, and whatever time was left after studying she spent with me. Zoe was aloof and rarely mentioned school. I'd heard her tell Tegan that she wished she could go to dance classes seven days a week, a statement that made me feel oddly jealous—like she was describing a stranger with whom she was obsessed. Naomi was insatiable in conversations. Zoe's eyes drifted from my face, her attention slipping through my fingers. Was it possible to have a crush on someone when you were supposed to love someone else?

Sitting underneath the window in Zoe's bedroom, I memorized each detail. She was tidy. It seemed she'd had the same bed since childhood; the wood was worn and scuffed at the corners. Her bookshelf was filled with Bob Marley and Björk CDs. There was a single photograph of her at a dance competition on the wall near her bed. Her eyes were rubbed black with mascara, her body frozen in a sculptural pose. I tried not to stare for too long at anything and forced my eyes to move from object to object calmly.

"How's Jonathan?" I asked.

"We broke up," Zoe said.

"He's boring," Stephanie added, flipping through the CDs on Zoe's bookshelf.

"Actually, he's had a really interesting life. I loved his stories . . ." Zoe trailed off.

My jaw clenched at the tenderness in her voice.

"What about you? Are you dating anyone?" She turned her eyes to mine, and I felt my mouth drop open. Cartoonish swirls seemed to pop out from her eye sockets and drill into the back of my head. I wanted nothing more in the world than to fall into a black hole in her carpet so I wouldn't have to answer this question.

"Can we put makeup on you guys?" Stephanie said, jumping up from the carpet.

"Sure!" I said. I ignored the look of shock on Tegan's face. Neither of us wore makeup, but I would have agreed to anything to be out of the hot seat. When we were all on Zoe's narrow mattress together, Stephanie combed my hair into a ponytail, and I sat facing Zoe as she applied soft brushes and her fingertips to my lips and the lids of my eyes. I thought about how many hours had passed since I'd brushed my teeth. I held my breath. When Zoe finished my makeup, she turned me toward the mirror.

"You're so pretty!" Stephanie said.

I shyly accepted the praise. But in the mirror's reflection, I saw a rush of blood spread across my cheeks. I didn't recognize the girl staring back at me.

Stephanie and Zoe had a large crew of friends that Tegan and I met in the student center on the following Friday afternoon. I was acutely aware of how attractive they were, and joining their circle emboldened me with confidence. I wanted to belong with these girls. Penny had a gap between her teeth, and she was the first girl I'd seen with short hair in our high school. Her side part was held in place with colorful barrettes, magnifying the symmetry of her remarkable face. I was envious of her flat chest and narrow hips. With her midriff exposed, my eyes were drawn to her belly button, and farther down to her belt. Her best friend, Jodi, was captivating, too, at nearly six feet tall. Her blond hair was chopped into a bob and she wore a tight choker of lace cut across her throat. She was always dancing in place and chewed hard on a piece of gum buried in the back of her mouth. They referred to themselves as "ravers" and seemed cast from the film *Kids*.

"Come with us to a rave this weekend!" Penny suggested.

"Yes!" Stephanie clutched both my arm and Tegan's. "That would be so fun!"

There was no way in hell that our mom was going to be persuaded to let us stay out until 6:00 a.m. with a group of girls she'd never met.

"We could tell Mom we're staying at Christina's dad's house," I suggested to Tegan.

"Or you can say you're staying at my house," Zoe offered.

My heart raced at the intimacy implied in her suggestion.

"We'll figure it out," Tegan said. "We're great liars."

On Saturday night before the rave, Tegan and I sat on Christina's unmade bed watching as she tore her clothing from the hangers in the closet.

"This one?" She held a blue hoodie with red cursive across the chest.

I shrugged.

"I don't have clothes for a rave!" She moaned and dropped onto the mattress.

"And we do?" Tegan asked. "Just be yourself!"

This made us crack up.

Christina pulled a hoodie over her head. "I'll wear this."

"We need to call and find out the address," Tegan said.

Christina let out a sigh. The cord of the phone she and her sister, Heather, shared was pulled taut under the crack of Heather's bedroom door.

"I need the phone, Heather!" Christina cried and pounded her fist on the wall. Heather's reply was muffled but unmistakable: "FUCK! OFF!"

This battle was one I recognized well; Tegan and I waged similar assaults almost every night.

Heather's door banged open, and Christina dialed the seven-digit phone number that Jodi had scribbled on my hand at school the day before. She passed me the receiver and moved to head off Heather in the hallway. The line rang until an answering machine clicked over. The message was a woman reading an address out slowly, two times, in mono-tone. I jotted it down and hung up. Tegan checked the bus times, and we zipped up our heavy coats and headed out.

On the bus ride across the city, we nervously discussed the evening's plans. We would arrive at the rave at 10:00 p.m. and meet Stephanie, Zoe, Penny, and Jodi, where they'd introduce us to their friend who would sell us speed. We hadn't done the drug before, but Stephanie convinced us it was better for dancing all night.

When we got off the bus, I heard bass thumping in the distance.

"This breaks a lot of Mom's rules about safety," Tegan joked as we looked around the industrial wasteland we'd entered. At the door, we each handed a woman five dollars and stepped inside. The room we entered was dark. A few figures stripped off coats and stuffed them into backpacks. We moved toward the lights and the music. Down a long hallway lit only by a red exit sign, we passed a restroom crowded with girls and then entered a small room where a DJ was spinning, a single row of lights twirling out of time with the beat. We stepped toward a group of people in the far corner, and I strained to see if it was anyone we knew.

"Do we dance?" Christina asked me, her mouth close to my ear. I shrugged. A few people were dancing, but I was too nervous and sober to join them. I pointed back to the hallway, "Bathroom?" We retraced our steps and entered the bathroom. Sitting on the counter with her back to the mirror was Penny. She was wearing only a sports bra and no shirt, the skin of her chest and neck sparkling with sweat and glitter.

"Hi!" She pushed herself off the vanity and hugged each of us. There were boys there, too. Everyone was using the stalls to distribute and openly consume drugs. Penny directed us to a guy with bleached hair whom we'd seen on the bus.

"This is my boyfriend, Nick," she told us. The metal barbell in Nick's mouth clicked the back of his teeth, causing a heavy lisp. "I hope you girls have a good night," he said, and placed the pills in the palms of our hands. I hadn't snorted anything in my life, but the three of us shuffled into a doorless stall, and on the tank of the toilet I crushed my pills into powder.

"Wow," Christina said. "So, we're doing this?"

"Fuck!" I said. "Yes, we are." I inhaled the pile of dust into my nose like I'd seen people do in the movies. My head shot back in shock, my eyes filled with tears.

Christina crushed her pills and followed my lead. We looked like pros. When Zoe and Stephanie arrived in the bathroom, my pulse raced, and it was hard to know if seeing Zoe was the cause or if it was the drugs. She had her own pills and expertly crushed them and snorted the dust right off the tile on the bathroom counter. I met her eyes in the mirror. She was so confident and sexy that I actually gasped out loud. Everyone seemed to know one another, and there was a friendliness that both soothed me and made me want to dart from the building and back to the bus stop.

"Why are we still in this bathroom?" Stephanie yelled.

We followed her down the hall and into the rave. The entire room seemed to absorb our bodies, and I watched our friends confidently break into movement. I busied myself with my backpack, crouching down for cover. When I finally stepped across the floor, my thoughts raced as I considered—perhaps for the first time since childhood—my arms and how to move them. Tegan, always more confident, had found a rhythm and was chopping at the air with her eyes closed, her feet shuffling a two-step. Some people were shifting their hands into angles and shapes; others were voguing. I swung my right arm diagonally across my body as if pulling a sword from my hip. My feet slid sideways in a motion like the one I used when ice-skating. I had no idea what was happening, but I went with it. My gaze shifted back to Zoe. She moved effortlessly, and the precision of her dancing took my breath away. I relaxed when I realized that I was the only person in the room who had their eyes open. I shut them. I stopped thinking.

There were long stretches of time when the music galloped. Then during swirling breaks of sound, people paused and gathered themselves, or let their hands shoot up above their heads as if reaching for the music in the air. When the bass and kick returned in surging buildups, there were rhapsodic cheers from everyone in the room. Ecstatic samples of ghostly trumpets and familiar vocal melodies screamed from the speakers; short phrases became stuck in my mouth. A hand grabbed my arm suddenly, and it was as if I were being woken from a dream. Christina stood bug-eyed, her nails digging through my sweatshirt.

"I need your help." She dragged me back toward the bathroom. In a stall, she turned and revealed her predicament: a snarl in her hair. Gum.

"How did that get there?" I laughed.

"I need your hat; I can't get it out!"

I removed my hat and stood in the mirror with her as she pulled on the red felt rim, turning it in circles, and adjusted it until it covered the sticky lump. Under the fluorescent light, I looked blotchy, and the frizz of my hair was an ugly halo.

"Ready?" I asked.

She turned and led us back to the main room, but I couldn't quite regain that sense of euphoria that had swept over me earlier, so I found my backpack and slid down the wall to the floor.

"Are you having fun?" Zoe asked, crouching down beside me. Her warm arm pressed against mine. "Yeah, it's really cool," I said. She didn't seem to hear me, so we sat for a long time not talking. "I love that photo of you in your room," I shouted in her ear. "The one of you dancing." She looked at me, nodding. Her unbroken eye contact, her serious face—I wanted to kiss her. My brain turned in a maddening loop. I stood up and indicated I was going to go back to the floor. She didn't follow me.

When the buses started running again at 5:00 a.m., Christina, Tegan, and I pulled our hoods over our heads and walked back to the bus stop. My teeth chattered in my skull, but the rest of my body felt hot. "That was cool!" I said when we were finally on the bus.

"*You* don't have gum in your hair," Christina said, fidgeting with the hardened glob.

"Oh, come on, a mohawk will look great on you," Tegan offered.

Sinking into the seat, I stared out the window of the bus. Zoe's name looped in my mind like a song.

11. TEGAN TEGAN DIDN'T GO TO SCHOOL TODAY

One afternoon while Mom and Bruce were out, Sara and I were rooting around in the storage under the stairs when we found a guitar case tucked between two towers of office supply boxes. I can't remember what we were actually looking for, what item was worthy of trespassing the only space in the house that was designated for Bruce's things. But once we saw the guitar case, we forgot about what we were searching for and that we were breaking his cardinal rule: never mess with his stuff.

"Bruce has a guitar?"

"So weird. I've never seen this before."

"Here," Sara suggested as she clumsily hauled the guitar over her head. "Help me, grab it." She passed the bulky laminate wood case over her head into my waiting hands. Bruce was particular about his things and would notice any slight disturbance to his stuff, so we covered our tracks before we turned out the light and closed the door. We were deferential to Bruce's belongings in a way that we weren't with anyone else's, ours included, and so my heart pounded as we moved the contraband out of its hiding place and brought it to the office. I trailed behind Sara, watching her labor with the long neck of the case as she navigated his gym equipment.

"Careful," I sang behind her.

"You be careful," Sara said.

In the office, she placed the case on the worn gray couch, left over from Bruce's bachelor days, and popped the gold locks along the perimeter. I stood alongside Sara and felt a jolt of excitement flood my bloodstream as the yellow body of the guitar was revealed. It was a Fender. Sara looked at me, twisting her mouth open, raising her eyebrows.

"This is so random," I said. "Why does he have a guitar?"

Sara shook her head. "I don't know. Obviously, he wanted to be a rock star, or he was at some point and never told us."

I reached out and grabbed the neck and pulled it free of the black fur-lined case.

"Wait!" Sara shouted. "Maybe we shouldn't . . ."

"Why not? He won't be home for hours. It's fine. Relax." I folded onto the floor, crossing my legs, and laid the guitar across my lap. Its thick body pressed into my thighs, I wrapped my right arm around it like I'd seen other musicians do a million times on TV and in music videos. Though neither of us had held a guitar before that afternoon, finding the guitar felt exhilarating, and the desire to play it felt instinctive.

At this point in our lives, Sara and I had taken nearly a decade of piano lessons from a grandmotherly woman named Lorraine. We both loved Lorraine, even if we didn't particularly love the piano, or at least not the classical pieces she forced us to learn, or the theory we studied twice a week in her rumpus room. Half of our weekly lessons were spent talking, something Sara and I both liked to do a lot more than playing the piano. I think Lorraine let us chatter because she knew we didn't practice. Eventually, she'd suggest we review whatever piece of music she'd assigned the week before, and my stomach would knot. As I stumbled through it, I would promise myself I'd practice more the next week. I never did. And Lorraine never reprimanded me. She only doled out compliments and tips for how to improve.

"Did Lorraine call your bluff this week?" Mom would ask from behind the steering wheel as we climbed into the Jeep after our lessons.

"No," we'd reply, smugly.

"This is hard," I said, plunking the fingers from my right hand along the strings of Bruce's guitar while my left hand tried to hold the neck in place. The sound it made was less than inspiring.

"No, I think you'd do it this way," Sara suggested after a second, pulling the guitar from me into her own lap. But she had the same result. "We need something to like, play the strings with."

"Like a pick?" I opened the case and found an orange Dunlop plastic pick. "Got one." I handed it back to Sara, sat down across from her, and watched in amazement as she strummed.

"It works."

We smiled at each other. After an hour we carefully returned the guitar to its case and replaced it in the space under the stairs, checking and double-checking we'd left it exactly where we had found it. Neither Sara nor I mentioned finding the guitar to Mom or Bruce that night when they got home. I also didn't mention to Sara that when she went to Naomi's after school in the weeks that followed, I stole the guitar from under the stairs and played it secretly in my room. I don't know why I kept my interest in the guitar a secret from Sara, or why I didn't just reveal to Bruce that we had found it and that I wanted to learn and take lessons. For some reason during those first few weeks, I kept the guitar and my desire to hold it to myself. Instead of smoking pot and falling asleep, I watched MuchMusic quietly in the basement with the guitar in my lap, trying to mimic the shapes I saw Kurt Cobain and Courtney Love making with their hands in their music videos. Slowly, I was able to start holding power chords that didn't sound half bad. And almost immediately, without thinking, I began to hum melodies along with them.

Sara and I had sung in the choir in elementary school. Though neither of us was a prodigious talent, we joined school productions and loved being onstage. I loved lip-syncing along to my favorite bands in my room and longed to stand in front of a mic. But I only ever sang in front of other people if everyone else was also singing: drunk at a party, in the mosh pit of a favorite band, lying in sleeping bags in the tent trailer in Grace's (a friend from the Frenchies) backyard. Never alone.

The only time I could recall having done so was in grade eight when a friend named Dawn called our house. After I finished a long monologue about my love of Green Day, she somehow coaxed me into singing "She," her favorite song. At first, I had laughed nervously at the strange request. Stalling, I tried to figure out if I was being tricked—a reasonable theory since we hadn't exactly been close friends in junior high. But as she encouraged me from the other end of the phone line to sing, I started to warm to the idea.

"Come on," Dawn begged.

"I can't."

"But you have such a good voice," she cooed.

Finally, I agreed. "Alright . . ."

Starting quietly, I mumble-sang the first few lines. As I started to sing, I liked it. I liked the butterflies flapping frantically in my stomach as I managed the notes and the words and worried about what Dawn was feeling on the other end. I liked having an audience. After I sang out the final note, Dawn purred, "Sing it again." I was awash with an untamable desire to perform for her. Her request quenched some part of me I hadn't even known existed five minutes earlier. "Okay," I agreed. And then I sang it again. And again.

I had never created my own songs or original melodies before. But the instinct was there. As the first attempts at original melody snuck out of my throat, I felt high. After that, time flew. I stitched words to the notes ringing out from the guitar with no awareness of the time. It was just luck that I noticed the clock in my room; I'd had the guitar out of the basement for over an hour. Reluctantly I returned it to its case and then back to the storage room in the basement. That night as I lay in bed, I hummed the beginning of the song I'd been writing earlier. In the dark, I felt a glow of purpose as I drifted off.

What I didn't know was that Sara was doing the same thing when *I* wasn't around.

I stopped dead in my tracks on the stairs when I heard her through the closed door of her bedroom one afternoon.

"Tegan didn't go to school today . . . ," she softly sang.

The first notes of her melody made the hair on my arms stand up.

"Left me all alone to play . . ."

It was good.

"Got up, thought everything was fine . . . found Tegan was walking that fine line between schooooooooool and home . . ."

She held the word "school" out longer than the rest, and

I laughed quietly to myself. *Holy shit*, I thought, *she's really good.*

Discovering that Sara was writing songs felt seren-dipitous—almost as magical as discovering the guitar. A few days later I was in my room doing homework when Sara appeared in my doorway. "Do you want to hear what I'm working on?" she asked.

"Yeah," I said. I had no idea how she had known I'd also been playing the guitar alone, and I didn't care. Every moment before that one became irrelevant.

Back in her room, she sat cross-legged on the floor. She started singing the song I'd heard through her door a few days earlier: *"Took her purple shoes when she went back to bed. Could have kicked Tegan in the head. Got to school, forgot my name. Got all flustered, acted lame. Where's Tegan?"*

I burst out laughing.

She stopped. "Bad?"

"No, it's really fucking good."

She played the song a few times, and I clumsily sang along during the choruses. We interrupted each other to make suggestions, and when we finally arrived at something that felt finished, I went in search of a blank tape so we could record it: another instinct.

"Ready?" I nodded to her when I had the stereo aimed at her guitar.

"Yes."

I pressed Play and Record together. We both exploded into laughter.

I hit Stop and said, "Come on. No laughing."

"Okay, I'm ready."

It took a few tries, but eventually, we made it through

the entire song. Listening back after, I couldn't believe how good it sounded. How good *we* sounded.

"Let's try it one more time," Sara said. "Don't sing until the chorus."

That afternoon we were so enthralled by our process we didn't hear when Bruce and Mom arrived home, snuck upstairs, and stood outside Sara's door for who knows how long. But at some point, they knocked, and we both froze in place on the floor of Sara's room. I stood, my legs half-asleep, and unlocked Sara's door. Instead of looking angry or displeased catching us with Bruce's guitar without permission, their faces lit up, not at all upset by our deceit.

"Let's hear it," Bruce said.

Stopping, again and again, tripping through the song, we played them "Tegan Didn't Go to School Today." When we were finished Bruce said, "It's pretty good." And Mom, smiling wide, clapped wildly next to him.

12. SARA HULA-HOOPS AND CHAIN SAWS

Strumming those first chords made the whole body of the guitar vibrate against my chest, sending waves tingling up through my wrists and along the veins in my arms. The weight of the wood felt intimate, touching almost all of me at once.

After we'd been caught shuttling the guitar between the basement and our bedrooms, Bruce gave us permission to use it. Alone in my room, I'd sit on the carpet with my back against the bed, plucking and strumming with my right hand, humming a little under my breath. Sometimes in the morning before school I'd sit with the guitar on my knees and try to remember little melodies I'd thought of before I'd fallen asleep. My thumb was red and swollen from dragging it along the thick ridges, so I cut up the plastic cards in my wallet and made myself a little pile of guitar picks.

The day that I wrote my first song, Tegan stayed home from school, claiming she didn't feel well.

"You're not going to school?" I asked flatly from her doorway.

"I'm sick," she said, pulling the covers back up to her chin.

"Can I wear your shoes?"

"Whatever." She closed her eyes.

That afternoon when I came home Tegan was cured of her headache and sore throat. She followed me from her bedroom to mine, flopping down onto the bed.

"Anything interesting happen today?"

"No, same bullshit."

"Did anyone ask about me?"

"Nope, I don't think anyone noticed."

She tilted her head. "Come on."

"Here." I handed her a stack of notes from friends.

"Don't forget to put my shoes back in my closet."

"Yes, yes, your precious shoes."

I reached for the guitar in its case and started strumming chords lightly. I didn't ever sing loudly, or with much confidence, but because I was just joking around, I adopted a kind of British whine, and wailed like a kid might. The words were simple. I was only trying to make Tegan laugh, but they spilled out easily as I shifted between chords.

> Tegan didn't go to school today
> Left me all alone to play
> Got up, thought everything was fine
> Found Tegan was walking that fine line between school
>   and home
> Took her favorite shoes when she went back to bed
> Could have kicked her in the head
> Got to school, forgot my name
> Got all flustered, acted lame
> Where's Tegan?
> Tegan didn't go to school today
> Tegan, I missed you!

"We have to record that!" she said, grabbing a blank tape from my bookshelf. She popped the deck open and stuck the cassette inside, pushing it closed.

"I don't even remember what I sang!"

She pulled a piece of paper from my binder and started writing down what she could remember.

For years we'd been going to see punk gigs on Sunday afternoons at a community center downtown. We never recognized the band names on the fliers but they all sort of sounded the same, so it didn't matter who was playing. There was no cover charge to get in, but you had to bring canned food for the Food Not Bombs hamper outside the entrance. We didn't dress like the kids at those shows, and sometimes in line or just inside the door, I'd see people giving us dirty looks, if they looked at us at all. The regulars gelled their hair into mohawks and moved through the pit like tropical fish you knew were poisonous just from looking at them. Some of the girls had shaved heads with a single row of bangs or sideburns grown long from above their ears. No one was friendly, but we weren't there to make friends. In the main hall, bare fluorescent bulbs flickered greenish light on the linoleum and the bands set up right on the floor where the audience stood. Tegan and I usually threw our bags down against the walls and marched straight to the pit, swinging our arms out at a ninety-degree angle. The inner rings would collapse into violent pushing that we mostly avoided, preferring to just bounce off each other like bumper cars at the edges of the pit. Sometimes after a show, I couldn't even remember what the band looked like, and I'd never felt interested in their instruments. What I loved was the atmosphere, the permission the music gave us to unfurl our insides out.

I was ashamed to think about us playing Bruce's acoustic in front of those snotty punks. Even if we found some way to stand up with the guitar, I felt like my body wasn't shaped right. The women in bands that I idolized had flat chests and electric guitars that they swung around their hips like Hula-Hoops and over their heads like chain saws. If we were ever going to be in a real band, we needed an electric guitar. I'd figure out how to deal with my body later.

The following Friday night, Tegan, Christina, Naomi, and I were making prank calls in Grace's bedroom when we heard her older brother, Daniel, playing guitar and singing in his bedroom. We sank into silence, our ears tilted toward the wall they shared.

"He sounds really good!" I said to Grace.

"He is, right? But he's so shy." Grace looked back toward the sound of his voice, pulling at the two dark braids of hair hanging over her ears.

"If I could sing, I'd be like Courtney Love!" Christina said, standing up and taking a rock star–like posture. She held an invisible mic and thrashed her long blond hair.

"No one should ever hear me sing," Naomi said. "I can't carry a tune to save my life."

Christina collapsed back to the floor, out of breath. "It's hard work being a rock star!"

Grace said, "Let's knock and see if he'll let us listen." She went to her closet and pulled a small bottle of vodka from under a pile of clothes. "But first." She splashed the clear liquid into our Slurpee cups with a mischievous grin. We filed out of the room, standing in a huddle outside Daniel's door, chewing on our boozy straws.

"Danny?" Grace touched the door lightly.

"Yeah?"

"Can we listen?" Naomi asked. I pinched the back of her arm. She turned and smiled, winking at me.

There was a pause and then the click of the door unlocking. We followed Grace into the room. Daniel shut the door behind us and locked it. The blinds were closed tightly, and the only natural light refracted on the floor and wall through a bent piece of plastic near the bottom of the window. Daniel turned on the bedside lamp and lit a cigarette. The walls were covered with band posters and psychedelic artwork. I could smell the skunky weed from the plastic bag near his stereo. I sat on the floor in the corner, next to Tegan.

"We want to hear you play!" Christina, always the bravest among us, blurted out.

"Yeah?" Daniel smiled, revealing a set of small sharp teeth. He pulled his hair from its elastic band and let it fall to his shoulders. He picked up his electric guitar and sat down cross-legged in front of his amp. His fingers were pale and fine, and they climbed on the strings like the legs of an insect. His vocals sounded shredded and strained, then sorrowful and tender.

When he'd finished, Tegan said, "You're really great, Daniel."

His face blushed scarlet. "I'm not that great." He took deep breaths through the filter of his cigarette and blew smoke up toward the closed window.

"Sara and Tegan write songs, too," Christina said, when Daniel leaned the guitar against the amp. Then, realizing she'd revealed a secret, she mouthed "Sorry" in our direction.

"Let's hear one," Daniel said.

"Yes!" Grace echoed, sitting up and crossing her legs.

Tegan and I locked eyes. My heart was racing. Daniel extended the neck of the instrument to me. I put my Slurpee cup on the carpet, wiped my hands on the knees of my jeans. I placed the electric guitar across my lap. It felt like a weapon, sleek and dangerous. I held it to my chest, ran my fingers along the strings. Little squeaks rang out of the amp. Tegan and I had spent weeks writing songs on only two strings. The rest had snapped when we'd wound them too tight. I didn't dare touch the tuning pegs on Daniel's guitar. Instead, I shifted my fingers into a familiar shape, struggling to make use of the extra strings.

I strummed Daniel's pick against the strings and began to sing. I was dazzled by the energy bouncing between the walls. My face throbbed with heat. Every time I made a surprising switch between quiet and loud, sad and happy, the air cracked around us like it had been whacked with something solid. Tegan's voice in the chorus split the song into stereo. *I'm alive! Look at me! She screams, I'm alive! Hello, it's me!* When we finished, I felt tipsy and buoyant. I turned the neck of the guitar back in Daniel's direction, but his hands didn't move.

"Are there more?" he asked.

That night in my bed, Naomi watched me in the near dark for a long time. We lay on our sides facing each other.

"I didn't realize you could do that," she said.

"Do what?"

"You know what," she said, sitting up. "You write and play songs!"

I laughed. "I guess so."

"But how did you learn to do it?"

"I don't know. I just tried, and I could."

I wasn't sure how to explain it. It was instinct but also mimicry. Hold your hand this way, move the other fast or slow, open your mouth and sing.

She squinted hard at me, shaking her head. "You're really good." Long after she had fallen asleep, I lay awake replaying her praise, grinning at the ceiling.

summer 1996

The month of July Dad was house-sitting for our aunt and uncle. He offered to let us stay at the sprawling lake house in southwest Calgary the first weekend of summer without him. The affluent neighborhood where the house was might as well have been a different city; it felt so exotic compared to northeast Calgary, where we lived. We were ecstatic. It was the closest thing to a summer vacation we were going to get.

"Invite some friends," Dad said over the phone. "I'll steer clear, just don't burn the place down."

Sara invited Naomi, and I called and invited Alex.

Naomi had met Alex during the second semester of grade ten. She mentioned her to me one Sunday while she and Sara were studying at our house. "There's this girl in my social studies class that I think would make the perfect best friend for you."

I'd blushed, assuming the suggestion was motivated by the lingering guilt Naomi had.

"I talked to her," Sara said, not looking up from the assignment in front of her. "*Alex.* She has a sexy voice."

"Oh, does she?" Naomi giggled, tickling Sara's side while she did.

I sighed deeply. "I don't know, it feels . . . weird. Like a setup or something."

"It's not weird. I already told her all about you, *and* that you need a best friend."

"I thought you said the Aberhart kids were all stuck up? Snobby rich kids who aren't allowed to come to the northeast?"

"She's not like the other Aberhart kids, she's like us. She's really cool. You're going to love her."

Eventually Naomi and Sara talked me into having a conversation with Alex on the phone. "Just trust me, you'll like her," Naomi said sweetly from next to Sara.

"Fine." I was intrigued.

The following day I was hanging out in my room when Sara yelled to me, "Tegan, pick up the phone!"

"Hello?"

"Oh, hi!"

The line clicked as Sara hung up.

"Hello?" I repeated.

"Hi, sorry. It's Alex. Naomi's friend from Aberhart . . ."

"Oh, hi! Um . . . nice to meet you?"

"It's nice to meet you, too."

We both waited in silence.

"This is weird," I said.

Alex burst out laughing. I liked her laugh.

Staring up at my ceiling and listening to her talk, I found myself relaxing, my shoulders sinking deeper into my bed. Naomi was right—Alex was funny, sweet, not snobby or stuck up at all. We liked a lot of the same music, and she offered to take us to a Value Village in the northwest sometime.

"They have so many striped sweaters there," she said.

"Cool."

After we hung up, I let out a breath of air I had no idea I'd been holding in. I lay there for a minute with the phone off the hook, the receiver still in my hand.

"Tegan, hang up the fucking phone. I need to call Naomi back!" Sara yelled from her room.

"Fuck," I said, floundering to get the receiver back on the hook.

That Friday we met at McDonald's downtown. I spotted Alex as I made my way toward the back corner where she was sitting with Naomi and the Frenchies. Between the waves of shoulder-length brown hair falling loosely on either side of her face was a set of brown eyes rimmed in thick lashes. A bright smile spread as I approached. Balancing the two-cheeseburger meal piled on the plastic tray in my hands, I awkwardly slipped into the plastic booth next to her.

"I'm Alex," she said, extending her hand.

I laughed. "I know everyone else here, so I assumed. But just in case you weren't sure, I'm Tegan."

"Oh, I know," she said seriously as we shook hands. "I can already tell you and Sara apart. You look really different, actually."

"Thank you for noticing." I tugged at the sleeves of my jacket to take it off. She grabbed at the end of the bright orange cuff closest to her and yanked.

"Thanks," I said, blushing.

"I love this," she said, pawing the neon nylon in her hand. "Where did you find it?"

"Value Village."

"Oh, I love it."

Unwrapping the yellow paper from my burger, I asked her about her siblings, school, and speed skating. Naomi had told me she trained twice a day, six days a week.

"Yeah it's a lot," Alex said. "But I love it. I started skating when I was little. Practically at the same time as when I started to walk."

"Wow, how do you have time for homework or friends?"

"I don't." After a pause, she threw in, "But don't worry, I'll make time for you."

And she did.

That winter, Sara and I would meet Naomi on Friday afternoons after school, and the three of us would take the bus to the track Alex trained at to watch her skate. In person, she could be self-deprecating, awkward, nervous. But on the ice, she was confident, at ease, smooth. We'd cheer and wave as she flew past, forgetting for a second that we were flanked by serious sports moms in tracksuits, there to watch their kids build bright futures for themselves. We stood out in the stands in our rainbow sweaters and shapeless pants. But when Alex would finish and change, rushing to meet us by the exit, her own secondhand sweaters and skate shoes exposed her differences from the kids she practiced with. She was more like us than them, and as we bundled ourselves up and pushed into the cold, I felt like she belonged with us, with me. From there we'd take the CTrain with her to a Pizza Hut near her house and sit for hours, eating and talking. Her appetite for details about my life, our school, and the neighborhood we grew up in seemed insatiable. I felt interesting, unique, worthy of study under her curious eye.

"Didn't I tell you she was perfect for you?" Naomi said to me one night on the train back to the northeast.

"She is," I said, turning toward the dark glass to hide the blush rushing across my cheeks.

By spring, Alex called me almost every night. And in the dark, pressed against the receiver, I found it easier to talk to her than anyone I had ever known. She pried without being pushy, unraveling me slowly. Unsatisfied with an answer I might give to a personal question she had asked, she'd laugh and press me to be more honest. Her directness was disarming, and I wanted to be disarmed. Bit by bit, I passed pieces of myself to her through the telephone lines connecting us, and she did the same.

Dad offered to drive the four of us to the southwest. He dropped us off in front of my aunt and uncle's bungalow just before lunch: "You know the number for 911?"

We waved as his gray Honda Accord sped off. Inside the house, Sara and I gave Naomi and Alex a tour. In the days leading up to the weekend away at my aunt and uncle's, I had become consumed with the details: Where would the four of us sleep? Two to a bed? All four in one? Sleeping bags in the living room? What kind of bathing suit should I bring? Could I get away with wearing a T-shirt over it? Would Alex think we were rich because our aunt and uncle were? Would she be disappointed later that summer when she saw our house? How much smaller it was? Would she be horrified when she saw our dad's small two-bedroom apartment? But mostly I worried about Naomi and Sara. How much did Alex know about what was going on with them? And how would two days in close quarters go if she didn't know?

"This is really nice," Alex said as we moved through the airy, comfortable rooms, peeking into closets looking for towels to take to the lake. I offered to carry all the striped towels so I could hide my body and the black suit I'd borrowed from my mom. I tossed them down and dove into the water as soon as I could.

"Nice form," Alex said from the dock when I surfaced. She cannonballed in, and we exploded into laughter when she popped up next to me.

We swam all afternoon, self-consciously sunning ourselves on the wooden deck; the paint was peeling off and it left tiny ticks of brown on our suits.

"In the winter we come here and skate the whole thing," I said, pointing toward the horizon from the dock later. "There's a clubhouse on that side of the lake. And they make a skating rink in the winter and serve hot chocolate."

"That's really fancy."

"Yeah, our dad always jokes that it's the one day a year where they let us 'poor folks' in." I blushed as I said it. I didn't want Alex to think we were poor, even though compared to our aunt and uncle we kind of were.

"My uncle's family took my dad in after his mom abandoned him," I explained. "They were his foster family."

"That's so sad. How old was he?"

"Eleven or twelve, I think," Sara said.

"Awful." Naomi shook her head. "Your dad is so sweet. I like him a lot. He's funny. He talks to you guys like you're adults."

"Wait until you meet Sonia," she continued. "She's so cool. She doesn't even seem like a mom."

It was nice not to feel like the third wheel; with Alex there things felt balanced. It felt easy, relaxed between us all. That night we ordered pizza and then applied aloe vera to our sunburned skin and fell into a tired quiet as we watched *My So-Called Life* in the sunken living room, our tanned limbs stretched out in front of us. As the sun slipped behind the trees and the room got dark, Sara stood and wordlessly headed toward the guest bedroom. Naomi followed. My stomach lurched.

"Have a good sleep," Naomi called over her shoulder. Sara was already out of sight.

"Should we stay out here?" Alex asked, confused. "Or . . . follow them?" We'd been to sleepovers at Alex's and Christina's quite a few times. But those group sleepovers were crowded affairs where everyone packed into sleeping bags on a bedroom floor together. I wasn't sure what we should do.

"I'll get sleeping bags from the basement. We can just stay out here if that's okay?"

"Fun."

I felt relieved to be past what I had worried might be an awkward moment. But the second the light was off, the energy between us shifted.

"Is it hard for you?"

My stomach dropped. "What?"

"You know, Naomi and Sara."

"Which part?"

"That they . . . do that. Leave you."

"No," I answered quickly.

Alex stayed quiet. I felt compelled to explain further, but was terrified to reveal Sara and Naomi's secret, especially when they were just down the hall. I felt loyal to them. But I also felt torn, because I didn't want to keep anything from Alex. I labored over what to say, then realized she'd fallen asleep. I knew I would eventually tell her everything. I needed to unburden myself. I hadn't realized how heavy the secret weighed on me until someone had asked.

Alex didn't bring up the subject of Naomi and Sara after we went home. I wondered if maybe all the awkwardness and tension that night had just been in my head. Then Alex left for Japan with her family for the rest of July. She promised me that the second she was back she would come over for a sleepover.

"I promise. I *have* to see your room before you move."

The month Alex was away with her family crawled by. I was stuck babysitting my little cousin Ashley and was back to feeling like the third wheel with Naomi and Sara. The two of us fought more than we had in months, and I felt miserable in their company without Alex to balance things, and even more miserable when they stayed at Naomi's to avoid me. But, as promised, the second Alex was home from Japan, she made plans to sleep over. Naomi came, too, and we waited anxiously on the front lawn for her to arrive. Ushering Alex into the house after her mom dropped her off, we dragged her on a tour and eventually landed in my room, where we spent hours looking at photo albums.

"I love this one," Alex said, slipping out one of me at seven, hamming it up for the camera in a green T-shirt on a camping trip. "Can I take it?"

"Of course," I said, blushing. I would find a way to replace the missing photo later. Bruce kept the albums meticulously organized in his basement office.

Mom took us to McDonald's for dinner, and after, around the table in our kitchen, we played songs on the vintage jukebox my grampa had restored and drank Coke from large mason jars as we extracted information from Alex about her trip to Japan. None of us had set foot off the continent, so we sat in rapt attention as she dispensed even the smallest details of her trip.

Before bed Alex pulled a necklace from her backpack. It was a Japanese coin on a nylon string. Pulling down her shirt collar, she showed me the duplicate she wore; she'd crafted them herself. "They're best friend necklaces," she said proudly.

I watched myself blush in the mirror as she tied mine around my neck. "I love it, thank you," I said, flinging my arms around her.

Though I had known since Naomi had first mentioned her that we were supposed to be becoming best friends, we'd never said the words until that night. I would have never dared to say them first and I felt happiness gushing inside me as I played with the coin around my neck. It had taken sixteen years, but I finally had a best friend of my own.

"Should we sleep in my bed? Or downstairs?" I asked after we'd changed into pajamas.

"Your bed," Alex said, tossing herself onto it as she did. "Oh my god, I've been dreaming of this famous bed of yours. It *is* the most comfortable bed ever."

I turned out the light and climbed in next to her. And then I told her everything—how hard it had been to lose Naomi and Sara, how confusing, how lonely. How I had hoped Kayla might become my best friend again when school started, but then she hadn't. When I cried, she held my hand, and when I stopped to find the right words, she waited. As we talked I felt the weight I'd carried all year lift from my body. Later, after we fell silent and Alex fell asleep, I realized Mom had been right. What I had needed all along was a best friend of my own.

Naomi and I spent the summer before grade eleven sleeping at each other's houses five or six nights in a row. My body pulsed with an urgency to touch her. If I woke in the night and found she wasn't near me, I'd slip across the mattress and curl around her in the dark. When we were apart, I felt heartsick, preoccupied with all the ways she might die before I saw her again. There were no more discussions about if she *was* or *wasn't* into me, no more panic attacks that we had to be "just friends." The more time we spent together, the less time she had to *think* about what we were doing.

At sleepovers, comments from our friends about who was going to sleep where sent bolts of strange electricity down my arms. "Sara and Naomi will *obviously* take the bed," someone would say, smirking. If Naomi suffered from their gossip, she didn't show it. She even started to hold my hand when we were out with our friends, swinging it for everyone to see. We were in love.

In the final week of August, the new house in Renfrew was nearly finished being built. It was a long, skinny house with hardly any back or front yard. "Modern" was what Mom called it. Tegan and I spent weeks covered in dust, sanding baseboards and painting shelves in the closets. We didn't mind pitching in, especially when the painters were there. We sucked in the fumes to get tipsy while we worked, laughing and singing so that our voices echoed through the house. After work Bruce took us down the street to Peters' Drive-In for burgers and slipped us each a twenty-dollar bill. Sitting at a picnic table in the parking lot, throwing French fries at the seagulls, I felt happy. This was our new life.

The night before the move, the workshop benches in the garage were stacked with boxes, half labeled in Bruce's capital letters, and the other half in my mom's bubbly cursive. Tegan's bedroom had been packed up for months. Mom had requested she make the walls "less crazy," but Tegan had gone overboard, removing so much of herself that it turned the space into something institutional.

"I said to clean it up and make it look *normal*," Mom said when she saw what Tegan had done.

Naomi and I finished packing up my bedroom. All that remained was the guitar and my mattress. We spread out on it, soaking up a few more hours until she had to go to work. I played her my new songs, and then some silly lyrics, trying to make her laugh. I adored the way she pursed her lips and focused intensely on my face while I was performing. She was my favorite audience. She pulled the guitar out of my hands and we lay on the bed, facing each other. I had a bad habit of staring over her shoulder at the red numbers on my alarm clock, calculating the time that remained.

"Stop looking," she said, covering my eyes with her hands.

"Maybe you can call in sick?"

"I can't."

"But I'll die if you leave."

Her face scrunched up. "I have to tell you something." She sat up, resting on her elbow. "I got accepted into an exchange program. I'm going to live in Montreal for three months next year."

I'd become so accustomed to her surprise attacks of guilt

about our sexual relationship that when I realized that she wasn't breaking up with me, I felt light-headed with relief. I pulled her back down onto the bed with me.

"You're not upset?"

"No."

"I didn't want to say anything until I knew for sure," she said. "I didn't think I'd actually be accepted."

"What about your parents?"

"They're fine about it."

"What about Christina?"

"I've only told you so far."

I was struck by how afraid I would be if it were me transplanting to a city where everyone spoke a different language, where I didn't know a single soul. I thought about Tegan and the way she'd suffered at leadership camp in elementary school, the daily phone calls home during which she couldn't stop crying. After each telephone call, I'd curl into the fetal position on the couch, immobile, devastated that I couldn't do anything to help her.

"Aren't you afraid to go alone?" I asked.

"No, I'm excited! Plus, I'll be with the exchange student, Isabelle."

I'd failed to consider the stranger that would complete the exchange. Isabelle was set to arrive in Calgary at the start of the school year and would live at Naomi's house. I imagined the hours they'd spend together on the bus, traveling to and from school, speaking together in a language I didn't understand. A hollow feeling opened up in my chest.

"We're never going to see each other."

"Of course we will." She curled up against me.

"I just don't get why you would do this." My eyes watered with tears and I pushed my palms against my face.

Naomi sat up, pulling my hands off my face. "Please, don't cry."

"You said that Aberhart was a *great* school!"

"It is." She stopped. "It's not about school. I want to experience something *new*."

I twisted away, turning my back to her.

"Nothing's going to change between us!" she said, moving closer to me on the bed. "We'll write each other letters and talk on the phone!"

"That's not enough."

She pressed her face onto my shoulder. "It has to be," she whispered.

The next day, after the moving truck was empty and had pulled away, Mom, Bruce, Tegan, and I took to our corners of the new house, tearing open boxes and scurrying with our belongings from shelf to shelf. Tall stacks of flattened cardboard were bound in the garage next to dozens of black garbage bags stuffed with bubble wrap. I loved the newness of the house. It smelled like paint and plastic, and a chemical scent wafted from the carpets. A clean slate.

The walls of my bedroom were painted lilac, and the carpets were a deeper plum, colors that Tegan and I had been allowed to pick for ourselves. I flopped down onto the bare mattress and stared up at the ceiling fan I'd helped Bruce install the week before. There were three huge windows, and a walk-in closet with another window in it, that looked out onto the street. The room was big enough for a couch, a TV, a stereo, and the electric guitar and amp that Mom had bought us as an early sixteenth birthday gift. It was the best bedroom I'd ever had.

In Tegan's room, I stood in the doorway as she dragged her mattress from one wall to the next, searching for the perfect spot. She always picked the smaller, darker room. Examining the wooden bench seat near the window, we agreed it would be a terrific place for us to hide drugs. She'd already marked up her ceiling with glow-in-the-dark stars.

"Is Naomi sleeping over?" Tegan asked, flopping down onto her bed.

"I don't know, maybe."

"Alex told me Naomi's going to Montreal next year."

That Tegan and Alex were talking about Naomi gave me an off-balance feeling in my legs.

"Are you sad?"

I shrugged. How could I explain how afraid I was that Naomi might meet someone else without acknowledging the fact that we were dating?

"Alex told me there's a French girl coming to live with her."

"Yeah," I said. "I hope she likes the same music as us."

"And the same drugs."

I laughed.

When I'd told Naomi my worries that Isabelle was going to be a stuck-up preppy girl who'd figure Naomi and me out and tell on us, I'd hoped she would dispel my fears. Instead, I'd watched her face stiffen as she considered for the first time the risks this living arrangement might pose. In junior high when rumors about girls kissing other girls at sleepovers spread through the school, I immediately felt implicated. It wasn't me at the center of the drama, but it could have been. There could be nothing worse than being called a lesbian.

Especially if you were one.

GRADE ELEVEN

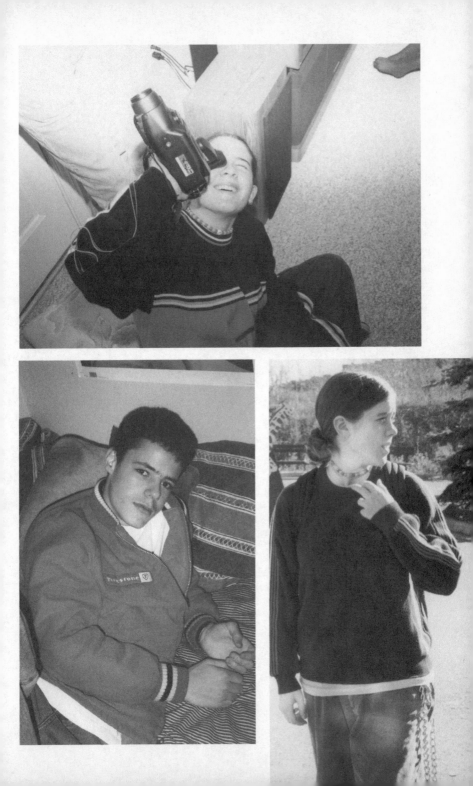

It was a ferocious start to the school year. Bruce was ornery, constantly stomping around the new house with his tools and muttering about stuff that still needed to be done; he was generally disruptive when he was awake. He and Mom were testy with each other, and it wasn't uncommon to wake up to Mom asleep on the couch in the living room. In the basement, Bruce would play U2 as he worked out in his gym, while on the main floor Mom would blast Melissa Etheridge and Sarah McLachlan on her jukebox.

While a gender war raged in the bottom two floors of our house, upstairs on the second, Sara and I were creating an unhappy cacophony of a different kind. Slamming doors and cranking our music to drown out each other, we fought over the usual stuff: clothes, friends, chores, who was going to carry the guitar to school and back. But now we also bickered in our rooms over which songs needed more work and which ones we should record. We accused each other of hogging the phone and using up the prime hours in the evening. We wore in the new wooden stairs of our house racing up and down them from our rooms to tell on each other to whatever parent happened to be home, when one was. Blaming each other for everything and anything, nothing was sacred.

The one place we experienced a reprieve from all this fighting was at our dad's. We'd never fought in front of him in all the years we'd been going to his house. No matter what was happening between us at home, when we got to his apartment, Sara and I put it on the back burner for the twenty-four hours we were with him. It was easier to get along with Sara at his house; I grew up feeling like with Mom, we were at home, but at Dad's, we were guests. He provided meals and entertainment, clean linen, and towels the way a host would. And like polite visitors we walked on our tiptoes, replacing items we used in their precise former positions, as if a cup out of place would throw the whole balance of the apartment into a tailspin. If Sara and I did disagree, we did it in hisses, not howls. Digging our sharp elbows into each other's forearms while his back was turned, we'd stifle cries so he didn't catch us disagreeing. Though he had never raised his voice, let alone a hand, to us as we were growing up, it was the mystery of what might happen if we misbehaved in front of him that made us work so hard not to provoke him. He was gone before we were five, and that ingrained in us a desire not to upset him, or risk making him disappear again. We adored him, and since his time with us, like ours with him, was in short supply, when we were visiting him we were ideal children who always got along. Until one Saturday that fall early into grade eleven.

Sara and I had been having a quiet disagreement in the living room while we thought Dad was out of earshot. Out of nowhere he appeared, grabbed both of our sleeves, and forced us to our feet. Stunned, Sara and I allowed ourselves to be walked to the front door of his apartment, where he shoved us both out into the hall. Our backpacks were already lying there waiting for us.

"Don't come here if you're going to fight," he said simply, then let the door close in our faces.

"What the fuck do we do now?" Sara asked me, lifting her backpack from the floor.

"I don't know. We can't go home. Mom will be pissed." I swept my bag up off the floor and onto my back. "Come on," I said to Sara after a few seconds. "Fuck this. Let's go to Christina's."

In Christina's living room we joked about what had happened until we shifted into the kind of laughter that becomes explosive. We gasped for air, holding our sides as we laughed.

"Imagine if Mom did that—threw us out every time we had a fight? We'd have to set up a tent in the backyard, permanently, to live in," I said.

"And she'd have to live out there, too," Sara said.

"It's like they're afraid to parent us," Christina commented of our dads. Her parents were recently divorced. "Without our moms, they're lost. They can't deal with conflict. They have no clue what to do."

When we got home Sunday, Mom didn't mention it. Dad hadn't called to tell her, or to figure out where we went. I felt simultaneously relieved and hurt. The next weekend he turned over a key to each of us to his apartment. "You can come over anytime you like. Even during the week if you want to get away from your mother, or each other. And you don't need to come on the weekend anymore. Go hang out with your friends if that's what you'd prefer. Your Saturday nights can be yours. But when you do come to my house, I prefer that you don't fight."

At first, I palmed the key excitedly, imagining the weekends I'd now have to spend entirely with my friends. It made me feel guilty, but I was glad I might not have to give up every single Saturday night for the rest of high school to sit with Dad and Sara in his apartment watching *Golden Girls* when I could be at Grace's drinking, or at Alex's watching movies in her basement. But then I considered that his time with us, already limited to one twenty-four-hour period a week, had just become less certain for him. I realized he wasn't simply giving us a key, he was giving up his time with us. As he'd done that past weekend when we'd argued, rather than parent us, he was sending us out into the hall again. I felt sorry for him then. I knew I'd probably return the next Saturday with Sara, and we'd go back to getting along, even if we were just faking it for him.

A few weeks later, Sara and I were rushing out of Mom's house with our guitar to go to school when I realized, only after I'd already pulled the back door closed, that I didn't have my key.

"Fuck," I said, grabbing the handle of the guitar and racing to catch up to Sara.

"Forget the key?"

"Yeah."

"Well, I'm going to Zoe's after school." Sara shrugged. "So, *you're* going to be locked out alone."

"Fuck." On the bus I dug around in my backpack, hoping I'd find the key after all. Instead, I fished out the one to Dad's apartment.

Mom worked until midnight, and Bruce had hockey that night. So, after school, Spencer drove me to Dad's. When I got there, I called him at work. "I'm here. I hope it's okay."

"That's why I gave you the key, babe. You don't have to apologize. See you at six thirty."

While I waited for him, I put on *Oprah*. Padding around his place I opened drawers and cabinets I wouldn't have normally if he were there. Snooping through the apartment, I pulled out a pair of red Converse I'd never seen him wear, still in the box in the front closet, and slipped them on my feet.

When he got home, it felt novel to have dinner alone with him, to talk about my day without interruption from Sara, to pick what he and I watched on TV before bed without having to negotiate with her. I called Alex at ten when she was finished with practice, long after Dad had gone to bed.

"It's amazing here," I told her. "It's like I'm an only child."

"Are you allowed to be on the phone?" she asked.

"Yes," I answered with equal amazement.

"Wow."

I felt strange climbing alone into Sara's and my bunk beds in the only room we'd ever shared there. When Sara stayed at Naomi's, her stuff, her room, and her energy had a presence that permeated Mom's house even in her absence. But at Dad's, all Sara and I had was each other. Though it had only been a few hours since I'd seen her, I realized I missed her a bit as I lay there in the dark.

The next morning, Dad gave me a ride to school with the guitar.

"Thanks, Dad," I said, jumping from the cab of his truck.

"Love you, babe."

"Hi, Teegy," Sara shouted as I walked up to her and our friends in the hallway before class. "Was it so fun being at Dad's during the week? What was it like?"

"Oh my god. It was amazing. He ordered pizza and went to bed at nine. And he said I could talk on the phone as late as I wanted as long as I got up at seven."

Sara shook her head in disbelief. "Oh my god, don't tell Mom that. She'll call him and make him change the rules."

We both laughed. Later that week, Sara went to Dad's without me.

Naomi and I had only been having sex for a few months when she suggested that we write down our sexual fantasies. She'd brought the first note to my house after school, telling me, "Do not read it until you're alone." After she left, I locked the door to my bedroom and paced around with the paper pinched between my fingers. Do I read it on the bed, the floor, in my closet, at the desk? Should I crawl out the window and read it in the park? Should I set it on fire? I settled on the chair and unfolded the paper while my pulse pounded in my eardrums.

No one's home so I invite you over. When you arrive, we decide that we're pretty hungry so we order food. The pizza man says it'll probably take about one hour. While we wait, I start kissing your body all over, paying close attention to "that place." The doorbell rings but neither one of us gets up cuz suddenly we aren't all that hungry for pizza. We both agree that a shower would feel great. In the shower, not surprisingly, we don't rest. We still go at it making each other feel unbelievably good. When we get out of the shower, we decide we're kinda hungry now so we each have a piece of chocolate cake. We have it all over each other and then lick it off. Good cake, especially the icing. We return to my bedroom still making each other feel wonderful. We fall asleep in each other's arms, naked.

Later, on the telephone, she asked, "Did you like it?"

Her voice made my whole body shiver.

"Yeah, it was cool," I said.

"Oh no. You hated it."

"No! I didn't, it was exciting."

"You owe me one now."

"I don't know what to write!"

"Anything!"

"I think you should write me another, so I know exactly what you *want*."

In her second letter she'd made a list of everything I did during sex that she liked. And there on the page was evidence that I possessed a knowledge of *how* to turn her on and proof that I did so regularly.

> #1 When you touch me in certain areas and then pull away, you make me want it so much more.
> #2 Put my hand somewhere on your body, that way I know what you like.

Those words vibrated through me like she was right in the room with me. I reread the note dozens of times. And when she called me to ask if I liked it, I was totally honest.

"Very much," I said.

"Now you really owe me!" she said before we hung up.

But I couldn't push beyond the frame of what we'd already done without feeling a rush of fear. *Sometimes I imagine your drama teacher is watching us when we have sex*, I wrote in my wobbly handwriting, then tore the paper into pieces, my face flaming hot. That was my fantasy. I wanted a witness. A year later, we finally had one.

Stephanie and I were in drama class when she handed me a folded piece of paper. I took the note from her, studying it briefly. I didn't need to open it; I had practically memorized both sides, the crease of the folds were soft with use.

"I read the whole thing," she admitted, brushing her hand over her shaved head. "It was jammed under the cushion of the chair you gave me."

"Oh." I swallowed, though my mouth had gone dry.

I'd given Stephanie the overstuffed chair from my bedroom when we'd moved at the end of the summer.

Stephanie's eyes bugged out. "Do you do that stuff for real?"

I shoved the note in my back pocket. I looked down at my feet.

"You don't have to talk about it," she said quickly. "But, you *can* if you want to."

I tried to ignore the panic welling up in my body. "It's nothing. We were just joking around."

"Whatever," she said, and returned to studying her script.

Stephanie was a notorious keeper of secrets. Friends were always making confessions to her. She didn't take advantage of what she knew, didn't ever gossip. But in this case, I felt like she had something on me. That the power dynamic between us was irrevocably changed.

I was ashamed I'd carelessly exposed Naomi's fantasies. Though the words in the note weren't mine, they implicated me as much as they did Naomi. The paper in my pocket felt contaminated. I felt like I was carrying pornography.

Throughout the day I compulsively patted my jeans to make sure it was still there against my thigh.

Once I arrived home, I returned the note to the cardboard box in my closet. I pushed it farther into the darkness and covered the whole box with a mound of clothes.

The ring of the phone sent me shooting across the room.

"Hello?" I said as I gasped for breath.

"Hello?" Tegan called out at the same exact time.

"Hi," Naomi said. "I have both of you!"

"I've got it!" I yelled into the air.

"Sorry that my sister is such an asshole, Naomi," Tegan said and hung up.

I waited to be sure that she was off the line.

"Hello?" Naomi said. "Did I lose you?"

"No, I'm here. You won't believe what happened." I lowered my voice, imagining Tegan with her ear pressed to the wall listening in.

"What?"

"Stephanie found one of the notes you wrote me last year."

"Which note?"

"Where you talk about your fantasies."

"Oh *god*, did she read it?"

"She read it."

I closed my eyes, waiting for her response.

"It's no big deal," Naomi said.

"Really?"

"It's obvious we're more than friends. Stephanie's not an idiot."

"So, you're not mad at me?"

"No! I just feel gross, like, she probably thinks I'm some sex-crazed weirdo. We used to be so into each other."

"And we aren't now?" I asked.

"It was different then."

And just like that, I knew we were drifting apart.

My next thought knocked the wind out of me: what I'd felt for Naomi the previous year, I'd feel again someday, but for someone else. It was like realizing for the first time that we all eventually die.

Before Halloween Emma called and asked flat out if I liked Spencer. I was not someone who gossiped about liking boys. In fact, I repelled such talk. The histrionics girls displayed for boys was a mystery to me. I just couldn't relate. So, I avoided all discussion of it. Which was why I was caught off guard. This was no casual inquiry from Emma. We didn't do boy talk. She was the nucleus of the Abbeydale crew, had grown up next door to Spencer, and was clearly calling inquiring on behalf of *him*.

"Yeah . . ."

"Is that . . . a yes?" I heard her husky laugh in my ear.

"Yes." I pressed my face into my pillow.

It's happening, I thought after we hung up. *Spencer's finally going to ask me out.*

Spencer and Kayla broke up in the second semester of grade ten. They remained friends, but eventually Kayla got a new boyfriend, gravitating to a table across the student center where he and his friends ate lunch. After that we saw her less and less, but in her absence, and with her blessing, Spencer and I grew closer. In the spring he briefly dated another girl from the Abbeydale bus stop named Corrine, but after they broke up, he started calling me more and more. After Spencer got his driver's license, Bruce agreed to let him drive Sara and me to school. And then over the summer, we hung out in the free time we had between his part-time job as a welder's assistant at the dump truck shop and my baby-sitting job watching my cousin Ashley.

I felt things change between us one afternoon when he offered to come along with Ashley and me to the wave pool. When we got there, we both admitted shyly we didn't want to wear our bathing suits in front of the other, so we paid Ashley's entrance fee and sent her in alone.

"I feel bad," he admitted. We were standing in the viewing deck suspended over the pool. "She looks so small."

"Yeah, I feel bad, too," I said as I watched Ashley's tiny frame hopping up and down in the crowded waves alone below. After a long pause, I added, "Maybe you should go in and swim with her? I can just watch from here."

"No fucking way."

We both cracked up, and he pushed me toward the edge, then pulled me back and threw his arm around my shoulders. He held me against him for a long time. My harmless crush, which had simmered throughout grade ten, began to boil.

Even though we lived within walking distance to school now, on the first day of grade eleven, Spencer offered to pick up Sara and me.

"My dad's letting me take his sixty-eight Mustang today. This one time only."

After that, it just became a thing. Whenever he drove us, I always sat in the passenger seat up front. And if I went to a friend's house or was busy after school, Sara would walk home. When we went to Denny's, Spencer sat next to me in the booth, pressed against my arm, even when we were the only two in it. For once I didn't avoid the intimacy sprouting up between us the way I had in the past when a boy seemed to like me. Convinced Spencer was different from other boys, I embraced the affection and familiarity that formed between the two of us that fall. I accepted the seat he saved at lunch for me, excitedly took the phone calls we had before bed, and when our friends joked that we were acting like we were dating, I didn't argue with them.

After Emma called, every second felt like the second before Spencer might ask me out. But he didn't ask for nearly another month. It was an unusually nice Sunday in October. He took me to the Crescent Heights student parking lot to teach me to drive standard. Placing his paw of a left hand over my right hand on the stick shift between us, I attributed the awkwardness of it to learning to drive and put it out of my mind as he patiently directed me through the impossibly difficult series of steps of shifting from gear to gear.

After, we sat in front of my house talking, leaning against his dad's maroon Nissan Maxima with our jackets off, letting the sun warm our skin. *This is the moment*, I thought. *It has to be.*

"I should get the car back to my dad."

I fiddled with my jacket impatiently and leaned in through the open window on the driver's side of the car. "Thanks for the lesson."

"Tell Bruce I taught you to drive standard. He'll be so impressed."

"Technically I still can't drive standard. I stalled it, like, a million times."

"Right," he said awkwardly, not making eye contact. "Don't tell him that part."

"I won't. See ya."

"Bye."

Upstairs in my room, I tried to start my homework, but

I felt deflated. I thought for sure he was going to ask me out. It had been weeks since Emma called. What was he waiting for?

Sara yelled, "Tegan, pick up the phone!"

"Hello?"

"Hey, it's Spencer."

"Sara, hang up."

We waited until we heard the click.

"Miss me already?" He chuckled but then didn't say anything for what felt like too long. *Come on*, I thought. "So, what's up?" I finally said.

"Yeah, so, um . . . I was wondering if you wanted to like, go out?"

"Go out?"

"Yeah, like . . . be my girlfriend?"

I squeezed my eyes closed and took a sharp intake of breath. "Obviously, Spencer. Duh."

"So, that's a yes?"

"Yes, it's a yes. Finally."

"Finally? I mean, you could have asked me out if you liked me all this time."

"No way," I said. "I wanted you to do the work."

"Right. Well, okay, cool. I guess I'll see you tomorrow? I can pick you and Sara up."

"Okay, thanks."

"Cool, see you at five to eight."

"Cool. Okay, bye."

"Bye."

Sara was already at my door. "Did he ask you?"

"Yes."

I blushed when she yelled, "Spencer asked Tegan out!" down the stairwell toward wherever Mom and Bruce were.

"Get out."

"You get out," she said, slamming my door.

I opened my books, smiled, snapped my pencil against the page, and sighed with relief. It was done.

The next morning, I sat in the passenger seat up front by Spencer like usual. Sara climbed in the back. During the drive, he didn't go for my hand, and I felt glad. It would have been weird since it was just the three of us in the car. At school as he locked his driver's-side door, Sara beelined for a group of our friends standing by the smoke doors. "Thanks for the ride," she called out, not looking back.

"Yup," he said. Then he reached out and took my hand, lacing his thick fingers through mine and smiled down at me. I felt self-conscious when he did; my fingers almost immediately fell asleep, they were so small compared to his. His hands felt rough, and as we walked toward our friends, the relief I had felt about finally being together escaped slowly, like air from a balloon. Standing around with our friends, my hand still dangling in the grip of his, something about the act of public intimacy felt false, performative. As our friends teased us, saying things like "Finally" and "I knew it," I didn't feel the obviousness of our connection the way they seemed to and as I once had. As our friends asked us questions about our new relationship, I was filled with ones I couldn't answer. The loudest was most familiar: *Why doesn't this feel right?*

Zoe cut her hair, and my feelings escalated from a harmless crush to obsession. Sitting behind her in English class, I wanted to run my hand along the soft buzz cut from her neck to the crown of her head. The urge became impossible to ignore.

"I like your haircut," I said after class. Zoe's eyes, so bare and scrutinizing, reflected and absorbed my gaze.

"Thanks." Her right hand drifted up to her neck. "My mom said I look like a dyke."

A wrenching feeling twisted in my stomach. "You don't look like a dyke," I said.

She shrugged. "I'll see you at lunch," she said, then sped off in the direction of the stairwell. I stood briefly at the big glass windows that looked down into the student center, hoping to catch a glimpse of her.

At lunchtime, I joined our friends in the school's main hallway. Diego, who'd started hanging out with us so he could flirt with Stephanie, brought a stereo from home, and we crowded around it like it was a fire, talking loudly over the music. Diego and his friends wore tracksuits, clean white tank tops, and sneakers buffed like new. He collapsed to the floor and began rotating himself expertly in circles, his legs and hips moving impossibly under his arms. I'd never seen anyone break-dance in real life; a crowd of students curiously watched him from a distance. We forced a bottleneck in the hallway, and students attempting to get by had to pass in single file.

Zoe arrived and sat down next to me, dropping a folded note into my lap.

"I drew you something," she said. "It's stupid."

I unfolded the page and saw an inky sketch of abstract swirls and ornate letters. My skin hummed. "Thank you," I said. "I'll do one for you this afternoon."

"Are you going to the rave on Saturday?"

"We're still trying to convince our mom to let us." That wasn't true. She'd actually forbidden us from going. She didn't understand that raves were the safest place for people like us. There were drugs, yes, but that fact produced none of the violence or risks she always warned we'd find there. Without gangs, or girls looking to start fights, or adults chasing us out into the cold, we could be ourselves. I loved those woozy nights of laughter and dancing, strange music that thrummed in my brain for days afterward. She couldn't keep us away.

The bolder our lies, the more attuned to them she became. It didn't help that she began speaking to our friends' parents behind our backs. Our intentions spread like gossip, and she set a trap for us.

She agreed to let us sleep over at Naomi's that next Saturday, asking us, "Just Naomi's? Not the rave downtown?"

We shook our heads no, assuring her that we were just going to a sleepover. Maybe to Denny's for coffee beforehand, or to listen to music at Stephanie's.

"If I find out you went to the rave, I will ground you for the rest of your life," she said one final time. Tegan and I pulled our backpacks over our shoulders and waved goodbye to her from the front door.

At curfew, Tegan called Mom to check in. She told Mom casually that we'd just finished a movie and might start a second. After she hung up the receiver, we waited for the return call, something Mom did from time to time, to check that we were where we said we were. Downstairs, Naomi promised her parents that our mom was well aware of our plan, and confirmed we'd be home at sunrise.

Spencer picked us up and drove us through the deserted streets downtown to an old hockey arena. Inside, a make-shift floor covered the ice rink. Drum and bass ricocheted off the domed ceiling. We'd spent time there as kids, watching Bruce playing goalie on Sunday mornings. When we were in junior high, he'd paid Tegan and me to run the scoreboard during weeknight games. We stuffed our bags and coats behind the penalty box and did a lap of the arena floor. Tegan and Spencer planted themselves in front of the subwoofer and smoked a joint, letting the vibration from the bass bounce their skulls violently against the boards. Naomi and I went looking for our friends.

"You made it!" Zoe said into my ear. She and Stephanie were dancing in a crowded locker room.

"Aren't you hot?" Stephanie asked, tugging at my sleeve.

I tried to imagine removing the thick hoodie I was wearing but knew that in a T-shirt I'd feel too self-conscious to dance. I pushed up the arms of my sweater to my elbows and hoped that would suffice. Warm house music oozed from the speaker, a respite from the battery of sound in the arena. Dancing in that small space, a feeling I'd lost in adolescence returned to my body. I was exactly where I wanted to be; I was happy. It occurred to me then that other people in that room might have lied to their parents in order to be there, might have stolen from their wallets or pockets to pay the admission. These thoughts comforted me.

Later, I watched Naomi swallow down a speed pill in the dark, hoping the drug wouldn't cause her to freak out the way she had after we'd shared a joint in her brother's bed. But, after I was high, it was me who was stricken with paranoia. My crush on Zoe felt magnified. The compartments in which I kept my feelings became distressingly overlapped. I withdrew to the edges of the room and danced alone.

At 6:00 a.m., when the lights came on without warning, the floor was revealed to be black with footprints and debris. Naomi's and Tegan's skin appeared green under the fluorescent bulbs. Outside in the parking lot, headlights blinded us as we searched for Spencer's car.

"I hope the battery's not dead," Spencer said as he sucked hard on a cigarette. We jogged to keep up. The cold air felt like glass in my lungs. In the back seat Naomi and I wrapped ourselves together, shivering.

"So cold, so cold, so cold, so cold," Tegan said, her teeth chattering.

When the car was warm, I nodded off against the window.

In Naomi's bedroom, I was too tired to even take off my coat. Tegan lay right on the white carpet at the foot of the bed, pulling the hood of her jacket over her head and face. Naomi's habits were too hard to break, and she took a shower and brushed her teeth. I was already asleep when she crawled under the covers next to me.

We were woken up by knocking at the door. Naomi's mom popped her head in. "Girls, your mom is on her way here to get you."

I looked at the clock. Had we slept hours already? It was only 8:00 a.m.

Tegan rose from the carpet.

"Shit." I pulled the covers over my head.

In the Jeep on the way home, my head felt swollen and my ears rang. In the daylight I still felt stoned, the drug jerking at my limbs and playing tricks with my eyes. Mom's silence unnerved me. I expected yelling, or an interrogation. She hadn't yet said a word to either of us.

As we turned onto our street, I saw the reason for her silence, the true symbol of our punishment. Dad's truck was parked in front of the house. His own father had died when Dad was only a child; he'd been driving while intoxicated. Dad had once made us sign a contract promising we'd never use drugs or drink. He kept it in an envelope on his coffee table. I couldn't bear to look at Tegan, too afraid to see my fear reflected.

Inside the house, Dad was sitting in the living room, his winter jacket unzipped. No one said a word, but once our shoes were off, we knew to sit across from him on the couch. Raves were a big part of the reason we'd stopped going to Dad's on Saturday nights. It was clear to me then that our deceit had hurt him, too.

"Do you want to tell your dad what you did?"

"We went to a rave last night," Tegan said. It looked like she was trying not to smile.

"Weren't you told that you were absolutely not allowed to go to raves? So, you *lied* to me and went anyhow?" she said.

"Yes, but—"

"There is no 'but.' You *lied*. You stayed out all night, you made Naomi lie—her mom is furious, by the way."

"Everyone we know is allowed to go to them!" I said.

"You're not everyone!"

"But they're safe. There isn't even alcohol!"

"Do you think we're stupid?"

We both stared back at her blankly.

"Do. You. Think. We're. Stupid."

"No, we don't think you're stupid," Tegan said.

"We know they don't sell alcohol there, but there are plenty of drugs to shove in your face."

"Nice," Dad said sharply. My blood ran cold.

Before Mom could respond I said, "It's not about drugs; we like the music. Dancing with our friends."

"I don't care what you like about it. Your father and I are not comfortable with you two lying and staying out all night."

"I'm very disappointed in both of you," Dad said, pulling the zipper on his coat up to his throat.

I felt ashamed, but defiant. Like we'd been tricked into doing the very thing they knew we would do.

"You're both grounded. For a month, at least," Mom paused. "And no phone, no allowance, no guitar, no stereo, no TV. And you're not going to bed. I'm not having you sleep all day."

"What are we supposed to do, just stare at a wall?" I asked.

She lifted her hand and pointed behind us. "Do your job."

Our "job" was a flier route that earned us each eleven dollars a month. We usually dumped the bundles in bins or hid stacks in our closets or in Tegan's bench seat in her bedroom. But on that hellish morning, we completed the route for the very first time, delivering a rolled bundle to every mailbox in the neighborhood. The rhythm and sound of our shoes cutting fresh prints through the snow in our neighbors' yards put me back into a trance. When the load lightened, I found myself slowing down, prolonging the punishment I deserved.

19. TEGAN YOU WON'T BELIEVE
WHAT HAPPENED

We arrived at my aunt Vivienne and my uncle Marty's house in Marietta, an affluent neighborhood a short distance from Atlanta, just before midnight a few days shy of Christmas. Along with Mom's parents, and her brother and his family, we descended on the house with a mountain of suitcases stuffed full of Christmas presents. I had mostly dreaded the holiday, preferring the comforts of home and proximity to friends to two weeks in one house with our entire family. But as I pressed into the grand entryway of their house, I felt like we'd entered a movie. Taking in the sweeping staircase and its banister lit with a million white lights, I watched as Mom embraced her sister and their mom, their eyes filling with tears. I felt some of my bad attitude dissipate. Maybe the holiday would be magical after all?

"You two are in the playroom," my aunt said cheerily to Sara and me. She was decked out in a black designer tracksuit with shoulder pads and elf ears on her head. She guided us through the kitchen and pointed us up the back stairs.

"We won't have any privacy," I whined to Mom when she came to deliver towels.

"Or our own bathroom," Sara added from atop her air mattress.

"Too bad," Mom said. "Would you prefer the basement with your four cousins? They're all sharing one room, but they have a bathroom down there. I can tell Vivienne to put you there instead if you like."

I rolled my eyes. "No."

"Then stop complaining and get in the Christmas spirit."

Putting her finger to her temple, Sara let off an imaginary round of ammo as Mom spun and walked off to find Bruce. As we unpacked, our cousins swarmed the room like locusts. Their incessant chatter and giddiness only grew louder when I pulled out the video camera I'd brought along.

"Oooh," my cousin Ashley, who'd also flown from Calgary, squealed. She pressed her face against the lens. "Can you see me?"

"Stop," I said, and pushed her back with a palm to the face. "Back up, you're making it fog up."

Seconds later, Caroline, who had thick glasses and nut-brown, shoulder-length hair tied up in a messy ponytail, appeared in front of the lens. The middle child of Vivienne's girls, she lifted their family cat into the frame and said, "This is Muffin," with great seriousness. "She hates to be picked up."

"Hi, Muffin," I said, zooming in on the black cat, who looked nonplussed.

Caroline's sister Madison, the baby of the family, bumped into the frame with a gray and white gerbil and placed it on Muffin's back. "This is George," she said, her glasses slipping off her nose, her short hair framing her pixie face.

"GET IT OFF HER, MADISON!" Caroline screamed, alarming both Muffin and George. "SHE STINKS! GET IT OFF HER NOW!"

The gerbil squirmed between Madison's tiny fingers, its sharp, protracted claws grazing the black fur of a now squirming Muffin, whom Caroline was trying to hang on to.

"MADISON!" she screamed a second time. Madison

lifted George, and Caroline fled with Muffin still in her arms up the hall. Madison and George followed, with Ashley close on their heels. Sara and I were finally alone in the playroom and could finish unpacking.

"It's like *Home Alone*, but instead of the McCallisters it's the Albertsons," I said to Sara, pressing my hands around my neck and pretending to squeeze.

"I *wish* we'd been left behind."

The next morning at breakfast our aunt announced a family trip to Target to shop for last-minute gifts. Christmas Eve was the following day, and we all excitedly donned Christmas hats and piled into the vans parked on the garage pad.

The second Sara and I were over the threshold of the store's automatic doors, we sprinted away from the rest of our family, tucking our festive hats in the ample, deep pockets of our baggy pants.

"Come back!" Madison and Ashley yelled.

"Oh my god, they have it," Sara cheered, holding up the self-titled record from the Murmurs, one of our favorite bands, in the music section.

"And it's only eighteen ninety-nine!"

"What did you find?" Bruce asked from a few aisles over.

"*You suck*," I said to Bruce, straight-faced as I ducked into the aisle with the CD.

"What did you say?"

"Relax, it's the Murmurs' big song," Sara said, motioning to the CD.

He threw his meaty forearm around my neck and pretended to suffocate me in the aisle.

"Do it," I said. "Save me from the rest of the holiday."

"No way, we're in this together," he said, releasing me.

On the van ride home from the mall, we played "You Suck" on repeat. By the time we pulled up to my aunt and uncle's house, we had our littlest cousins singing,

> *Right now, there's dust on my guitar you fuck.*
> *And it's all your fault.*
> *You paralyze my mind, and for that, you suck.*

In the fading afternoon light on Christmas Eve, Bruce admitted to me, on camera, that the men had gone to Hooters for lunch while out running errands. Around us, Mom and our aunts immediately jumped into attack mode.

"Grampa," I said, zooming in on him amid the chaos of voices. "Whose idea was it to go to Hooters for lunch?"

Eventually, from behind a soap opera magazine he'd suddenly taken an interest in, Grampa grumbled, "Marty. He suggested it."

"Oh sure, blame the *one* guy not here to defend himself," my uncle Henry, Ashley's father, snorted.

"Oh, I'm sure it was him that suggested it." Vivienne laughed about her husband from her spot on the couch next to Mom.

"The Georgian Pig was *closed*," Bruce said, exasperated. He looked at me pleadingly, as if I could somehow undo this. I laughed from behind the camera.

Vivienne rolled her eyes. "Did you see the closed sign, Bruce, or did Marty just tell you that?"

"They have good wings," Grampa said.

"Would you like it if Madison or Ashley were using their tits to sell Hooters wings?" Mom asked.

At the mention of their anatomy, the cousins, who'd been

uninterested in the conversation up to that point, started giggling.

"I've been to Hooters," Gramma answered, defensively. "The food's nothing to write home about. I don't see what the fuss is about."

"The *fuss* is that the women have to dress in a certain way to sell the food." I zoomed in as I said it.

"And men go there to watch them do it," Sara added. "It's *gross*."

"I didn't even want to go," Bruce said, almost shouting now.

"Were you kidnapped?" Mom asked, not looking up from her book, refusing to meet his eye. Beside me, Henry snickered.

I looked over and saw Grampa was asleep. His superpower was napping through conflict.

"Look at that Roseanne on TV," Gramma said. "In her bra, she's so gross." My Gramma's superpower was deflection.

"Gramma," I scoffed. "Hello? Double standard?"

With us distracted, my uncle and Bruce jumped up and left.

"Can't stand the heat?" Vivienne asked as they fled.

Most arguments in our family ended this way, with the men fleeing, claiming the women were too emotional to have a rational conversation. But the older I got, the more I saw the men leaving as irrational, and the women's emotions as the only sensible reactions. From the women, I learned to speak up about the things that were important to me. To brandish my emotions with pride. My voice mattered.

Sensing Sara and I were restless, missing our friends back home and going slowly crazy, Mom and Vivienne suggested a shopping trip downtown to spend our Christmas cash. Only Sloane, our twelve-year-old cousin, Vivienne's oldest, was invited along. The three younger ones cried when the trip was announced and they were told they'd have to stay back with Ashley's parents, our uncle Henry and aunt Lynn.

"Oh, come off it. You hate shopping," Vivienne said to Caroline and Madison.

"Let them go," Aunt Lynn said to Ashley. "We'll make cookies here instead, girls," she said, gathering up the kids.

I waved with delight as my aunt Vivienne backed the van down the driveway, and I saw the kids in the front window. Their sad tableau made us all laugh.

"Downtown, here we come," my aunt shouted as she aimed the van toward the Atlanta skyline.

As Sara and I scoured store after store in Little Five Points, a hip neighborhood my aunt had found for us to shop in, we looked for things we would never find in Calgary: Bugle Boy sweaters, JNCO jeans, indie records of bands we'd only heard of but never actually heard.

"I remember when you two hated shopping," my aunt said after a few hours, all of us weighed down with plastic bags full of our purchases. "Do you remember how we used to have to pay you to dress up for family photos?"

"Yes, and you'd still have to pay me to wear a dress," I told her.

"I don't think either of us imagined you two would be the kinds of girls who'd like shopping," my aunt said to Mom. "Hey, Sonia?"

"God, no. They were just like their dad. Impossible to shop with. It was a nightmare taking them to get school clothes every year."

"Think of all the money we saved you," Sara said. "Can you buy me an extra shirt today to make up for it?"

"No," Mom answered.

Before dinner Sara and I walked the runway, a small stretch of space between the TV and the coffee table, modeling our new clothes for Gramma, Aunt Lynn, and the cousins who'd stayed back.

"How was the big adventure downtown?" Uncle Marty asked Sloane after dinner.

"It was fine."

"Did you buy anything?"

"No way. The stores Sara and Tegan like are weird."

"You're weird," I teased her as I passed, taking my plate to the dishwasher.

"I saw a girl with pink hair," Sloane added.

"Interesting." My uncle chuckled.

"Yeah, and she was kissing another girl."

My heart stopped. Everyone in the kitchen froze in place. Next to me at the sink, my aunt Vivienne was totally still, a plate in her hand stopped under the stream of water from the tap.

The first to speak was my uncle Marty. "Where was this?"

"Junkman's Daughter," Sloane answered.

"*What* is Junkman's Daughter?" my uncle asked, twisting his blond mustache, his face already turning a bright shade of red.

"A store Mommy and Aunty Sonia took us where they play loud music, and Sara and Tegan bought striped sweaters."

As Sloane prattled on to Aunt Lynn and Gramma, Uncle Marty turned to my aunt and narrowed the space between himself and her. "*Vivienne*, where were you when this was going on?"

She kept rinsing dishes and stayed silent, choosing to ignore him. I slunk away nervously.

"*Vivienne?*" When he spoke her name, it sounded like he was spitting out a sunflower seed.

"Oh Marty, stop being such a prude," Aunt Lynn said, dropping a dish in the sink as she passed.

I gathered placemats from the dining table and noticed every man who wasn't Marty eyeing the door, plotting his escape.

"*Vivienne*, what kind of place did you take our twelve-year-old to today?"

"It was just a clothing store, Marty," Mom said, annoyed now.

"Stay out of this, Sonia. I want to know where my wife was and why she wasn't protecting our daughter."

"Protecting her from what? Gay people?" I came alive. "Seriously?"

"*Calm down*," Mom mouthed at me. Behind her, Bruce looked on with interest.

I felt hot. As if the screws holding the hinges of me together were about to come loose. "*Why?*" I mouthed back at my mom.

"*Vivienne*," Marty hissed for the tenth time.

"*Marty*," Mom hissed back at him. "You're starting to show your true colors."

As they argued back and forth, Gramma asked Sloane if she knew what it meant for two girls to kiss. Sloane answered, "Of course, Gramma. It's no big deal."

"Exactly," I shouted. "Apparently a twelve-year-old is the only open-minded person in this family. Why is everyone acting so messed up about this? We've been watching violent movies for ten days. Marty, you take your kids to Hooters. How is Sloane seeing two girls kissing such a big deal?"

In the corner, Grampa joked to Uncle Henry, "Well, the women don't kiss at Hooters. Wouldn't mind, though." They chuckled. I felt sick.

"The girls are not a big deal," Marty answered, annoyed. "It's that Vivienne wasn't there, that my daughter was seeing . . ." He was almost purple in the face by this point. My aunt was still silent.

"Seeing *what*?" I was yelling now.

"ENOUGH!" Gramma yelled, stunning us all back into silence. "That's enough now. We're playing cards and you men are going downstairs; the conversation is done. No more talk about this. Right, Sloane?" She said it cheerily, but I knew Gramma was upset.

"We've been banished, men," Uncle Marty announced, grabbing his beer and darting for the basement stairs, Uncle Henry and Grampa close behind. Bruce was the last one out; he threw a sheepish, resigned look at me over his shoulder as he did. I shook my head, disappointed. Why hadn't he spoken up? Why hadn't Vivienne? Why had it felt like the entire family was tossing around a hot potato? For once the women *had* banished the men. But I felt angry they had. I wanted Uncle Marty to answer for his discomfort around homosexuality. Discomfort I could see in him because I had felt my own earlier at the store when I had seen the girls. They'd been holding hands when we walked in, and I'd felt personally exposed by the act. Though I suspected plenty of girls in my own life to be carrying on with each other behind closed doors, seeing it in the open had made me want to hide. Seeing my uncle's fear, my own returned. What were we all so afraid of?

Our last afternoon in Atlanta, Marty came to the playroom where Sara and I were reading on our air mattresses. "You girls want to call your friends, wish them a happy New Year before the party?"

It felt like an olive branch, and I took it.

"Yes!"

"Got a pretty good long-distance plan—your mom and Vivienne sure can talk."

"Thanks," I said, hopping up and racing toward his office. With the door closed behind me, I called Alex. "Oh my god. I miss you so much. You won't believe what happened. Sloane saw two girls kissing."

20. HOMOSEXUAL

For their French 11 health class, Naomi and Alex created a project called "Les Homosexuels." In a series of interviews, they asked family, friends, and other students about homosexuality. Sara and Tegan agreed to be interviewed for the project. This is a full transcript of the interview.

NAOMI: Okay, the camera's on!

(Sara and Tegan both look to the camera, smiling.)

ALEX: *(From off camera)* Do you know or associate yourself with any homosexual people?

(Everyone laughing)

SARA: As much as possible.

(The tape stops and starts multiple times.)

ALEX: Okay, it's back on.

(Laughing)

ALEX: Do you know any homosexual people?

SARA: Yeah.

ALEX: Do you ever feel uncomfortable around them?

SARA: No.

(Tegan turns and looks at Sara, smiling.)

ALEX: Would you ever ask them or talk to them about their sexuality?

SARA: No.

TEGAN: Yeah!

SARA: *(Looking at Tegan)* What?

TEGAN: *(To Sara)* We do!

ALEX: *(To Sara from off camera)* You wouldn't ask them questions or anything?

SARA: *(To camera)* Normal questions about life, yeah, but not, "What's it like to be gay?"

ALEX: Okay.

(Silence)

SARA: *(To camera)* It's just a normal part of life, you know? I wouldn't want to exclude them or make them feel different in any way.

(Discomfort visible on Sara's and Tegan's faces)

SARA: *(To Alex)* Are you okay?

ALEX: Yeah. What do you believe causes a person to become homosexual?

SARA: *(Turning to look at Tegan)* I believe that they are born that way.

TEGAN: *(To Alex)* What an asshole!

(Tape stops and starts again.)

ALEX: Do you know any homosexual people?

(Laughing)

ALEX: *(To both Sara and Tegan)* Fuck you.

(Tape stops and then starts again.)

ALEX: Do you know any homosexual people?

SARA: Yeah.

ALEX: Do you ever feel uncomfortable around them?

TEGAN: No.

ALEX: Would you ever ask them or talk to them about their sexuality?

TEGAN: Yeah.

SARA: No.

TEGAN: Yeah!

SARA: No.

TEGAN: *(To Alex)* We would.

SARA: *(To Tegan)* No, we wouldn't. Maybe you would. I don't.

TEGAN: We do! We do talk to people about it. *(To Sara, quietly)* What are you talking about? We do.

SARA: *(To Alex)* Can you give an example?

ALEX: Just like, maybe ask them, I don't know, about experiences about being homosexual? Or like, effects that it's had on their life. It doesn't necessarily have to be like a sexual question.

TEGAN: Yeah, we have.

SARA: No, we haven't.

ALEX: I don't necessarily mean a sexual question, like "What's it like to have gay sex?" or something. Just ask them about their homosexuality.

TEGAN: Yeah. Generally.

SARA: We've come to a consensus. Generally, we may talk about their sexuality.

ALEX: What do you believe causes a person to become homosexual?

SARA: Born!

ALEX: You think they're born that way? You don't think it has anything to do with environment or life experience? We've had a lot of answers about like, um, people saying, like, bad experiences with men.

SARA: That doesn't necessarily mean you're gay. It might mean you don't like the opposite sex.

ALEX: Okay. Based on your upbringing how do you feel about homosexuality? Like, based on what you've been taught.

TEGAN: Open-minded about it. My mom's always had lots of gay friends and stuff, so.

SARA: Tegan's gay.

(Tape stops and starts again.)

ALEX: How do you feel about slang such as "faggot" or "dyke" toward homosexuals?

SARA: I think that it's mean, it's like using a racial term.

TEGAN: Yeah, you might as well be calling someone . . . I won't say it, but to me, it's the same thing.

ALEX: Okay, racial. Do you see a difference in our society in the acceptability of gays versus lesbians? Can you explain it?

SARA: *(To Tegan)* You be the boy. Typical boy, ready? What do you think of gay people and stuff?

TEGAN: *(Pitching her voice low)* It's gross! It's gross! It's nasty, man! It's nasty, gross! Girls are okay!

ALEX: *(Laughing)* Why do you think guys feel that way?

TEGAN: They're really close-minded about it. They get all freaked out that people are gonna think they're gay. Like, asking two guys to kiss each other . . . girls do it all the time, but guys are all concerned everyone is going to think they're gay. I don't think girls care.

SARA: *(Straight to camera, Naomi)* Some girls care. But they're gay, too.

TEGAN: *(Surprise annoyed face, mocking voice)* Everyone's gay.

ALEX: Do you think that homosexuality has become a trend in the artistic world?

SARA: No.

ALEX: Do you believe as teenagers we're old enough to know about and understand our sexuality?

SARA: No.

ALEX: A lot of adults hear about a teenager deciding that they're gay, or thinking that they're gay, or worrying that they're gay and they'll be like, "Oh, they're just confused. There's no way they're old enough to understand."

SARA: They might know, but they might not have had the experiences to know what exactly they decide for their life or whatever. It is trendy to be, in some groups of people and in some different areas, it's trendy to be bisexual or be experimenting or whatever. But, that's not necessarily how you live your life.

TEGAN: Plus, lots of people come out at forty. You can change your mind. That's one of the things that people should be encouraged not so much to say, "I'm straight or I'm gay." You can be anything you want. You shouldn't set yourself that one thing and say that you're going to be that 'cause when you're forty, coming out of the closet will be a more traumatic experience for you.

(Sara smiles at Tegan.)

TEGAN: What!

(Sara grabs Tegan and kisses her on the cheek.)

ALEX: How would you react if you discovered that a homosexual was attracted to you, had a big crush on you?

TEGAN: Compliment!

SARA: Rock on.

TEGAN: The coolest thing I ever heard was a guy say, "Not only do girls like me but guys like me." I think that's a cool thing to say. If someone finds you attractive, who cares who they are. That they can find something good about you, that's great.

ALEX: Do you see homosexuals as having a stereotype?

SARA: Yeah.

ALEX: What do you think the stereotype of them is?

SARA: Guys are supposed to be all girly and not mannish, and girls are supposed to be boys.

TEGAN: And butchy.

SARA: *(Pitching her voice down)* Into sports and stuff.

ALEX: Do you ever think or worry about your sexual orientation?

(Laughing)

SARA: No.

TEGAN: No, I was just going to say how different it must be because you get up to all the stereotypes, you get up to all the people who hate you, you get bashed in public, not seen as a citizen, you don't have the same human rights. But every day you get up, and you continue to go out with this person, or you continue to live that life. Can you imagine doing all those things just for this one person or just for your sexual orientation? Maybe they don't choose it, but that they actually choose to be open about it. If you're doing all that stuff for one person, who would walk away from that? Who cares? Here's this perfect person, but I'm going to walk away from them because I'm too afraid? If you're really going through with it, putting up with all that stuff, who would turn away from that? That would really be love.

21. SARA MY GIRLFRIEND HAS A BOYFRIEND

"I don't want you to go," I said.

"I'm going to write you a letter on the airplane and I'll send it as soon as I land in Montreal," Naomi said, wrapping her arms around my neck. She left me one of her favorite hoodies and a few of her T-shirts. I thought of my mom at boarding school when she was a teenager, burying her face in a sweater her mom knit for her, desperate for the faintest trace of her mother's scent. I spread Naomi's hoodie across my pillow at bedtime, closing my eyes and imagining that we were together.

Naomi promised we'd speak on the phone after she'd settled in, and a few days later she called my house, describing in exuberant detail the Montreal suburb that she now lived in and all the new friends she'd made. She told me that Isabelle was being an amazing host, and then Isabelle took the phone and told me in her broken English how much her friends loved Naomi. Listening as they flipped the phone between them, I felt my first pang of jealousy.

When her next letter arrived, scattered through the pages of her swirling cursive was a name: Frederic. *"Isabelle's boyfriend brought his friend Frederic to the party! . . . Frederic and I went downtown and got tattoos! . . . I slept at Frederic's house last night."* The letter burned in my hands, a betrayal. Even more distressing was the short stack of photographs that she'd tucked inside the envelope. In one, Naomi's arms were draped across the chest of a thin boy with ratty blond hair, her lips planted in a kiss on his chalky skin. Frederic.

Christina confirmed what I feared: "Naomi's got a boyfriend already."

"I know. She sent some photos of him," I said calmly. I wanted to burn them all.

When I next talked with Naomi over the telephone, she admitted that she and Frederic were having sex and that she was on birth control. She told me these details unashamed, as if I were her best friend, which I was. But she said it like I was *only* her best friend. If she felt bad about cheating on me, her voice betrayed nothing. Everything I'd feared had come true. Naomi was having sex with a boy. She was irreversibly different from me.

"You there?" She paused. "I miss you."

I was determined to hide how deeply I was hurt. Silence swallowed me whole.

"My phone card is going to die, it just beeped."

"But we just got on the phone!" I said.

"I know, I'm sorry. We can talk longer next time."

As I pulled the speaker from my ear, I heard her say, "I love you!" Another twist of the knife in my heart.

I drank myself blackout drunk at Grace's house the following Friday. On Saturday morning a lightning bolt of pain woke me up.

"You fell," Tegan told me when I asked what happened to my wrist.

She and our friends filled the gaps in my memory with embarrassing details. I'd broken a wine cooler; I'd run away.

They'd found me in the park down the street, hands bleeding, smoking a joint with a group of boys none of us knew.

I walked across the hall to the bathroom and tried to pull my clothes off without moving my left arm. I climbed into the shower, finally letting myself cry as the water poured down over my skinned knees. Pulling my shirt back on, I noticed in the mirror that there was puke caught in the tangles of my hair. I removed as much of it as I could using toilet paper and my one good hand.

"I tripped," I told Mom over the phone. "We were running to 7-Eleven."

This was the story I rehearsed with Tegan before dialing our home phone number.

"Don't give her too many details," she told me. "Just act like it was no big deal."

"I think it's broken," I said, using Tegan's script carefully.

"Really?" She sighed.

"Yeah."

"Okay, I'll come grab you."

Tegan stood in the front window like a worried dog watching for Mom's Jeep.

"You sure you don't want me to come?" she asked when Mom arrived.

"No, it'll be fine."

I stepped out into the cold air without saying goodbye to the rest of our friends.

"See you later," I said, closing the door.

"Good luck," she called after me.

I climbed carefully into the car, wincing when the seat belt brushed my injury. I started crying as soon as the door was closed. Warm tears spilled off my chin and onto my winter coat.

"So, tell me again what happened?" she asked, pulling away from the curb.

"We were going to the store to get chips and we were just racing each other, and I tripped on the sidewalk."

"Why didn't you call me last night?"

"I just thought maybe it would feel better in the morning."

When we stopped at the first red light, she turned and faced me.

"You sure you weren't drinking?"

"No, we were just running. It was stupid," I said.

"You look white as a ghost."

There was something so specific about the comfort I felt when Mom took care of me. She pressed her foot to the gas, ran through yellows like an ambulance, and pulled into the parking lot of the hospital like I was bleeding to death.

Only when the doctor rolled the final piece of fiberglass over my wrist a few hours later did I realize how impossible it was going to be to play guitar.

"Let me wash your hair," Mom offered when we got home from the hospital.

"Okay." I carried the green apple shampoo from our bathroom down to the kitchen sink.

She leaned my head over the porcelain, twisting my hair in her hands under the stream of warm water.

"I used to do this when you were a baby," she said.

"Smells like spaghetti sauce down here." I inhaled deeply, trying not to cry.

Upstairs, I crawled into bed with my clothes on. I hugged the cast to my chest. I wished I could have my entire body encased in one. I felt hurt, inside and out. The lingering feeling humming at the center of my hangover was fear. The black holes in my memory from last night unnerved me. What would have happened if Tegan hadn't come looking for me? What the fuck was I thinking?

After a few weeks I could wedge my cast around the neck of the guitar without difficulty. Melodies poured out of me in a terrific wave. I wrote lyrics that sometimes felt too close to the bone. I found it liberating to sing as if directly to Naomi: *You* did this to me. *"You go away, but I'm still here. You lie, but I still miss you. You lie, but I still need you."* To date, my songs had mostly been written about other people, characters, or abstractions. I moved the words I couldn't say to Naomi in my letters or over the telephone straight into my songs.

"Can I hear what you're working on?" Tegan asked one afternoon.

I was embarrassed to play it for her. I realized that, for the first time since we'd starting writing songs, I hadn't designated anything for her to sing. It was important for these words to remain mine, and mine alone.

She sat down on the carpet, and I nervously slid my notebook with the lyrics across to her. She scanned what I'd written, her brow furrowed.

"So which part is mine?"

"The verses will just be me, and maybe you can sing the chorus with me?"

"Okay," she said, underlining the words as I sang them.

"I don't owe you. No, I don't owe you anything."

She quietly mumbled along, getting comfortable with the melody and the timing. When it felt locked in, I stopped playing. "Okay?"

"Cool," Tegan said, smiling. "Then what?"

"I do this next section alone," I said, jumping back into the song.

"That's not right, that's not the way it's supposed to be! That's not right, that's not my destiny!"

I built up the strumming like I was going back into the chorus, but instead I dropped out suddenly, picking single notes quietly on the electric strings.

"I gave up love tonight. I waited up all night, I can't be wrong this time. I waited up and I don't owe you. No, I don't owe you anything."

When I returned to the words in the chorus, I banged out big, distorted chords on the guitar, letting my voice go hoarse. *"I don't owe you! No, I don't owe you anything!"* Tegan joined in, her voice matching my ferocity. We repeated the lines again and again. When we finished, I felt lighter.

When I wasn't working on music, I dialed the phone numbers of my crushes, one by one. When I hung up with Veronica, I called Grace and then Zoe. I felt buoyant and flirty. I loved their voices in my ear, the sugary high of making them laugh, and the quiet, awkward moments when I sensed a secret on their lips. I read my lyrics and poetry into the telephone until I felt high on their attention. At parties I let myself linger too long and too near them in hopes that someone would be as brave as Naomi. And, finally, someone was.

It was a Friday night, and Stephanie was throwing a

party in the basement where she and Penny shared a large double room. Tegan and I liked to bring our guitars with us everywhere we went. Even if we were competing with a stereo and the drone of conversation, we'd tuck away in a corner and play our new songs for whoever wanted to listen. That night Zoe and Diego both leaned up against the wall where we were sitting on the carpet. The heat on my face grew warmer each time we finished, and Zoe was still there listening. It never mattered to me how many of our friends stayed, as long as she did.

"What was that last one about?" she asked me when our guitars were back in the cases.

I shrugged.

"Never mind, it's none of my business. I just liked it."

It was one of the new songs I'd written about Naomi. I wondered if Zoe knew, or suspected something was going on between Naomi and me. Or did the words make her think of a relationship in her own life? I was too shy to ask.

We returned to drinking, dancing together to Björk in the near dark.

With one eye closing, and the room spinning, I headed for the bathroom. Turning the knob, I popped my head into the harsh light. Stephanie and Zoe were sitting on the floor, facing each other. Stephanie's hands were flat on either side of Zoe's face, her thumbs were hooked around each of her ears. They were kissing. I stepped inside the room and closed the door, sliding down hard onto the floor next to them. Zoe leaned awkwardly toward me, slipped a hand around my neck, and replaced Stephanie's lips with mine. Stephanie sprang up and squeezed past me out the door.

I briefly worried that Stephanie might be angry with me for interrupting, when Zoe snapped the fluorescent light off and found my face again in the dark. Twisting my hips, she pushed me down onto the floor and spread my knees, pressing her full weight into me. My head hit the porcelain toilet.

There was a knock at the door, and once again the light overhead was on. Zoe backed off me and pulled us both up in one swoop. We stepped into the dark hallway and I turned toward Stephanie and Penny's bedroom, unsure if Zoe would follow. The bodies of my friends were a blur in the soft blue light. They were dancing near the stereo and I went to join them. My heart was hammering as I swung my arms around their shoulders. I tried to move with the music but knocked the whole group off-balance. Crawling into Stephanie and Penny's room, I passed out on one of their beds.

When I woke up sometime later, there was no movement in the room, and the music was off. Zoe was lying beside me, her eyes wide open, staring at my face. Everything was in focus. Our faces met. She pressed her thigh between my legs, and I felt her hand pull on my zipper. I had wanted this for months. Zoe's tongue was in my mouth, her hand in my jeans. There was no talking, no flirting, no hesitation. But when I woke up in the morning, she was gone.

22. TEGAN   LOOKING FOR A HERO IN ALL THE WRONG PLACES

We met Tess through Leah, a friend from junior high. They went to high school in the southeast part of Calgary, at a vocational school focused more on trades than grades. She brought up Tess constantly, the way someone with a crush finds any opportunity to talk about them every chance they get. The more Leah talked about Tess, the more I wanted to meet her. We finally got our chance in late fall.

I was outside in my socks at Grace's waiting for Leah to drop off some weed for the party. When she finally appeared, she invited us to her friend Rick's house. She told us he was throwing a party. "You guys should come. Tess will be there."

"We have to go," I insisted to Christina when we were back inside Grace's. We were sitting at the long wooden table in the kitchen.

"What's wrong with this party?"

"Nothing, but it could be fun to do something different. If it sucks, we can leave."

"Come on, Christina. We'll stay an hour," Sara interjected. "Don't be such a mom."

"Fine," Christina agreed. "But we *have* to be back for curfew."

Around ten we all headed to Rick's. As we walked through the front door, into the wall of bodies, my eyes were already burning. The air was thick with a mix of body odor and cigarette and pot smoke. The mashed-down green carpet was littered with beer bottles, cigarettes, and guys who looked to be in their twenties. Posters on the walls were half torn and hung at different heights. I felt out of place and *really* young. I was immediately too hot in my army jacket, but I didn't take it off; this seemed like the kind of place where if you put something down, it wasn't yours anymore. "Let's go find Tess."

We found her outside the bathroom at the top of the stairs, with a cigarette dangling from her lips. Her dark brown eyes were friendly, her hair was tied back in a slick ponytail. She wore a mask of dark foundation, and her eyes were rimmed in thick black eyeliner. "FUCK YEAH," she yelled, slamming Leah into the wall in a sort of hug-like greeting as we approached.

"I've heard a lot about you," Tess spit toward Sara and me after Leah introduced us. "This one over here never shuts the fuck up about you two."

"Fuck you," Leah warned. "That's not true."

"What did you say?" Tess pushed Leah against the wall, and the two play-wrestled until Leah yelled for mercy. "That's what I thought," Tess said in a mocking growl at Leah. Sara and I shot each other nervous looks, but we both laughed as Tess started teasing someone else.

People vied for her attention as we trailed behind her, the sea of bodies parting to let us through as if we were famous, untouchable in her wake. I gulped down the devotion for Tess and my beer as we moved past. "Where the fuck are you going?" she yelled from the top of the front steps when she caught us leaving an hour later.

"We have a curfew," I yelled.

"You better fucking come back next week!"

We did. We went the Friday after that, too. And then the one after that.

The more we went to Rick's, the more I found myself bringing up Tess any chance I got, as Leah had before me.

"Someone has a crush," Alex joked one night on the phone.

"No," I said, but I did.

Looking for Tess in every corner, longing to be near her when she was far, I let her grow up around me like a weed. With one arm slung over my shoulder she would move us through the crowded house parties at Rick's as if we were a pair. If a guy got too close to me, Tess would sense it and come barreling out of whatever corner she'd been holding court in. "Fuck off" was all she had to say, and they'd scatter like mice. Eventually our friends stopped going to Rick's with us.

"It's so dirty."

"The guys are old."

"My parents would kill me if they caught me going there."

"I'm shocked you haven't gotten scabies yet from those people."

"It's not that fun."

So Sara and I went there alone. And Tess acted as a custodian, offering attention and protection for us both.

The night Tess turned eighteen, Sara and I needed it more than ever.

"Those bitches are always looking for trouble," Leah warned Sara and me as a crowd of unfamiliar faces arrived just after ten. "Steer clear of them."

Within an hour the girls had pissed off half the party.

After they dumped a slick path of dish detergent on the kitchen floor to create a slip and slide of sorts, Rick had ordered Tess, the resident bouncer, to get rid of them. I'd watched her usher all three out of the kitchen, pointing them toward the front door in a firm but friendly tone. On their way out they tried to shake Sara's hand, but she refused.

"She's got a thing about shaking hands." I raced over to explain when things started to get heated. "I'm her sister. We're *twins*." I motioned to her face and back to mine. "See? So here." I extended my hand. "Shake with me instead."

The tallest of the three looked between Sara and me and seemed okay with the deal I was brokering. She took my hand. "Alright."

I went back to my card game and didn't see the glass bottle hurtling toward me in time to move. When it hit the back of my head with a thud, I flew forward off my seat onto the filthy carpet. Half the party was already on the front lawn by the time someone had helped pull me up off the floor.

"Are you okay?"

"I'm fine," I said, dizzy and dazed, already halfway out the front door to find Sara. On the lawn Tess was slamming punches into one of the girls, who was lying flat on her back in front of her. I searched the dozen or so people scattered in the front yard, looking frantically for Sara. She and Leah were sandwiched between a few of Rick's friends next to where Tess was hitting the girl.

"What's going on?"

"She's the one that threw the bottle at you," Leah answered. "Are you okay?"

"I think she thought you were me," Sara said, wobbly

from alcohol. "Boy, did she pick the wrong person to pick a fight with at this party."

Tess dragged the girl to her feet and shoved her toward her friends. Someone had called a cab for them, and as they staggered away Tess grabbed me by my shoulders and forced me back inside Rick's.

"Are you okay?"

"I think so." I was shaking.

"Fucking bitches," Tess said, but she looked excited, not angry.

"TESS!" Leah's guttural cry ripped through the screen door. Tess dropped her hands and pitched herself through the open door and down the steps. This time I was on her heels.

Everyone still outside was crowded near the cab stopped at the curb. As I got close, I saw all its doors were open; the driver, half in and half out, was yelling incoherently. The three girls Tess had just ejected from the party had Sara pinned facedown on the back seat with their knees. They were punching her back and screaming for the cab driver to "Go!" Tess was next to an open door and had hold of one of the girl's legs, which were kicking wildly. Next to her, Leah was trying to untangle Sara from the bodies on top of her. I could see Sara's cast from her broken arm dangling, unmoving, off the edge of the seat.

"Help her," I screamed.

"Get out of the way," Tess yelled. Leah stepped back, and Tess leaned in the car, grabbed the girl on top and dragged her out, tossing her into the snowdrift behind her like a doll. Then she hauled out the other two. Leah and I grabbed Sara's legs and helped her out of the cab; the driver took off. As we helped Sara across the lawn, I saw Tess swinging brutally at the girls she'd dragged from the car. They were crumpled on the ground, not even bothering to fight back. I felt sick.

"ENOUGH!" Rick yelled from the top of the front steps. "Tess, get the fuck inside before the police show up. All of you get inside. NOW."

"Are you hurt?" I asked Sara when we were back inside.

"No, I don't think so."

"Is your arm okay? Why were you in the cab?"

"Leah and I were helping them to the cab when they pushed me in and started hitting me. It happened so fast."

Someone offered Sara a fresh beer and asked what happened. She jumped up and took the drink and started retelling the story. I felt guilty watching her. I knew I should insist we leave, make her walk with me to Grace's where we belonged, with our other friends, out of harm's way. But I didn't think Tess would be okay with us leaving, and part of me didn't want to. Even after everything that had happened.

"Tess wants you," Leah said, interrupting my thoughts. "She's upstairs in the bathroom. She said to bring her some ice."

Tess was next to the grimy tub, a giant bottle of beer between her legs when I came in. I knelt and dumped the ice into the water, gasping when I saw her knuckles, which were already bruised and swollen. "Fuck," I said. She didn't react. I sat against the bathroom door and watched Tess slide her right hand into the tub. Outside the door, I could hear Leah and Sara telling the story to anyone who would listen. "You're a hero."

"Yeah, a *real* hero," Tess scoffed. After a beat, she looked over at me and gave me a crooked snarl of a smile. I *was* terrified of her, but there was nowhere and no one else I wanted to be with more in that moment.

"Tess said we should bring a guitar over and play at Rick's house this weekend," Tegan said on our walk to school.

"Really?"

I tried to imagine us carrying our acoustic guitar into the bedlam of that house, singing campfire-style on the couch pocked with cigarette burns or the rotten carpet stained with beer. The only music I ever heard coming out of the speakers was thrash punk and occasionally No Doubt, if Tess threw punches and blocked the guys from changing it. I was afraid we might cross paths with the girls who'd beaten me up a few weeks earlier. Tegan didn't seem nervous at all. For once I let her confidence fill me up.

The night we took our guitar to Rick's it was frigid. The kind of cold where every car and bus on the road exhales great plumes of smoke. The hems of our pants dragged under our heels and became soaked and muddied, our feet completely numb. Leah carried the acoustic guitar from the bus stop with her hand wrapped in her sleeve, telling us, "Save your precious fingers," in a monotone.

She was dressed even less appropriately than us in only a hoodie, which she'd tightened around her head and face. When we crossed through the entryway at Rick's, I saw a dozen eyes turn and stare at the guitar case in her hand. We were often razzed by the older boys who hung out there, but the guitar seemed to provoke something crueler.

"Oh-ho!" a guy named Phillip bellowed. "Since when is this a coffee-house?" He reached his hand down to the stereo next to the couch and turned up the volume.

"You sure you know how to play that?"

"'Free Bird'!"

"Play Nirvana!"

"Look at those groupies!"

When Tess came down the stairs, she flipped her middle finger up at them like a switchblade.

"Fuck you. And you!" She leaned in, sneering close to their faces. "AND FUCK, FUCK, FUCK *YOU*!" She finished with her finger dug into Phillip's chest.

They went pale and turned their eyes back to their video game.

Upstairs, Rick sat in the corner of his bedroom, stoned, his skin washed with blue light, his eyes cut like slits across his face. Tess closed and bolted the door. Tegan opened the case, and our friends found spots to sit on the mattress. Rick lit a joint, and generously passed it around. Leah pulled frozen bottles of beer from her bag. Tegan started noodling on the guitar, twisting the pegs, trying to bring the guitar's tuning into focus. Then she started to sing. The jeers and hollering from the boys in the living room rose, but we shifted our bodies closer to hear Tegan's voice. Tess, in particular, seemed transported. The energy that vibrated through her like a seizure all but stopped. She could have been asleep.

While Leah and Sara made awkward small talk on the landing at the top of the stairs at Rick's, I casually pretended to sip my warm beer next to them. Though the blinds were drawn in Tess's room, I could see she was on the bed, facing away from us. The longer she refused to acknowledge us, the more we squirmed. It felt like we were trapped in quicksand with her; a miserable, slow-moving death that had been in progress for about a half hour.

Leah had begged us to come: "One last party at Rick's before the end of the school year."

We had agreed, but only out of guilt.

After the fight at Rick's, Sara had been reluctant to return again. Leah and Tess had convinced us to play a gig and some of our routine returned, but things didn't feel the same as they had before. We instigated a slow disappearing act in the months that followed, showing up for only a few hours, then an hour, then not at all. I made excuses to Leah and Tess when they called.

"We're grounded."

"Alex has a competition I have to go to."

"Stephanie's having a party."

Soon one week turned into four, and then six, and then I lost count of how many weeks had passed since our last visit.

Tess and I had kept talking, though. She had been expelled for fighting and was living at Rick's and I felt bad for her for having to stay there. She'd call after school, and we'd discuss my classes and the books I was reading. She was smart and loved to read. They were the first sober conversations the two of us had ever had, and I enjoyed them immensely.

One night when we were on the phone, I was in Sara's room playing *Mario Kart* when Tess said, "You guys should come over to Rick's. I'm so fucking bored."

Sara shook her head no, but I said, "*You* come over. It's a school night. We can't leave, our parents are here."

"Okay." Then the line had disconnected.

"Shit."

"You're on your own," Sara said, ushering me out of her room and locking the door securely behind her, as if she were afraid.

From the living room window, I watched Tess's shadowy frame hustle up the street just before midnight. I scampered to the front door silently to greet her with a sick feeling in my gut that I'd be caught sneaking her in. I warned her to be quiet in a hysterical whisper on the snowy front porch before I led her to my room. Sitting next to each other on the couch at the foot of my bed, Tess offered me a small bottle of whiskey she'd brought along with her. I shook my head no and fixated on the snow melting off her army boots into my purple carpet. Seeing her in my bedroom, among my things, was discombobulating. I was used to seeing her in the chaos of Rick's house, not the tidy orderliness of mine. Even when she was silent, her presence in my room felt oppressively loud.

"I didn't expect you to live somewhere so . . . nice."

"Oh . . ." I shuffled on the couch, trying to hide my awkwardness. "We just moved here . . . My stepdad, he builds houses . . . He . . . he built it."

"Why the fuck do you guys hang at Rick's?"

It felt like a statement, not a question. I shrugged, hoping not to come apart entirely in her eyes. Did she feel like we misled her somehow? Why *did* we hang out there?

We talked until she finished the last of the whiskey and I suggested we go to bed.

"I have to get up in a few hours for school."

She wore her clothes, and I wore the pajamas I'd awkwardly changed into while she looked away. I could make out the faint sound of her mascara-thick eyelashes opening and closing in the dark, and at some point her hand brushed my leg. I turned over casually, my heart thumping in my chest, and edged myself to the farthest part of the mattress I could without falling off. Neither of us spoke or moved after that. I barely slept, and just before six I got us both up and snuck her out the back door without a word. That afternoon, after the longest day of school I'd ever lived through, I stripped my bed, washing away all evidence Tess had ever been there.

When I told Alex about the sleepover that night, she snickered. "I knew you were into her."

"I'm not."

"She's into you, too."

"No, she's not."

"Who takes the bus across the city to go to someone's house at midnight, drunk? She wasn't bored. You're kidding yourself if you think that's why she came over. Do you like her? Is that it?"

"Oh my god. No. What are you talking about?" I tried to laugh it off. But I flushed and pressed my forehead into the wall beside my bed in shame. All of a sudden everything about me and Tess felt so obvious and I felt so embarrassed. Alex had come to Rick's only once, but she'd been disgusted that we were hanging out there. Like Tess, and now me, she had wondered, "Why do you hang out there?" It sounded to me as if she were saying, *I would never hang out here, so maybe you shouldn't either.* Like a caught cat, I arched my back and skulked away from any mention of Tess after that.

Tess kept calling for a while after the sleepover, but things felt different between us when I would take her calls, which wasn't often. We never addressed the awkwardness that transpired that night at my house or in my bed, just like we never discussed the violence the night of her birthday at Rick's. As the pile of unsaid things between Tess and me grew, her grip on me loosened and I slipped from her hold. Then she stopped calling.

The next time I saw her was in late winter when she and Leah surprised us after school at Sunridge train station and offered us each a tab of acid.

I'd sworn off acid, and so had Sara, after I'd taken a nasty fall down two flights of concrete stairs at the same station a couple months earlier.

Sara had told my parents about the fall that night when they got home. Though I'd been livid that she had told them, she left out the fact that I was on acid when it happened, which I felt grateful about. She watched guiltily from my doorway as Mom and Bruce examined me, asking if I had a headache or any pain when they poked and pressed my back and neck.

"I thought you might be bleeding internally," Sara said later. "If you died, it would have been my fault. If you were me, you would have told, too."

In the mirror later that night I gasped when I saw the plum-colored bruising covering the backs of my arms, legs, and shoulders from the places where I'd hit the concrete stairs as I fell. Alex sounded alarmed when I told her about it, and looked even more distressed the following weekend when she saw the yellowing bruises on my body in person.

"I wish you'd stop" was all she said.

And we had. Like Rick's house, acid didn't seem to fit Sara and me anymore, so we had tried to leave it behind.

That was until Leah and Tess surprised us with the acid. Then we decided we'd do it—one last time.

Sara and I were picky about who we did drugs with, and the second I placed the paper on my tongue I regretted our quick decision to take it with Tess. She didn't have the right energy for acid. In the fading daylight on the bus she seemed cagey and kept saying she wasn't feeling it.

"It takes a bit of time to work," Sara said, rolling her eyes at me and Leah as Tess paced in the aisle on the bus. "When we get to their friend's house, let's make an excuse and leave," Sara whispered to me.

I nodded in agreement.

Inside the guy's house we were told to sit by his room-mates; the guy wasn't there yet. They were watching a hockey game and drinking La Fin du Monde, which was fitting, since our world felt like it was ending. Tess was toddling around with a giraffe Beanie Baby she'd found upstairs clutched in her hand, claiming she still wasn't feeling it. I was peaking, and *definitely* feeling it. Sara called Christina, and, mercifully, an hour later Sara announced we had somewhere to be, and we escaped while Tess was upstairs. As we fled down the front walk toward where Christina was waiting for us, Tess gave chase with the giraffe still in her hand. "Fuck you for leaving me here."

"Sorry," we shouted.

She left me a message the following day letting me know how hurt she was. I was too scared to call her back. We haven't spoken since.

As I waited at the top of the stairs at Rick's, I accepted that things between me and Tess were never going to be okay. An hour of small talk and warm beer later, the reconciliation I was hoping to have with Tess by agreeing to attend Rick's year-end party never happened.

"Sorry," I said to Leah when I heard Christina's booming "hello" through the screen door, exactly sixty minutes after we arrived. She and Grace had refused to come to the party with us, but agreed to come get us after an hour.

"If you try and get us to stay, I will leave you there," Christina warned.

"See ya, Tess," Sara called into the dark room where Tess was still sitting silently with her back to us. Tess didn't respond.

"Nice to see you, Tess," I added weakly, then I turned and walked down the stairs. I felt sorry then that we'd never get the chance to say all those things left unexpressed between us.

As we walked down the front pathway with Christina and Grace, I heard the screen door behind us slam. In the glass of the car parked out front I saw Tess had come outside.

"Go, go, go," I said quietly to the girls, my stomach churning in fear.

"Fucking ditch pigs!" Tess yelled.

Taking my arm, Christina hissed, "Don't look back."

I didn't.

From the other side of the bedroom wall, Tegan's voice climbed notes of a melody, her guitar cutting strokes through each word. I resurfaced from a dream. I could see the song forming behind my eyes—black lines of music as unique as fingerprints. When she returned to the chorus, there was a rush of the familiar and the pleasure of hearing her repeat a hook I had memorized after listening to it only once.

My eyes fluttered open. I stared at the Smashing Pumpkins poster on my ceiling. It wasn't quite life-size, but big enough that I could look straight into each band member's eyes. I leaned off the mattress and grabbed my electric guitar. I bent my fingers back toward my wrist, recirculating blood into the joints before I twisted the volume knob on the guitar halfway. There was a steady hiss of static from the amp. I took my first big gulps of breath and let out a cry between the changing chords. When I finished, my body tingled like it did in the first seconds after a drag of a cigarette.

I heard Tegan outside my door. "Wanna play something?"

"Sure."

She sat down on the couch with the acoustic guitar and said, "I've been thinking. What about calling our band Plunk?" Immediately, I knew it was right.

"Yes," I said. "But what is it?"

We laughed.

"Well, we're punk, but we don't have a drummer so we're kind of—light punk."

"*Plunk.*"

"It's cool, right?" She smiled.

"Yeah, I like it."

We plucked the fattest string on our guitars slowly, twisting the pegs to tune. I bit down hard between turns, anticipating the snap of the oily bronze E string winding tighter.

"Don't break it," said Tegan. There was no way we could afford a new package of strings. If one snapped, we had to play with a gap tooth or replace it with a less important string, which worked but sounded weird. Tegan called out names of songs we both knew. I wanted to ask her about the new song that woke me from my dream, but she bent her fingers into the shape of a power chord and began to crash through the intro to "Smurf Revolution." I slid my thumb along the back of the guitar neck and dug my ring finger into the skinny high E string. As I plucked out short notes with my pinky, my other fingers started to burn. I dropped out as Tegan started the first verse.

"*I stand alone and she knows tomorrow I will go on without her. I know the world we created is fading . . .*" She held a long, raspy "Ohhh" before I joined her in unison, shifting to the chorus.

"*If I hold my breath until I die, I'll be alright.*" I kept my voice slightly quieter than hers because I sometimes lost track of which part came next.

Tegan shouted through the outro, and I tried filling her pauses with the last half of the chorus melody and lyric:

"*She hurts my head!*"
"*I'll be alright!*"

"She hurts my head!"
"I'll be alright!"

When the front door of the house slammed closed, we stopped singing.

"I can hear you two screaming all the way down the street!" Mom shouted up the stairs into the hallway.

"We're practicing!" we yelled back.

We were preparing to record our first album.

The radio broadcasting classroom at school was cluttered with pieces of audio and video equipment; hulking VHS camcorders, drawers jammed with tangled cords and adapters, and shelves of dusty VCRs. It seemed our teacher, Mr. Kim, was uncomfortable letting us girls handle the machines unchaperoned; we weren't afforded the same freedom for our projects as the boys. In the editing bay and at the sound console, he'd often push our hands off the controls and make the desired adjustments himself. If he was too busy to copilot, he'd assign a trusted male student to ensure we didn't "fudge anything up."

Before his class, it had never occurred to me to learn how to operate objects more than superficially. I was impatient with technology, anxious for the result and the pleasure of what they produced more than the accomplishment of understanding how they worked. He inspired me to prove him wrong.

"This isn't just you goofing around, right?" he asked us when we pitched the idea to record our songs for our final project.

"It's very legit, Mr. Kim," Tegan said.

"We're going to use all the skills and knowledge you've bestowed upon us this year," I chimed in.

He squinted at us, tapping the ends of the pen laced between his knuckles on his desk.

"Mr. Kim, you could be the one responsible for helping us make a Grammy Award–winning album," Tegan said.

Finally, his face broke into a smile. "I knew them when . . . ," he said. "Alright, but you have to record after school. Last time you had your guitars in here, I got a noise complaint."

On the day of the recording, Mr. Kim had Tegan and me run a dozen black cables from the back of the mixing console through the door of the sound booth and out to the main room. We pressed microphones that looked like miniature flashlights into clips and pointed them to the front of our guitar amp. Mr. Kim showed Spencer and Christina how to set the faders on the recording console so that the squares of digital color stayed green, and not orange or red.

"Maybe we should sit? Like we do at home?" I asked Tegan, who was pulling the couches and chairs littered around the room into a semicircle around our setup.

"Just do what feels comfortable. We can always move the mics around if you want to sit," Tegan said.

Standing with my black electric guitar on my shoulder in front of our friends and Mr. Kim, I felt a spike of jitters. The sunlight from the large second-floor window was like a too bright spotlight, and every gesture felt magnified.

"Rolling!" Christina shouted.

"Okay, we're starting!" Tegan said into the microphone, launching into the power chords of "Liar's Club": *"I don't know what I want anymore. I don't know who I want anymore. I don't know who I am anymore."*

When she hit the chorus, I watched Mr. Kim's face sink.

"Fuck you, fuck me / it'll never be! FUCK YOU!" Her voice cracked into distortion and Mr. Kim walked quickly into his office and closed the door.

I saw a flurry of activity behind the glass and Christina stuck her head through the door, waving her hand at us. Spencer stepped across the room and whispered, "It's way into the red! You're blowing it up!" His eyes darted to the corner where Mr. Kim was hunched over his desk.

"Pull the faders down, it's fine," Tegan said off microphone. Spencer and Christina returned to the booth and we started the recording again.

"Instamatic" was a new song of mine, so Tegan put her guitar down and sat on the couch between our friends while I played. As soon as I began, my hand started sliding around on the frets. Hesitating about where the next chord should go, I kept glancing down, and then forgetting the lyrics. I dug my fingers into the strings during the chorus, pushing harder than I usually did at home. Leaning into the microphone, the weight of the guitar shifted from my shoulder to my left hand and I closed my eyes. *"You go away, go away! And I don't mind. You go away, go away! But I'm still fine. You lie, lie, lie, but I still miss you! You, lie, lie, lie but I still need you! It's your mind that matters most. It's your mind that makes you mine!"*

"Woooo!" Tegan shouted at the end. "Rock star!"

"Rock star," I said into the mic.

Afterward, we listened back to a few of the songs on the big speakers. It sounded so much better than the songs we'd recorded at home on our stereo. Mr. Kim even seemed excited that we'd pulled it off.

When we climbed into Mom's Jeep later, Tegan and I talked over each other, recounting every minute of the recording.

"Can you take us to the mall?" Tegan asked. "We want to buy blank cassettes and make copies for everyone at school."

"And we need a photocopier!" I said.

"For what?" Mom asked.

"For the album cover and track listing! It'll make it more legit," Tegan said, putting "legit" in air quotes. "We promised Mr. Kim we'd take this very seriously."

"We'll pay you back once we start selling them," I added.

"Selling them to who?" Mom laughed, turning in the direction of the shopping mall.

After we recorded the Plunk demo, we submitted it as our final project for Broadcasting and Communications class before the end of the year. Mr. Kim gave us a perfect grade, and Mr. Russel asked if we'd make a duplicate for him, which we agreed to do.

"Stephanie told me Mr. Russel is getting one, can I get one?" Zoe asked at lunch.

"Me, too," Christina said. "I was the one who recorded it."

"Um, I should get one if Christina is," Spencer said.

Though our group of friends had increasingly become divided about what music we all preferred to listen to at parties—throwing on Mariah Carey and Usher more often than Rancid or Hole as the year came to a close—they'd started asking Sara and me to play more and more. Even the least alternative among us would cheer after we performed. Our friends began requesting our songs by name, and it seemed like they were becoming actual fans of the music we were writing.

"Yeah," Sara agreed in the hall. "We can make copies for you guys."

"Sure," I said. "No problem."

"We'll pay," Zoe offered.

"Cool."

Word spread that we were going to make copies for people and by the end of the day, nearly all our friends promised they'd buy one if we made them one, too. Sara and I went to work on fulfilling our first order of cassettes.

"Does it have to be so loud?" I yelled over the stereo at Sara, who sat among piles of tapes. I was pacing by her window, walking off the pins and needles sensation in my legs from sitting in one spot for four hours. I watched the wheels of the tapes spin as our voices were transferred onto the cheap cassettes Mom had bought us.

"Yes," Sara shouted back.

"Why is there no 'i' in 'Johnny My Frend'?" I asked, annoyed. Sara had written out the track listing, since her handwriting was better than mine. We argued over the names of the songs as we dubbed. Some still didn't have proper titles, and some we just couldn't agree on, not even their spelling.

"Because it's cool."

"What does 'Condamnnation' mean?"

"It's condemnation, but with 'damn' in it instead."

"Right."

On the cover, Sara wrote out our band name, Plunk. "We need to call this album something."

"*Who's in Your Band?*" I said without thinking. It was the first thing everyone asked when I told them Sara and I had a band.

"Fuck, yes," Sara said, laughing. "Who's . . . in . . . your . . . band?" She wrote it down, and spun the paper to show me.

"Awesome."

Mom agreed to make copies of the track listing and cover art at work the next day. They were barely in our hands that night before we were racing up the stairs to put them into the cassette cases. When Mom and Bruce poked their heads in later, they laughed at the mess of paper and tapes taking over Sara's bedroom floor.

"Imagine if they applied this much effort to homework or school," Mom said. "They'd be on the honor roll."

I grabbed a red-and-white tape from the pile between us. Dropping it in the case, I delicately slipped the artwork inside and handed it to them. "Five dollars, please."

"Ha," Bruce said, snapping it from my fingers. "I paid for those tapes."

"Uh, *I* paid for them," Mom said, grabbing the tape from him. "Get your own."

That night when I turned out the light in my bedroom, I put on *Who's in Your Band?* and turned it up as loud as it would go in my headphones. Like almost every other night I could remember, while everyone else slept, I listened to music. I had spent hundreds of hours mouthing silently along to the songs of other bands, working myself into a frenzied state flat on my back, in the dark of my room. I'd spent a lifetime projecting myself onto other singers' bodies, in front of their audiences, on the lip of their stages while locked behind my bedroom door. But that night it was my voice, my songs, my music I heard; my stage, my audience, my body I saw.

At school the next day I swung my backpack around at lunch and unzipped it in the hallway. "Who wants a Plunk tape?"

Our friends crowded around Sara and me, jumping up and reaching to take the tapes from our hands.

"Oh my god, this is so cool," Grace squealed.

"I can't believe we can finally listen to all your songs anytime we want," Zoe said.

"Is 'Missing You' on here?" Emma asked. "That's my favorite."

"Who's in your band?" Diego asked.

"Yeah." I smiled.

"No, who *is* in your band?"

"It's just them," Stephanie said. "They don't need a band."

"Well, that's not *really* a band, if it's just them."

"Yes, it is."

"You guys wanna buy it or not?" I interrupted.

Diego handed back the tape and dug around in his front pocket. Then he passed me a crumpled-up bill. "Of course I do. I'm going to tell everyone I knew you guys before you were famous."

Naomi slipped further from my mind during those three months that she was in Montreal. Our infrequent phone calls and letters scattered with mundane details about the new songs I'd written and my fights with Tegan were the only exchanges we had. I refused to ask her about Frederic, and, when she called me once from his house, I drunkenly argued with her until she cried. In the morning I wrote a long apology, begging to be forgiven. When she received the Plunk tape I sent her she either didn't notice or care that all my new songs seemed to be about her.

Now she was back. Standing at the front door of her house, my pulse dashed in my throat. I rang the doorbell and took a deep breath. Naomi pounced through the door, throwing her arms around my neck.

"Oh my god, I'm so happy to see you!" she said.

Her skin smelled spiced and familiar. I'd spent hundreds of hours with my face pressed in that exact spot between her shoulder and neck. I stepped into the entrance and pulled my boots off. We made our way up the stairs to her bedroom. With the door closed, she kissed me full on the mouth.

"I've really missed you," she said.

I sat on the bed, biting at my lip.

Her brow wrinkled with concern. "I thought we were okay."

"I just feel . . . shy," I said.

I hoped that seeing her after three months would return to my body the feelings that had consumed me the previous year. But, fumbling through that awkward kiss, I felt a growing insecurity that she might be comparing me to Frederic. How did he kiss her? Touch her? How did I compare? Imagining them having sex filled me with shame; I wanted my body to look like his.

"Your parents must be thrilled about Frederic," I said, pulling away.

"They said he could come visit."

I nodded, but I could feel the skin on my face tightening, my jaw pulsing.

"He hasn't called me much since I got back."

"You got home last night!"

"I guess." She sighed. "I'm worried about him meeting someone else." She leaned closer. "Is it okay to tell you that?"

I was only willing to tolerate their relationship so long as it stayed in Montreal. I shifted my weight back on the bed, away from her. "Did you promise him you wouldn't hook up with anyone?"

"I promised him I wouldn't hook up with another boy."

"What about hooking up with me?"

"You're a girl, it's different."

I hated that difference, the undisputed truth of it.

"And Zoe? How's your little crush?"

I felt my cheeks burn red. "She's not my 'little crush,' she's just my friend—*our* friend."

"You're blushing! It's okay if you like her. I get it. She's beautiful."

"I don't *like* her."

"Did anything happen between you two while I was gone?"

"No!" I said forcefully.

I wasn't yet ready to admit that my attraction to girls existed outside of the sexual relationship Naomi and I had. An instinctive warning flashed in my mind that what had happened while Naomi was away should be kept a secret to avoid hurting her, but also to protect Zoe.

"Are you still attracted to me?" Naomi asked me then. Like, *prove it*.

"Of course." I kissed her but felt decapitated by the absence of feeling below my neck. I let myself think about Zoe, about our kiss. Was Naomi imagining someone else, too?

"We should get ready, everyone is going to be here soon," I said, sitting up on the mattress.

Naomi stood up, gazing into the mirror that hung on the back of her bedroom door.

"I look fat in this," she said. I felt her eyes rest on my face in the reflection.

"You don't look fat!" I stood and wrapped my arms around her, rested my chin on her shoulder.

"I just feel like you'd rather be with Zoe."

I recoiled from her angrily. "Stop saying that! She's my friend! She's *your* friend!"

"I just feel gross." Her chin quivered. "I just wish you would tell me the truth."

"There's nothing to tell," I said.

"I don't believe you."

"You were the one fucking some guy for three months!"

"And you're the one making me feel like shit about that guy!"

"Am I supposed to be happy for you?"

"I like him," she said, "but I like you, too, and it seems like you don't feel the same about me anymore."

She opened the door and went into the bathroom. I followed behind her and grabbed at the handle, but it was locked.

"Fuck. Naomi. Please open the door." Pressing my ear to the wood, I heard the sound of her retching into the toilet. My skin went cold. "Naomi!"

The flush of the toilet, water running in the sink. When the door opened, she pushed past me, and I followed her back into the bedroom.

"What's going on? Are you sick?"

"No, I'm just . . . I'm upset."

"I heard you," I said.

"It's nothing."

"I heard you throwing up." The words felt dislocated from their meaning. Throwing up was the result of a flu or a night of too much drinking. My mind scrambled. She was pale, the whites of her eyes were bloodshot.

"Sometimes I feel better if I—if I do that."

"You *made* yourself do that?"

"Yes," she said.

I was dumbfounded, trying to comprehend how our argument could cause Naomi to make herself sick. I'd heard rumors about girls at school who threw up to control their weight, but I'd never heard of someone purposely throwing up because they were upset.

"Don't ever do that again!" I grabbed at her arms, above the elbow. "Is this also a thing people do in Montreal?"

Her eyes filled with tears. Her mouth went slack.

"I'm sorry," I said. "I didn't mean that."

Tears slipped down her cheeks. I tried to hug her, but she went straight to her bedroom mirror and dipped her head backward like she had a bloody nose.

"Please, Naomi. Just don't throw up like that again, okay? Promise me!"

She caught her tears before they fell. "I won't," she said, then straightened up.

After that night it was impossible to shake the feeling that I was to blame for everything going wrong between us. My failure to fix it was a second kind of erasure. What sexual attraction remained between Naomi and me felt sullied by my fear that I was making her sick. I lingered outside the bathroom each time she locked herself inside. When we were out with our friends I overcompensated, treating Zoe coldly, sometimes ignoring her completely. Naomi and I were both suspicious, tracking each other for evidence, which we weaponized in our frequent arguments. Desperate to be freed from her secret, I threatened to tell her parents what was going on. When she admitted to me that they'd booked her a ticket to Montreal that summer, I was relieved.

Summer 1997

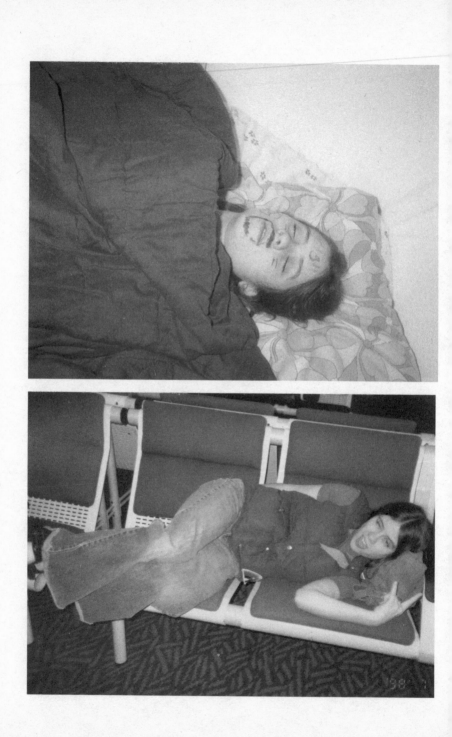

"Have you and Spencer had sex yet?"

Emma and I had grown apart in grade eleven. We were still friends, still hung out at school. But we'd long since stopped writing notes, sleeping at each other's houses, and talking on the phone like this. There was no one reason for it; we'd just been absorbed into a larger group of shared friends, she'd gotten a boyfriend, I'd grown close to Alex, and we'd moved and no longer saw each other in the mornings before school. After Emma asked if Spencer and I were having sex, she took a drag off her cigarette and I tried to figure out how to answer her question. While I did, I imagined her in her kitchen, the long, tangled tan cord of the phone knotted on the floor in front of her. I felt dizzy with nostalgia for a time when Emma and I were headed toward the kind of friendship where I might have readily shared something so intimate, without it having to be pried from me.

A year earlier we'd edged right up to that kind of intimacy, but it hadn't happened. We'd been together in her bed after a party, coming down off acid, and she had started talking about two girls we hung out with who I assumed were hooking up but had never admitted it to us. I'd frozen the second Emma brought them up, shocked by her candor but also enticed by what she was dangling in front of me in the dark. It felt like an opportunity.

"I don't know why they don't just tell us they're getting it on. It's not like any of us would care or be bothered by it."

I had wanted to tell her about Sara and Naomi then. To explain that these friends of ours weren't the only ones hiding in plain sight.

But then she had surprised me even more, adding, "Why don't girls like *me* that way?"

I'd wanted desperately at that moment to confess that *I* did, that I had a crush on her. And that it wasn't the first one I'd had on a girl. I'd barely allowed myself to even think such a thing, but I'd felt the truth crowd my mouth as I watched the red tip of Emma's cigarette light up her face as she talked.

"Come on, everyone has a crush on you," I managed in a hoarse whisper thick with suggestion.

"That's not true."

I breathed in her vulnerability, drew my own into my lungs from deep inside me. I was about to spill everything when she leaned across me to put her cigarette out. Overwhelmed with the desire to kiss her, my heart jackhammering so loud I was sure she could hear it as she pressed into me, I swallowed the truth. I went silent and stayed still after she lay back down. The next morning, I woke up relieved I hadn't said anything to her about how I felt. We'd been high, and the lines of reality were hazy to me. Stoned and caught up in the moment, I'd felt sure of my feelings, but sober in the light of day, I felt less sure. For a while after our talk we had felt even tighter than before. But soon I withdrew from the line I'd come close to crossing with her, and the intimacy between us eventually faded like the memory of that night in her bed.

———

Emma calling about Spencer a year later to inquire about our sex life, or lack thereof, reminded me of the intensity of the feelings I'd had for her in grade ten. If I could tell anyone about the lack of intensity between Spencer and me, it was Emma.

I switched the phone from one hand to the other and took a deep breath. "Um . . . well—"

"You don't have to answer," Emma said flippantly, cutting me off. "It's none of my business if you guys are having sex. I was just wondering."

"No, it's not that—"

"No, you know what . . . ? Just forget about it."

I shifted on my bed, closed my eyes, and pictured Emma on her bottom bunk. Wringing the words from myself, I finally managed, "No. We are *not* having sex. Not even close."

"*Oh-kay*," Emma said, punctuating the syllables with a pause long enough for me to curl up and die from mortification between.

Though she didn't come right out and press me for an explanation of why Spencer and I weren't having sex, she circled it like a patient vulture for the next hour. I eventually admitted to her that it hadn't come up, that Spencer and I never talked about sex.

"Not even once."

"Really?"

"I don't know if we're ready," I said, immediately regretting it. I sounded lame, and it was a lie. I knew Emma was having sex. I knew Spencer had been, too, before me. It was a lack of desire I felt—not lack of readiness. I muttered, "I just feel like we don't really connect . . . that way." Emma stayed silent. "It's like we don't have any chemistry or something," I added quickly. I pressed my face into my pillow and rolled toward the wall, hoping to smother any further words that might try and slip out.

"Hmm, I see," she hummed knowingly, as if she'd come to understand something about me I couldn't, had discovered some detail in me I had overlooked in myself. "Makes sense."

I wanted to yell, *Why does it make sense to you and not me?* Why, if I liked Spencer, didn't I desire him? I wanted to open my mouth and have all the words trapped in my throat unspool like ribbon. I wanted to take her back with me to a year earlier, onto the mattress in her room, and be braver, bolder with her. I wanted to make her see, to really understand. But every time I opened my mouth to say more, the words didn't come. Eventually, Emma let me go. She sounded a bit hurt, as if she sensed I'd not been totally honest.

The next day I went to Spencer's thinking about Emma's question. About sex. About her. About what I was unable to say a year earlier, and what I had not been able to explain the night before.

"You're quiet," Spencer said. We sat next to each other on the couch.

"You're always quiet," I said.

He suggested we smoke a joint in his room, and afterward we lay down on his plaid comforter. I curled up next to him. He drifted off, and I felt a familiar relief, just as I had a dozen other times that summer when it seemed like something physical might happen between us and it didn't. Pressed against him, I thought back to when Emma leaned across me in her bed to put out her cigarette. As I replayed the memory in my mind, this time I didn't swallow the words that rose in my throat. Instead, I said them to myself: "My heart has never beat for you the way it did for her."

The next day Spencer and I went to Denny's for coffee. We were both quiet. Finally I said, "I think we should break up."

In the last weeks of grade eleven, Tegan and I walked home from school every day, even when the sky dumped summer rain in sheets without warning. It was liberating to strip off our jackets and lace them through the straps on our backpacks, lifting our arms to wave as friends' cars passed. On one of those soggy afternoons, Cameron offered to tag along, carrying our guitar the full twelve blocks home. Cameron looked like a surfer. His bangs sprang up off his forehead in a cowlick. He had wide-set eyes, and his skin was as soft as that of any of the girls I'd kissed. Even though he dressed a lot preppier than the rest of our friends, he often turned up at raves, his cigarette drawing red lines in the air as he danced.

When we arrived at our house, he lingered on the sidewalk. Tegan went inside.

We sat down on the front steps.

"We should start a band," he said.

"I'll ask Tegan," I said.

"So . . ." His eyes were bloodshot. He was a little stoned.

"So . . ." I said.

"You don't have a boyfriend."

"I don't have a boyfriend."

"I don't have a boyfriend either," he said, laughing.

"What about a girlfriend?" I asked.

"Nope." He grinned.

"I thought you liked older girls," I said. He pressed his

back up against the iron railing. "I just know that you might expect or want . . . sex."

"I just want to get to know you," he said, and then leaned in to kiss me. His mouth tasted like smoke. His blue plaid coat smelled of cinnamon.

I pulled away. "I don't know," I said. "Maybe."

The smile didn't leave his face as he pulled a cigarette from behind his ear and lit it.

"Let me know about the band," he said, standing up and flashing me a final grin before stepping off the curb and walking away.

Once inside, I went upstairs to Tegan's bedroom. The journal in which she kept her lyrics was spread out on her purple duvet, and the room was smoky with incense.

"Cameron asked to be in our band." I folded myself onto the bench seat next to the window. "And he asked me out."

"I think you should just tell him no. About the band, I mean." She sounded annoyed.

"Okay." I stared out the window, thinking about the kiss. I was more than a little flattered that he liked me.

"I might say yes, about the other thing," I said casually.

She shrugged. "Spencer and I broke up again," she said.

"Why?" I asked. I'd seen Spencer a few days earlier and he'd told me as much. They were kind of like Naomi and me, never quite settled or satisfied with each other, but not really ready to let go either.

"I don't know. He's boring me lately."

"You're being kind of mean to him."

"*I'm* mean to him? You're one to talk."

"What does that mean?"

"Naomi?"

"What about her?"

"Whatever."

"You don't know a fucking thing about me and Naomi." I stood up and left, slamming her bedroom door closed behind me.

At first Cameron and I didn't really refer to ourselves as boyfriend/girlfriend. He just started tagging along with Tegan and me to the movies and to our friends' houses, calling me every day, and showing up with extra of whatever he was drinking or smoking. He never seemed to tire of asking me questions. I couldn't think of a guy who'd ever really tried to get to know me. We talked about playing music and song writing, and he'd call me on the phone and ask me to play songs for him. In Broadcasting class he'd taught me to play drums, and he was always putting whatever instrument he had in his hands into mine. The boys we hung out with clammed up if you dared to ask them about their feelings, but Cameron went glassy-eyed more than once telling me about his. He was generous, affable. Everyone liked him, even Bruce.

Bruce had stared down every one of our boyfriends as if he might grab them by the scruff of the neck and eject them from the house. He'd grown up with three sisters and was always telling us stories about the losers he'd had to chase away from the dinner table when he was a kid. The way he planted his meaty forearms around his plate after he'd loaded it up seemed like an unconscious behavior left over from childhood. I understood that when it came to boys, Tegan and I were in that defended space between his arms.

Mom was more suspicious, eyeballing Cameron when he strolled bare-chested through our house with his T-shirt off and tucked into the back of his jeans.

"He's kind of a hippie" was my explanation when she mentioned it to me later.

There was a humiliating attempt to discuss birth control, which I shrugged off, but later felt relieved about. That she suspected I was having sex with Cameron ensured a respite from her probing questions about Naomi.

After a month of dating, I agreed to meet Cameron at the reservoir near his house. The trip took an hour and a half, and when I finally arrived he was waiting for me at the bus stop in sandals and a tank top, beach towels slung around his neck. He was like a golden retriever—always in a good mood, unashamed about his desire for affection. He picked me up in a bear hug and swung me around.

"You brought a bathing suit, right? You're going to love this spot. It's very remote." He seemed so pleased to be alone with me, for a day devoted to just the two of us. The park surrounding the reservoir was lush, and he guided us to a narrow path, which we eventually abandoned for the flat rocks along the river. The current carried teenagers on tubes and blow-up rafts. The sun was molten, but the breeze off the water was cold. We arrived at a bend in the river, where a deep pool was carved into the cliff. He spread our towels on the rocks and stripped off his tank top. I pulled my shirt over my head and bunched it self-consciously on my lap. I was still wearing shorts and a bathing suit, but I'd never felt more naked.

"You look hot," he said, kissing my shoulder.

We stepped into the water and he dove under, coming up seconds later with a guttural hoot. My legs went numb: the water was as cold as ice. I finally submerged myself with a scream. He pulled my arms around his neck, and shivering,

I wrapped my legs around his waist. It was a gesture that should have been sexual but felt paternal. When the sun split itself in half behind the mountain, we dried off and put our clothes back on. We walked back along the river, through the park and into the neighborhood where he lived. His house was a large ranch-style bungalow, spread out across a manicured lawn. Inside, each room was drenched in orange light from the sunset. The furniture and books were just so, like something from a movie. I felt like an intruder.

He flopped down onto his unmade bed. The door to his bedroom was open, and I reflexively turned and closed it, though it seemed no one was home. There were guitars strewn about, books stacked on the shelves and the floor. His room smelled like him, a mix of musk and the metallic tang of stale cigarettes. We'd never fooled around sober. I had the strongest urge to rest inside his frame like a nesting doll, to study him so I would know what it was to be him. I found the obvious pleasure he took in his body intoxicating. As if by osmosis, I adopted the same swagger and ease in my own just by lying next to him. We made out, and a light-headed urgency that often preceded sex with Naomi washed over me. I was surprised to find that I was turned on— evidence that I wasn't entirely what I feared. I pulled off my jean shorts and swimsuit, and he scooted back toward my hips and placed his mouth between my legs. The keen desire that had gripped me seconds before evaporated. It wasn't different from when Naomi did it, but it felt utterly wrong. I pulled him up by the ears, hoping he caught the drift that what I wanted down there wasn't his face. He kissed me, and then rested his full weight on the bed; his arm stretched across my hips. His face was flushed, serious.

"It seems like, maybe . . ." He got quiet. "Like you want to go further than we normally do."

"Maybe."

"I just don't think you should do anything you're not ready for."

Did he think he knew more about what I wanted than I did?

"We should talk about it more. Like, before we—or if we ever . . . You know."

"Yeah, I guess we should," I said.

"Dad should be back with the pizza soon."

"I should really get going."

"Really?"

"It's such a long way back, and—"

"I'll take the bus with you!"

"No, that's crazy." I grabbed my clothes from the floor and dressed quickly, keeping my eyes down at the carpet. I went out into the hall and ducked inside the bathroom, closing the door behind me. I braided my hair and straightened my clothes. My cheeks and the tip of my nose were sunburned. The person in the reflection didn't look like me. Was he right? That I wasn't ready? He was with the wrong girl. He should be with one who knew when the right time to have sex was, who wanted to spend a day alone at a secret swimming spot and laugh with his family over pizza. I felt like an interloper, a bad fit.

When I finally got home, it was almost midnight. My body felt like leather, toasted. I sank down onto my bed and called Cameron to tell him that I was home safe.

"Thanks for coming all the way to my house. I really loved spending the day with you," he said.

"It was fun," I said.

"Hey, I wanted to say, I hope it wasn't weird, what I said about—"

"It wasn't."

"I just don't want to rush."

"Okay."

He was quiet, and I stared out the window at the street.

"Is what we did today as much as you've ever . . . done?" he asked.

Because he was a guy, I knew it wouldn't threaten him if I told him the truth, however wrongheaded that idea was. Plus, his best friend, Zach, was gay, and I'd heard him tell people off for using the word "fag" in front of him.

"I've done that with Naomi," I said, listening hard at his breath on the phone.

"Oh."

"I haven't really told anyone that—"

"Hmm."

"We used to do stuff with each other a lot, actually."

"And you liked it?"

"Yeah. Are you grossed out?"

"No! It's hot. I mean, not like, 'It's hot,' but like . . . Whatever."

"I think it's cool that you're so accepting of . . ." I paused. "Zach. A lot of guys wouldn't be." I had wanted to say "accepting of *me*." The line got quiet again.

"I don't care that Zach's . . . gay. Like, at all."

I was unsure what to say next.

"Can I ask you something?" he said.

"Yeah."

"What we did today—how did I compare to Naomi?"

I buried my head in my pillow. "Oh! Yeah, it was great."

"Cool." He sounded relieved.

Cameron's indifference about what I'd told him had an unnerving effect. I was uncomfortable that he could accept about me what I couldn't accept about myself.

Before school started again, I broke up with him.

GRADE TWELVE

Everything changed when grade twelve started. First, Alex told me she was going to go to university abroad. All of a sudden we realized we had only one year left together. We committed to making the most of the time we had, promising to spend every second we could together before the year ended and she abandoned me to go away to school. The imminent threat of being apart dominated every conversation, influenced every plan we made, and crowded every room we were in together. We became inseparable, codependent, bound together like chain. And everyone noticed.

"Why don't you girls get up and get some air?" Alex's mom suggested nervously from the doorway to Alex's room one Sunday. It was midafternoon, and we were still shoulder to shoulder in Alex's single bed.

"Haven't seen Christina or any of the girls around here recently," Mom commented one afternoon after Alex had left to go home after a weekend at our house.

"You guys are so gay," Sara scoffed on another afternoon when she'd grabbed something from my room while Alex and I were studying on the bed together, our textbooks and binders spread between us. I'd bristled when she said it, worried Alex would feel uncomfortable, that it would cause her not to want to be close to me. But Alex hadn't said anything, hadn't seemed hurt or disgusted.

On another night when Alex was studying at Naomi's,

she called me. We were on the hundredth "No, you hang up first," "No, you hang up first" when Naomi yelled, "Say goodnight to your girlfriend already!"

"Goodnight, girlfriend."

Every hair on my arms had stood up when Alex said it. I knew she was joking; she always took the teasing and taunting in stride. But afterward, I sat for a long time, blushing and bathing in the feeling it had generated in me to hear her say it.

Even Spencer seemed to notice. One night I asked him for a cigarette at Grace's birthday, and Alex told him not to give it to me.

"She can decide what she wants for herself."

"Yeah." I smiled, a cigarette dangling from my lips as I did.

Alex had stormed off after he leaned into me to light it.

"Better go find your girlfriend and apologize," he'd quipped, a little hurt showing behind his eyes.

When I asked Alex to explain what made her feel so upset in these moments, she would cry, become frustrated, admit she wasn't sure. "I just feel so crazy sometimes. I know I overreact. He just . . . makes me feel jealous. I don't know why."

I would try to console her, to be patient. Though I'd kept it to myself, I'd struggled with the same kind of irrational emotion.

When Alex had gotten a boyfriend over the summer while she was at camp, I'd felt sick with jealousy when she told me—and then fat with relief when she called crying a few weeks later, telling me they had broken up. But even after they broke up, it still bothered me that he'd been worthy of her tears. I'd felt like the most important person to her, and it nagged at me that she'd let a boy close to her heart. When she showed me photos of him when she got home, I'd felt a rising pressure in my chest; the sight of him with his arms around her in her bathing suit made me feel displaced, as if I didn't belong anywhere, not even in my own body. When she cried about Spencer or acted jealous, I felt like I understood the feeling, even if I didn't understand where it came from or what it meant. I tried to find the words to tell her all this, but they always seemed to fall short of making her feel better.

The biggest shift between us came one afternoon in late fall. Alex changed in front of me in her room, and I accidentally glanced at her at the moment her shirt was off, and then our eyes met. I blushed and looked away. I felt crushing embarrassment and fear. It had been an accident, but I felt sick because maybe she'd think otherwise. But she just laughed and said, "Whoops." We never mentioned it again. Still, I couldn't forget what I'd seen. That night on the phone as she rambled on about something, almost without thinking I found myself writing to her about it in the journal we shared. I wanted to go back to that moment and not look away, not let her pull her shirt down and cover herself. In our journal, I wrote out what I had become consumed by: her. Printing the words felt exhilarating and terrifying at the same time. I grew convinced that what I felt wasn't just inside me. I was sure I wasn't the only one who felt this way. She must, too. It explained so much: the jealousy between us, the fact that we'd only grown more interested in each other, not less, as our friendship had developed over the last two years. I wanted desperately to rip the page out later but forced myself not to. I wasn't going to mess this up like I had with Emma and all the other girls I had become close to. This time was going to be different.

Later that week as we waited for Alex's mom to come pick her up after a weekend together, she went to the bathroom and I grabbed the book from the bench seat in my room where I'd hidden it. I opened it to the page where I'd confessed how I felt about her. Dragging my finger along the words, I felt sure I was going to faint. When I heard Alex come out of the bathroom, I ripped the page out and shoved it in my back pocket, snapping the book closed just as she walked through my open bedroom door.

"What are you doing?" she asked.

"Nothing, just . . . grabbing the book. I actually forgot to write in it. I started but messed up. I owe you twice as much next week." I was talking too quickly. Acting too nervous.

"Oh, want me to throw it out for you?" she asked, extending her hand toward me, a smile sneaking out as she did.

I smiled back. "No."

We both started to laugh at the same time. Then, she lunged at me. I darted around her, dropping the book, and tripped toward my bed. I landed hard on my mattress and flipped onto my back, putting my body between Alex and the note as she pinned me down.

"What are you hiding?" she asked.

"I'm not hiding anything." I giggled, twisting and squealing, already out of breath.

"Really? You're putting up a big fight over nothing."

Sitting astride my hips, her fingers pecked at my sides. The more I laughed, the weaker I got. She managed to wedge her knees into the soft part of the underside of my upper arms, pinning me to the bed. I bucked; hysterical laughter scored our struggle. We kept it up for a full minute and then she stopped, sat up, and stared down at me.

"What did you rip out of the book?"

"Nothing."

"What does the note say, Tegan?"

I shook my head. "Nothing."

"Tell me what it says."

"It's nothing."

"If it's nothing, show me."

"No."

She stared at me without saying anything. Then without warning, she leaned down and kissed me. She held her lips to mine for no more than six seconds, but those six seconds rearranged me, completely.

"Tell me what it says," she said, a smile spreading across her face as she sat up.

"No."

"Tell me."

"No." I grabbed her sweater and pulled her toward me so I could kiss her again.

When Alex's ride arrived, she left me with the note and a hickey the size of a nickel. I gasped when I saw it in the mirror of the plywood changing room at Value Village an hour later. Pressing my finger into the bruised skin, I leaned in, immediately paranoid someone had seen it. How would I explain a hickey after a weekend alone with Alex? My fingers drifted back and forth over the misshapen purple spot; I imagined Alex's mouth where my fingers were. I leaned against the cheap wood and raced through excuses I could give if Mom or Sara mentioned it.

"You done in there?" Mom called from outside.

"Almost," I said.

I locked eyes with myself in the mirror, tugged my hoodie up, and felt relieved to see it mostly covered the hickey. I knew I'd have to figure out how to cover up the bruise when I got home. But for a minute, I let the hickey, and what it meant, sink in. She liked me. She kissed me. She hadn't seen the note. She had no idea how I felt about her, and yet she knew, had likely known all along. I placed my palm over the mark, let myself feel Alex's mouth one more time before I unlatched the door. Smiling at myself in the mirror, I felt the happiest I ever had in my entire life.

"What are you doing!" Tegan shouted from the other side of my bedroom door. I was pushing against it, trying to close it. I straightened my legs, driving my body harder into the wood. "Fuck off!" I said. I lunged forward again, and the inches between us disappeared as I slammed and locked the door. She punched at the door with a fist. I lunged for the phone that was sitting on top of my bed. I could hear her rushing back to her bedroom. I picked up the receiver and dialed Naomi's number, the seven digits blurring under my thumb. Nothing. No ringing, just Tegan's heavy breath on the line. I slammed my phone down into the base. In the hallway, I could hear the metal end of a coat hanger being jammed in the doorknob. She was trying to pop the lock on my door. I rushed to it and leaned against it with all my weight.

"It's my fucking turn to use the phone!" I said.

She ignored me, patiently moving the object inside the doorknob.

"Why are you such a fucking bitch?" I yelled.

Suddenly the door burst open against my shoulder.

"Who are you going to call anyway?" she said through clenched teeth. "Nobody fucking likes you."

I pitched my shoulder against the door, closing it in her face.

"If you slam the goddamn door again, I will take it off the fucking hinges!" Bruce shouted up the stairs.

"It's my turn to use the phone!" Tegan screamed back.

"I don't give a damn whose turn it is!" Bruce yelled.

These fights happened constantly. Almost every other day. We'd been caught in this kind of territorial battle since we could lift our chubby arms and throw each other's toys down the stairs. Shoes, clothes, a chord change, the last drop of Coke in the bottle. It didn't matter what it was; everything was a battlefield.

I raced back to the bed and picked up the phone. Tegan had already dialed a number and it was ringing.

"Get off!" she said.

I ran my fingers vertically across the glowing white keys, beeping out her conversation. I could hear Tegan in the other room shouting in between the monotones. When her friend hung up, Tegan rattled my door and kicked at it with her feet in frustration.

"You're so fucking embarrassing!" she said.

Then I heard Bruce stomping up the stairs. I couldn't see what was going on, but Tegan was protesting. I maintained my defensive stance with my forehead pressed to the door. There was a single knock and I sighed.

"Open it," Bruce said.

I did. He pointed a screwdriver at the silver hinges on the door frame.

"See these?" He deftly set about pushing and pulling at the pins of the hinges and popped the door off the bracket.

"You can't do that!" Tegan said, crying from the doorway of her own room.

"Where are we supposed to get dressed?" I added.

He swung his arm down the hall, pointing to the bathroom. "Right there." And he turned back to my door, his fingers poking at the bottom hinge.

"We won't slam them anymore!" I said.

"You can't take our doors," Tegan said.

"I can. And I will."

Without a door and a lock, I had nothing. He might as well have taken the walls around me.

"We won't slam them again," I said calmly. I shot Tegan a death stare.

"Figure it out," he said, relenting. He put the door back on the hinges. "I'm tired of the two of you arguing over the telephone."

Tears of frustration stung my eyes as he spoke. I wanted him to pick a side, even if it wasn't mine. When my door was back on the hinges, I closed it gently and locked it.

After Bruce went to bed, I slipped down the stairs to the basement. Line 1 on the telephone was lit up, red. Tegan was on the phone with Alex. I hit Line 2 and dialed Naomi's number.

"I hate my sister."

"You don't."

"I do."

"I hate when you two fight."

"It's ridiculous. She and Alex just sit there for hours saying nothing!" I said.

"We used to do that, too," Naomi replied.

"They're weird."

"They just like each other."

"Obviously," I said.

Tegan's attraction to her best friend was no surprise to me. I knew what a crush looked like. It wasn't the giggling or hum of conversation through my bedroom wall that revealed her feelings so much as the intensity of her fights with Alex. Suspicion, jealousy, feelings bruised and broken. That's what love sounded like. I was repulsed by her, threatened by her sloppiness, how easy she made it to suspect and confirm what was going on with her and Alex. Returned to our original sameness, even my secret shame was not entirely mine anymore.

"Do you think they're hooking up?" Naomi asked me before we hung up.

"Ugh."

She clicked her tongue. "Don't be like that."

"I don't want to even *think* about it."

When my love with Naomi was in bloom, we'd hidden ourselves behind locked doors. I felt the urge to invade Tegan's privacy the way she'd invaded mine.

"I should go," I said.

"Okay, well. Be nice to her."

The next day Tegan and I launched into round two of our battle. Careful not to slam the doors, our fighting was contained within the boundary of our rooms. We hovered just at the edge of violence. With my hands curled into fists, she dared me to punch her.

"You're going to hit me?" she taunted. "Do it, you psycho." Her mouth curled into a smile.

We didn't hear our mom open the front door or her steps on the stairs. Suddenly she crossed through my doorway and snapped the phone cord from the socket in the wall.

"I'm fucking done." She wrapped the cord around the phone as she spoke, pushing past us and toward Tegan's bedroom, where she took Tegan's phone, too. I heard the muffled bells of the telephones in the hallway as she carried them to her bedroom and closed the door. Now bonded together in a fight against Mom, Tegan and I went to her door and knocked.

"That's not fair!" Tegan yelled.

"They're our phones!" I said.

Silence.

"Mom!"

"Another word about it and you'll be grounded, too," she said through the door.

"Fucking bitch," I muttered under my breath.

Tegan turned, glancing only briefly at me.

"Fucking psycho," she muttered, slamming her door behind her.

The next day no one in the house was on speaking terms. Perhaps to avoid the unbearable meal we were having with Mom upstairs in the kitchen, Bruce was eating the dinner he'd made for himself in the basement. As Mom was cleaning up the dishes, Tegan asked her for our allowance.

"I already gave it to you. If you want more money, get a job."

"Dad gives you six hundred dollars a month for us in child support. Don't you think we're entitled to more than fifteen bucks a week?" Tegan asked.

I bolted up the stairs when the yelling started. Tegan was dead meat. Even I knew that she'd gone too far. Part of me was relieved to hear someone else express rage at her, while another part of me worried she'd be leaving the house in a body bag. When the fight arrived in the hallway outside Tegan's bedroom, I listened with increasing worry. Mom's voice was hoarse, anguished, outlining in excruciating detail our monthly expenses, and the sacrifices taking care of us required of her. I opened my door and tried to intervene, playing referee and then peacekeeper. Bruce joined me at the top of the stairs, calmly calling Mom's name as if she were standing on a high window ledge. She turned and pushed past him down the stairs. She returned with two garbage bags.

"Pack your shit. You can go and live with your dad," she said, throwing the bags at Tegan's feet.

Tegan argued, at one point she begged, but eventually she grabbed some clothes and books and stuffed them into the bags as I looked on. When she was done, Mom tied them up and dragged them down the stairs to the front door. I heard Tegan sobbing, and then the front door closing. The house settled into a terrifying quiet. I hadn't said a word but was afraid that I would be next.

At school the next morning, I saw Tegan in the student center. She had big, black circles under her eyes.

"Mom's a psycho," Tegan said. "I didn't mean that she should give us *all* of Dad's money."

I knew that she was regretful, I could hear it in her voice. I knew Mom had to run a full cycle of rage. Maybe she deserved to.

"She'll calm down," I said.

Tegan called Mom the following week and apologized, and Mom agreed to let her come home. For a few days after she returned, there was peace in the house.

32. TEGAN WE'RE NOTHING LIKE THEM

Alex and I spent the fall falling in love.

"When did you know?"

"Always."

"How did you know?"

"It was so obvious."

"Was it always there between us?"

"Yes."

"Why didn't we do this sooner?"

"I don't know."

Obsessing over the most minute details of our friendship and its ascension into romance, we got lost in the small things.

"I can't believe you like milk. How did I never know that?"

"I'm trying to imagine you on a bike, but I can't . . ."

"Really?"

"I'm trying, but I can't . . ."

"Try harder."

"I am . . ."

We cavorted and coalesced under the microscope of infatuation, making even mundane facts seem riveting and essential. A spectrum of colors and feelings and tastes and a kind of touch that I'd only just figured out existed surged through me. I had never considered what it would be like to be in love until I was in it. It was a concept that felt out of reach before Alex, just beyond the scope. Even my most intense crushes on other girls hadn't exercised so much dominance over me, and the boys even less. Truthfully, the boys had induced little but a constant desire to break up with them. But with Alex, I wanted to stretch out our beginning, I wanted to never reach our end. As I fell in love with her, I could think of nothing *but* her. I half listened in school, half studied for my tests, half completed my assignments, half lived when I wasn't next to her. My desire for her didn't make me sick, or sad about what it might mean. The way I felt about her helped me forget the stress I felt bricking itself inside me about university and my future, and the lack of clarity I had about both.

All week when we were apart from each other, Mom would nag me about my terrible grades, my lack of focus, my nonexistent plans for university. Her comments took small bites out of the secret desires I was storing up about playing music and what was happening between me and Alex. I only half listened to Mom as she tried to reason with me, pleading, "I want you to have an easier life than I did. I don't want you to struggle like I did. You need to try harder. You need to do better."

Reunited with Alex when the weekend came, tucked together in the dark of our rooms, she would reassure me, tending to the love between us, reminding me I was blooming, not wilting.

"You're destined for something more important than university," she said. "Fuck school. You're going to get a record deal. You're going to change the world."

Drunk on her vision of my life to come, my fears blurred,

and I felt soothed into seeing what she saw. I trusted her because she knew me better than anyone ever had. Having revealed myself totally to her, she took ownership of everything of mine, even my future.

In the meantime, Sara and I were fighting more than ever. She sensed what was happening between Alex and me, and for reasons unfathomable to me she started projecting an almost puritanical loathing at us. I screamed for Mom, demanding she intervene between us: "Get Sara out of my fucking room. Tell her to leave us alone!"

The happiness Alex and I exhibited only seemed to threaten Sara. It seemed like we were a reminder of what she and Naomi had lost. I burned with irrefutable confidence that she was just jealous of us. But a small part of me was worried Sara might be mad because she thought I was copying her. It nagged at me, and threatened to ruin the new love I was in. Alex and I spent a lot of time making up after fights that started when I'd brush Alex's hand away if Sara entered a room, or grew cold to her to mask our intimacy. I knew I was straddling a fine line between sharing an incredible heady secret love with Alex and hiding who I was becoming with her behind closed doors. I remembered my disgust when Sara demanded privacy for her and Naomi after they got together; their desire to hide what was happening between them had felt shameful to me. Now I languished, in love with Alex, wanting at once to be open about it while also fearing shame was staining us.

"We will *never* be like they were. *Ever*," I cried to Alex.

"Never," Alex agreed.

We promised each other a different outcome than they had succumbed to, as we winded closer and closer to the path they'd taken. In the dark, behind closed doors, en-twined in bed, we outlined the ways we'd always love each other; the lengths we'd go to guarantee we'd never fail as they had. How naive we were, so seized by love, to think we would end up any different.

To qualify for a high school diploma, it was mandatory to complete a semester of Career and Life Management (CALM). The curriculum was an array of topics including mental health, skill building in interpersonal relationships, career goals, and instruction on the proper way to fill out tax forms.

CALM wasn't taken very seriously. Most days I dozed off during the films or whizzed through worksheets quickly so I could read a novel under my desk. Our CALM teacher, Dr. Morgan, seemed especially hapless when standing slumped at the front of the classroom. The fine hairs left on the top of his head were swept across his perspiring scalp. His sweaters were pilling and his corduroys—the same kind worn by most, if not all, of my male teachers—were rubbed white at the knees and below the sagging pockets on his backside. He was soft-spoken, but firm. A doctor of what? I don't think he ever said.

The sexual education curriculum came halfway through the semester, once routines and decorum had been established. Perhaps to jolt us from our boredom, we were invited to welcome with enthusiastic applause a sexual education speaker from the Calgary Birth Control Association. Dr. Morgan briefly introduced a woman who looked to be in her early twenties. She had a voice that failed to quiet the murmur of conversation in the back of the room as she drew white chalk across the blackboard, outlining the day's topic, STDs. She dropped the chalk on the rail below the board and smacked the white dust from her hands.

"So!" she said, smiling brightly at us. "Let's talk about sexually transmitted diseases!"

"Can't get AIDS unless you're a fag," Troy shouted between his hands from the back of the room. Troy was one of those boys who bullied everyone, including his friends, but especially teachers. His good looks and charisma made it seem like he was doing you a favor. He was used to being looked at and took every opportunity to spin the heads of the class in his direction.

The guest instructor's neck stiffened, and she turned toward Dr. Morgan, who had taken a seat on a chair in the far corner of the room near his desk.

"Troy. Knock it off," he said, still looking down at his notes.

Recalibrating, our guest began to speak again. She was interrupted a second time.

"Seriously, why the fuck do we need to learn about this shit?" Troy said. "Nobody in here is a fucking faggot." I turned to look at him. His mouth was stretched into a lazy grin, his eyes nearly closed.

"Dr. Morgan!" I called loudly from my seat. Other students turned to stare at me, as if I were the disrupter.

"Troy, enough," Dr. Morgan said, with some force.

"It's true, though," Troy said.

I turned around and yelled, "Shut up, Troy!"

"I'll say whatever the fuck I want." His smile curled. "Fags get AIDS." He shrugged as if he were only stating a fact.

"Troy!" Dr. Morgan yelled, and then stood, tapping his clipboard nervously against his thigh. I heard coughs of laughter from the boys in the back row.

"Are you going to let him say these things?" I stood up from my seat; I felt the light-headed rush you get before you throw a punch.

"Let's just everyone calm down," Dr. Morgan said.

"Yes, calm down," Troy said. He was slouched in his chair, his eyes locked on me.

"What if someone in this class is gay?" The dangerous sound of my voice silenced the room. With tears blurring my sight, I picked up my chair and hurled it over my classmates' heads at Troy's desk. The legs smashed the laminate of his desktop, bounced, and then crashed into another desk. The sound was spectacularly metallic. And loud. Troy's hands jerked up across his face and he let out, "What the fuck!" as he stumbled from his seat, toppling his chair.

I grabbed my backpack and rushed to the door. In the hallway outside the classroom, I started to run. I didn't know where I was going until I arrived at the Pit. When I burst through the door, Mr. Russel was sitting in his small office, working. I collapsed in the plastic chair next to his desk. Through heaving sobs that gathered and broke in my chest, I explained what had happened.

"He said that only fags get AIDS," I cried. "And Dr. Morgan let him say it!" I cried into my hands. "He's fucking pathetic."

Mr. Russel's face drained of color. Then, over the loudspeaker came an announcement: my full name, repeated twice, and a request to make my way to the principal's office.

"Please, don't make me go up there."

Mr. Russel placed his hand flat on his cheek and another on his hip. Breathing out of his nose in one big huff, he said, "I have to tell them that you're here."

I nodded, and he lifted the telephone on his desk. "Yes, this is Mr. Russel. Ms. Quin is with me."

He hung up and turned back to me. "Dr. Morgan is in the main office and he'd like to speak to you." He rested his hand on my shoulder. "You're not in trouble."

When Mr. Russel and I walked through the doors of the main office, I felt self-conscious about how swollen and red my face was. I avoided the eyes of the secretary and followed Mr. Russel into a small room. Dr. Morgan was standing with another male staff member I didn't recognize. Mr. Russel closed the door behind us, and I began to cry.

"I . . . didn't mean to throw the chair."

Dr. Morgan lifted his hands. "Troy's been removed from the class." He paused. "And I'm so sorry. He shouldn't have said those things."

"But you let him. You let him!" I said.

He looked grim, his jaw pulsing. His next words came out hoarse, as if he, too, might cry. "You're right, I'm sorry."

I fell into sobs then. "I don't want to be in your class anymore."

"I think we should go back downstairs. It's enough," Mr. Russel said softly.

"Troy is *not* welcome in the classroom, but *you* are," said Dr. Morgan.

"I'm not coming back."

The male staff member standing with Dr. Morgan finally spoke, opening his eyes wide like an idea had just then popped into his head.

"Do you want to finish the year in the library?" He turned

to Dr. Morgan. "I imagine you could give assignments and she could do them independent of the class?"

Dr. Morgan's chin dipped to his chest. He sighed. "Of course, that would be fine."

I was hiccuping, and my sleeve was damp from wiping snot and tears from my face. My head felt scooped out and hollow. "Okay," I agreed.

We left the office, and I followed Mr. Russel through the student center and down to the Pit. He left me on a couch, where for the rest of the hour I pretended to organize the contents of my backpack. When the bell rang, I stood and thanked Mr. Russel. I found that I couldn't quite meet his eyes. I wanted to tell him that I knew he was gay, and that I probably was, too. But I couldn't. So I turned and walked out the door and back upstairs to my next class.

34. TEGAN DON'T BELIEVE THE THINGS THEY TELL YOU, THEY LIE

The rumpus room in Naomi's basement felt muggy. We'd been drinking greedily all night, exercising our freedom in the absence of Naomi's parents, who were away for the weekend. Sara and I had dragged along our guitars and were playing some of our new songs for Christina and Naomi and the other Frenchies crowded around. Naomi's older brother, Kevin, whose bedroom was also in the basement, came out at one point and leaned on the back of the couch, watching with interest. When Naomi's parents would go out of town, he'd supervise, which usually meant throwing a party where his older friends would ply us with alcohol and cigarettes. He played drums in a local band; their gear was strewn around the room. The four-year difference in age between us might as well have been ten. He had a job and went to university. We thought he was *so* cool.

"You guys are awesome. You should jam with my band sometime," he said. "We need a singer and you guys are good."

Few people aside from our friends and family had heard Sara and me play. And not many of them had been adults. His compliment fed the part of me hungry for validation from people older than us—adults who weren't also related to us. We desperately wanted to be taken seriously. And Kevin's offer felt serious.

"Sure," I said.

"Cool."

The first time we showed up to jam, Kevin suggested we play Justin, the bass player, and Corey, the guitar player, a few of our songs. They all nodded along, smirking and smiling to one another.

"I told you," Kevin said from behind the kit.

But Corey suggested we start with learning the ones they already had written and rehearsed. I felt off-balance, in part due to the beer I'd drank before while we waited for them to get off work, but also because it was weird to sing lyrics I hadn't written, and even harder to strum along to chords I didn't know the names of.

"Just sing," Corey suggested to me after I hit the wrong chords enough times. He wasn't cruel about it, but it stung. I could feel him growing impatient when I'd squint to watch his hand, trying to see where to move my own fingers. I had no technical knowledge of the guitar, not the way I did with the piano. I had no way of knowing what a C chord was when he called it out. Sara gave in before me. Opting to wrap the mic cord around her hand, she flopped on the couch, and I felt jealous of the casualness of the move. Eventually, I put away my guitar and joined her.

I wasn't sure I liked playing with them. On the phone the next night I told Alex they seemed a bit old.

But when Sara told me Kevin had invited us to come jam with them again and that Corey thought we were really talented, we caved to the shine of their attention.

A half dozen rehearsals later, Kevin announced our first *real* gig. "It's on Halloween at Travis's friend's house." Travis was the part-time trumpet player. He was twenty-five.

"Maybe we could play one of our songs there, too," I suggested.

Kevin perked up behind the drums. "Yeah, for sure," he said. "That's a good idea. Corey, let's let them play one of theirs."

Corey didn't say much, just lit a cigarette and mumbled, "Go for it."

"Ready." Sara nodded toward me. "This one's called 'Christ Comes Quickly.'"

Sara started to pick out the intro on her electric guitar. Kevin found the tempo and started to follow along with his kick drum. Then Sara started to sing. *"Late at night, when the stars are eating you alive. Does it make you sad, does it make you cry deep down inside?"*

I nodded to Kevin, trying to give him cues to show him we were moving to a new section.

"In your dreams when the blood falls in your arms. If I fall, will you catch me?"

I jumped in, yelling, *"Will you catch me in your arms?"*

We sang the chorus together, both frantically strumming power chords in unison as we built to the second verse. Kevin pounded away behind us.

"Does it bother you, does it bother you, does it bother you? Yes, it does," we yelled. *"She opens her eyes, there is no fire, she's a liar."*

When we finished, Kevin slammed down his drumsticks on the snare. "That was awesome."

Corey let a long plume of smoke out and smiled. "It *was* awesome."

We had to bargain with Mom to get permission *and* a ride to the party. "It's our first *real* gig," we begged.

"Are there going to be parents there?"

"*Mom.* No."

"It's Kevin's friend's house, Mom. They're all like, in their early twenties."

"You're not going to do any drinking? Right?"

"*No*, Mom. *Please*."

She dropped us out front. Even from the street, you could see the house was packed. As she waved through the front window, she looked nervous. I tried to look confident as I waved back, but I was nervous, too.

Kevin came bounding toward us. He was dressed as a surfer. He darted around other adults in costumes who were smoking and drinking in the living room.

"Where do we go?" Sara asked awkwardly. "I didn't realize we needed costumes."

"No, no, no. You guys look great. Here," he said, grabbing the handle of my guitar case. "We're set up downstairs. Corey's there tuning the guitars. Come on. You guys want a beer?"

"No!" we answered together.

When we were ready, Kevin got on the mic and shouted for everyone to come downstairs. The rumpus room filled quickly—it seemed like there were about thirty people. They looked so tall and drunk, but the costumes made it seem less serious somehow, and I told myself to relax. I felt my knees wobble a little as I stepped toward the microphone. When the crowd quieted down, I leaned in and cleared my throat. "We're . . . the Dragonflies."

Kevin counted off the top, "ONE, TWO, ONE-TWO-THREE-FOUR."

As we exploded into the song, I felt the adrenaline of the packed room of people who didn't know us propel me forward, eviscerating the nervousness I felt before we started. The sound system they'd rented was so loud my ears rang between the first two songs, but I was having fun. It was the first time I felt like I was in a *real* band. People were moving to the songs and smoking in the small space. If I squinted I could imagine we were in a bar or a club, playing a real gig, rather than Travis's friend's basement.

In junior high, Sara and I had gone to gigs at nearby community centers to watch local bands play, and I'd dreamed of standing on the stage where they were, singing into a mic over music that filled the space and people in front of me. We'd performed plenty of times now for our friends, but this reminded me how those gigs had made me feel all those years earlier: happy. We were doing it. We were in a band—a real one.

When we finished the last Dragonflies song, the crowd cheered and the five of us pretended to be done until they called us back for an encore.

Kevin leaned in and said, "You guys play one of your songs."

"So, we have one more song," Sara said. "Tegan and I wrote it. It's called 'Don't Believe the Things They Tell You, They Lie.'"

Everyone cheered.

As soon as we started, I felt a different energy fill the room; somehow there was still space for more. Goosebumps popped up, and I memorized their faces as we reached the pre-chorus where Sara sweetly sang the lyrics, *"I don't want to be a liar, but I do it every day. I don't want to be so tired, but I can't sleep anyway."* As she sang the last line she started to growl, *"Don't believe the things they tell you, they lie."* I spun the volume up the rest of the way on my electric guitar and slammed into the final word frantically. Behind me, Kevin was doing the same on the drums. When we stopped, the entire room lit up.

"They loved you guys," Corey said afterward.

"I think they were just being nice," I answered sheepishly as I locked my guitar case. It was obvious which song had gotten the largest cheer, and I felt guilty it had been ours.

"No, they weren't. You guys have something. It's special. Your songs are powerful."

My chest expanded as I absorbed the compliments. I trailed Sara up the stairs, and at the door, a friend of Kevin's stopped us. "What are you doing playing with these burnouts?"

"One day we'll say the famous Quin sisters played a gig with us," Kevin said, grinning with all his teeth showing. "Stay for a beer."

"We should go."

"Yeah, I guess it's no fun partying with a bunch of old guys, huh?" He chuckled.

"Nah, you guys are cool. But we promised our mom."

"Their mom," the friend said to Kevin, laughing. "How old are you guys?"

We shuffled outside into the cold without answering to wait for Mom.

"I don't think I want to play with them again," Sara said, eyeing me.

"Do you think Naomi will be upset if we quit?" I was glad Sara felt the same as me. And glad she said it first.

"No, she doesn't care what I do."

"Are you sure?"

"I think we should just do our own thing. The band's cool, but the way the audience reacted to our song—I don't know, it's something else. We just need to keep doing *our* songs."

"I think so, too."

We didn't formally quit the band, but after we turned down a few invites from Kevin to come jam again with the Dragonflies, he stopped calling. Naomi never seemed to care, or at least she never said she did. And when Kevin would appear when we were over at their house, he always stopped and asked how we were doing, what was happening with music, if we'd written any new songs. We returned easily to being his little sister's friends, and I put the Dragonflies out of my mind. Besides, Sara was right, what we had was different, unique, and there was only room in it for us.

"Don't have the party," we told Wendy, over and over. Only the naive or insane would offer their home to feral teenagers for an unchaperoned New Year's Eve blowout. Wendy's invitation to host seemed particularly suicidal given that her parents kept their home meticulously decorated. The impeccable ivory carpet and white baby grand piano seemed especially vulnerable. But how the party might advance her reputation must have proved too intoxicating; she ignored our pleas. And before the holiday break, word spread that Wendy's house was *the* place to ring in 1998.

"Do her parents *know* about the party?" Mom asked us when we told her.

"Of course!" Tegan answered, truthfully.

Wendy's parents had even organized to take her younger sister to a hotel for the night. What she hadn't told them was just how many people she'd invited.

"We don't have to go. There are *other* parties," Tegan said to me later.

"Maybe it won't be as bad as we think it will be," I said, knowing full well that it would be worse.

The first sign that things had gone sideways was that no one had removed their shoes. When Tegan and I arrived, the house felt damp with intruders; the muddy footprints at the top of the basement stairs seemed especially ominous. Already there was a large dent in one of the walls, the result of someone being pushed violently from behind. A crowd of students perched atop the baby grand with cigars hanging out of their mouths. They were rapping along with the hip-hop blasting from massive wooden speakers while their boots dripped ice and gravel on the floor below their feet. A trail of blood snaked its way through the upstairs, evidence of a knife fight that had started in the formal living room between the leather sofas. I floated through these scenes, recognizing almost no one. Tegan begged me to leave with her and Spencer, but I was conflicted about abandoning our friends.

"We should do something," I said.

"Like?" Her eyes opened wide, and her chin jutted toward me.

"Call the police?"

Tegan closed her eyes, shaking her head.

Upstairs, huddled in a bedroom, I dialed 911 and pleaded with the operator to break up the party. The dispatcher took the address, but she was far from empathetic.

Back downstairs we found that Christina and Grace had crawled under the massive dining room table with the cordless phone; Christina was hitting redial to 911 over and over, pretending each time to be a different neighbor calling in, unaware that the phone number betrayed her. Kids spilled into Wendy's parents' bedroom and onto a pullout couch, clawing at one another and disrobing, oblivious to any audience. Sloppy threats between exes quickly turned violent. It seemed sobbing girls had locked themselves in bathrooms on every floor. Scattered between the basement and the upper level, we drank with abandon, and occasionally refereed or offered moral support to heavily made-up girls with hoop earrings and blunted bangs who were crying or trying to fight one another. Cars loaded with teenagers circled the cul-de-sac menacingly and flashed their headlights through the windows into the crowded, darkened rooms. The house felt infested, every corner and hallway corrupted. A group of us finally abandoned the chaos, no longer convinced we were safe or able to help control what was full-on mayhem.

"I feel bad," I said as we closed the front door and carefully maneuvered over the icy sidewalks to Spencer's car.

"We warned her," Tegan said.

"But—" I looked back at the house.

"We'll come back, Sara. I'm not spending New Year's Eve with strangers."

In the back seat I awkwardly squeezed in next to Naomi and her new boyfriend. We'd met him at a party at Naomi's a few weeks earlier. I'd watched him drunkenly mime having sex with a male friend, while an audience of Aberhart kids I didn't know well laughed. He'd left his malt liquor sheathed in a brown paper bag, and I couldn't decide what offended me more—mocking gay sex, or a rich kid hiding his cheap beer like he was poor. Later I'd told Naomi that he seemed gay.

"You think everybody's gay," she said, and rolled her eyes.

Tegan directed Spencer to an affluent neighborhood in the northwest part of the city for the countdown. I sulked. I knew that invading the next party would feel as jarring as entering the previous one. Tegan had grown closer with Alex and Naomi's friends from Aberhart, and their excitement had an alienating effect. When we pulled up to the house, it was brightly lit. Inside, a dozen people were smoking pot, sitting cross-legged on the carpet, jamming on acoustic instruments. Alex ran over to greet us, and for the first time that night, Tegan looked happy. Our intoxication made us clumsy and loud, and we filled the air with shrill accounts from Wendy's party. At first, I reveled in their looks of genuine shock. Then I began to wish that the details of our night didn't line up so closely with the assumptions held by this group of people about what happened on our side of the city.

"I can't believe you had to call the police!" someone said.

We nodded our heads solemnly.

"Aren't you worried?"

"There was nothing we could do," I said.

Guilt about the crisis unfolding elsewhere weighed heavily on my mind, and after midnight I felt relieved to be back in Spencer's car, on our way to the northeast and back to Wendy's.

"I hope they're not pissed at us for taking off," I said from the back seat.

"They probably didn't even notice we were gone," Spencer said.

When we pulled up to the house, we could see through the windows that the rooms were emptied of people.

"Maybe the police finally came?" I said.

"Holy fuck," Tegan said, pointing at the garage door. A dent the size of a car had crumpled it like paper.

Inside, the destruction was immediately and frighteningly visible. There was dried blood on the carpet and sofa, and chunks of drywall and dust collected at the bottom of the stairs. I ran my hand along the hole in the wall; the shape was the size of a wrecking ball. In the laundry room, someone had defecated in the washing machine atop a pile of towels. A kid was attempting to remove it with garbage bags wrapped around his hands. The remaining guests were crowded onto a basement couch. Wendy sat drunk and bewildered in the center of them. Zoe was long gone, but Stephanie remained at Wendy's feet.

"It's not that bad," Stephanie reassured her.

Tegan and I piled back into Spencer's car, dragging Naomi and Christina with us. A car parked down the street flashed its lights at us. As we pulled a U-turn away from the house, the car followed. When we approached the entrance to the highway, the car was still following us—too closely.

"They're definitely following us," Christina said. The air in the car felt colder than outside; our breathing fogged the windows, adding to the confusion. Spencer stayed frighteningly quiet. At a stop sign, three men suddenly piled out of the vehicle, bats and pipes raised stiffly over their heads, clumsily lunging on black ice toward the back of our car.

"Go, go, go!" we screamed at Spencer. He stomped on the gas pedal, and we fishtailed, then shot across the intersection, the back tires letting off a screech.

"Oh my god, oh my god, oh my god!" Naomi gasped beside me. The scenario unfolded again at the next traffic light, and we had no choice but to run the red.

"The police station, at Franklin mall!" Christina called out.

"We should do that," Tegan said, clutching at Spencer's shoulder. In the dark, the angles of his jaw protruded as he clenched his teeth together.

"Spencer!" I yelled.

"I'm thinking!" he called out.

As each light turned from amber to red, a collective moan of fear would gurgle up from our chests, and Spencer would twist his head left and right without lifting his foot off the gas. We'd cleared half a dozen intersections when he suddenly jerked the steering wheel of the car to the right, making a harrowing entrance onto the highway. But the car followed, and the speed with which they pursued us became an additional threat.

"Please don't crash," I said, gripping my jacket collar.

"Hold on," Spencer said. "I'm going to take the exit to your house."

We skidded across the solid yellow line and onto the off-ramp. The car behind us couldn't follow, and we all let out a scream of relief. Spencer parked on a dark street and extinguished the headlights. We collapsed to the floor, the breath from our bodies labored and fogging up the interior windows. We stayed like this for what felt like an eternity. When it seemed the coast was clear, Spencer turned the key in the ignition and drove cautiously to our darkened house.

Tegan ran upstairs to our parents' bedroom and the rest of us remained downstairs on the couch, afraid to even turn on a light.

"She said it's okay," Tegan told us a few minutes later. On any other night, Spencer wouldn't have been allowed to stay over, but Mom and Bruce were concerned, and we were given permission to head down to the basement together. We stretched out two to a couch, feet to feet, and recounted the night's horrors. We were relieved to be finally safe.

In the morning, Stephanie and Wendy called the house to request empty bottles and cans for a fundraiser to help pay for the damage done the night before. The totality of the wreckage had provoked empathy from Wendy's parents, not rage, and the resulting punishment seemed illogically minor. There was little humility from any of us on these calls, but no one dared to say, "I told you so." Later with Christina, we bonded over how different our punishment would be if it had been one of our moms' houses that had been destroyed. Boarding school? Forced to live with our dads? Jail?

"I'm just not surprised," Tegan said finally. "They don't care about what happened to *us* last night. How fucking traumatized *we* are!"

"Sounds familiar," Christina said, rolling her eyes.

Our friendships with Wendy and Stephanie had been strained since a sleepover at Stephanie's in the summer. After we spent hours smoking weed and wandering through the empty tennis courts and parks behind Stephanie's house, she'd invited a few of us back to her place. While Veronica, Christina, Tegan, and I drifted off to sleep in piles of blankets on the carpet downstairs, Stephanie and Wendy had sat on the front steps outside drinking wine from long-stem glasses and gossiping in the dark.

When I woke up, it was blindingly bright. The overhead lights, which were never on in Stephanie's room, exposed a nightmare: Christina was screaming angrily at a group of men who were bent over our bodies. These men weren't boys—they were older, stronger, and no one I recognized. They were laughing, grabbing at our ankles, which were exposed by the blankets they'd tossed off us while we were still asleep. Christina intimidated them with her wild kicking; at five eleven she was formidable prey. I pedaled my legs defensively in the air. They turned away from us to focus on Veronica and Tegan, who despite their furious kicking and yelling were easily overpowered. With their fists tight around both girls' ankles and wrists, these strange men dragged them to the bottom of the stairs and then up to the main floor. Christina and I followed behind them, howling, helpless to do anything more than create a vacuum of panic and noise. When we arrived in the living room, the men finally released Tegan's and Veronica's limbs. Wendy and Stephanie were standing near the front door, blushing and laughing, still holding wineglasses. I'd been betrayed by girls for male attention before, but this set a new precedent.

After that night, whose side you were on was determined by whom you identified with most in the story. We fixated on the role each of us played in the incident, rarely considering the men who had participated in the attack. However unfair, the betrayal seemed to reveal something sinister about what girls would let boys do to other girls. Why had these strangers been permitted into the basement to scare us? Why hadn't Stephanie and Wendy come running when they heard our terrified screams? Why wouldn't they apologize for a prank that had spun out of control? There was a code that we had always adhered to, an unspoken promise to close ranks when any of us were at risk. These men introduced a permanent shift in our world, a danger that was impossible to dismiss.

When we returned to school a few days later, I recognized faces in the hallway that I'd never noticed before New Year's Eve. Perhaps even more jarring was that they seemed to know mine. Bound together as central characters in the story of Wendy's already infamous party, we snuck knowing glances at one another as we passed. Details were exaggerated in animated retellings across rows of desks in classes. Even the specifics of our car chase filtered through a school-wide game of telephone. In these versions, we crashed or were caught, were dragged from the car and beaten. Wendy herself heard tales of the unlucky hero who threw a party and was kicked out of her house and then sent to another high school by her furious parents. In that way, Wendy got what she wanted. The party was a legend, and everyone knew who she was. She seemed to bask in the glow of the newly famous. Maybe we all did.

I threw my fists against Sara's bedroom door so hard and fast I felt my face flinch as the door rattled in its frame. Tears blurred my eyes as I shouted, "FUCKING OPEN THE FUCKING DOOR, SARA! RIGHT FUCKING NOW!"

For a half hour I'd been trying to get her to give back a shirt of Alex's she'd taken out of the dryer without asking. Alex's sister was waiting in her car out front, and Alex was pacing wildly in the hall behind me.

"I have to go," Alex said, crying tears of her own. "If I don't go now, my sister's going to be mad. Tegan, I *have* to leave."

"SARA!" I yelled. I knew she wasn't going to open it no matter how loud I yelled. "Just go."

Alex gave up and headed toward the top of the stairs; her backpack, half unzipped, was slung over her shoulder. In a defeated whisper she said, "She's so fucking mean sometimes."

I locked the door to my room after Alex left and fell face-down on my mattress. I cried hot tears of frustration into my pillow. I didn't want to give Sara the satisfaction of hearing how much she'd upset me. When I opened my door to go down for dinner, Alex's shirt was crumpled on the floor in the hall. I hated Sara at that moment. I felt increasingly embarrassed by her open hostility toward Alex and me and hopeless to stop it.

Alex tried to combat it initially, showering Sara with praise when she played us her new songs, lending her clothes to Sara when she said she liked them. Alex claimed that when I wasn't around, Sara acted like a different person. Nicer. So I knew I was the problem, but I didn't know how to fix it.

"Your girlfriend's just sensitive," Sara would tease when I would involve Mom in the conversation.

"No, you were a fucking asshole to her. Because that's what you are. A fucking asshole."

"Alex *can* be sensitive, Tegan," Mom conceded.

"She's not sensitive, *Mom*. Sara took her toque without asking and then said she didn't know where it went. And then I found it in her closet."

"You shouldn't be in my room. Stay out of my stuff!" Sara yelled.

"Mom. *Mom*. Aren't you going to do anything? That's not fair."

"Work it out between you," she'd say, unpausing her show, blocking us out.

Sara smirked. "Yeah, Tegan. Stop tattling."

Alex had brought up my mom's reluctance to pick a side, too. She felt injured that no adult ever seemed to come to our defense when these altercations took place within earshot of them. Trying to explain to Alex that it was about me, not her, was impossible.

"You're just an extension of me," I would plead. "My mom thinks it's about Sara and me. So she doesn't get involved because it's not about you."

"It *is* about me because it's me she's mean to."

It was hard for Alex not to make it about her. Which I understood well.

I had a hair trigger about Alex's family, too. I was tortured by the fact that her parents didn't appear to know who I was, Sara or Tegan. After two years, they still seemed confused about which one of us was her best friend, leading to constant name mix-ups when I was over at her house. When we first became friends, it was amusing, but after we started hooking up, it became deeply hurtful. Though they had no idea that something had changed between Alex and me, some part of me wanted them to treat me differently. To know that I was special.

"How do they not know that your best friend is named Tegan, not Sara?"

"They aren't like your parents. They probably get my sister's friends mixed up, too. It's not personal. They really like you guys. Both of you."

"But *I'm* your best friend. *I'm* the one over there all the time."

Alex just sighed. "I don't know, Tegan. I don't know."

Our houses had become riddled with emotional potholes and situations with our families that could knock us out of alignment without warning. We were constantly changing our plans to go where people weren't. If Alex's family wasn't going to be home, we spent the weekend at her house. If Sara decided to stay at a friend's, we'd change our plans and stay at mine. If my dad went out of town, we'd invite ourselves to his apartment while he was away. We tracked privacy like hounds.

"Can I go with Alex to her family's condo this weekend?"

"Where is it?"

"Jasper."

Sara rolled her eyes. "Must be nice . . ."

"Yes, you can go," Mom answered. "I want you to call

when you get there. And be back to do homework Sunday by dinner."

"Thank you." Turning to Sara I added, "Try not to act so jealous all the time."

The next afternoon I felt high waiting for the doorbell to ring. It was the first time I'd ever left the city limits without a parent.

"Alex, you make sure you drive slow," Mom warned when Alex arrived to pick me up.

"Watch out for black ice," Bruce added from over her shoulder, his brow frowning in worry.

"Yup," I said rushing Alex out the door. "We got it. Slow and cautious."

On the drive up, Alex held my hand on straight stretches, taking it away only for the hairpin turns on the icy mountain passes. I felt giddy, grown up, in love as we sang every word to the Ani DiFranco record *Not a Pretty Girl*. When we arrived at the condo, it was past dark. The two of us padded around the simple carpeted two-bedroom, our hands webbed together, flipping on lights in the different rooms as we went. Its opulence was its emptiness, and I felt rich. In those rooms, those two days, the simplest of things felt pleasurable without the fear of being caught: cuddling on the couch, making out while we cooked, taking a bath together. We were able to have conversations in full voices rather than whispers about our family, our siblings, and our friends. For two days I didn't strain to listen for anything but sounds of pleasure from Alex—her laugh, her heartbeat, her sighs, and her breath against me. For two days I forgot about the messiness of our lives back in Calgary. The gloom that hung over Bruce's and Mom's heads. The anxiety and emotion that could overtake any conversation between them and us about school or grades or money. I forgot for two days about my friends who were slowly dividing themselves, every day becoming more like strangers to me as we prepared to move on from Crescent Heights, maybe even from Calgary. I felt lighter and happier those two days in the mountains with Alex than I had in a long time. More certain we were meant to be together; that all the conflict we faced on a weekly basis from our families was about them—not us. I knew the weekend couldn't last. That there was nothing about locking ourselves away in a mountain retreat that was realistic. But for two days I let myself imagine we were home.

Driving back Sunday afternoon, I lowered the volume on the stereo and admitted to feeling melancholy as we neared the city limits.

Alex agreed. "Back to real life."

"Back to reality," I sang in response.

We giggled. She took my hand as Calgary appeared on the horizon.

Garage Warz posters were hung all over the city. Our mom's cousin Tracy tore one off a bulletin board at Mount Royal College and brought it to dinner at our grandparents' house.

"You should submit a tape," she told us.

I scanned the flier.

Are you unheard? unsigned? unmanageable? Include tapes, press kits, and a letter of recommendation from your mom. Grand Prize: Gigs + Plenty o' Quality Studio Time.

"They'll never pick us," I said. "It's probably only for people who are in college, right?"

"Let me see," Mom said. "You're entering this contest." She slid it back across the table to Tegan. "'Free studio time.' Meaning, I don't have to pay for it."

"We do need a proper demo," I said, looking at Tegan.

We'd been fighting with Mom all year about our post–high school plans, and the contest stood as a test of our seriousness about a music career. A truce seemed plausible if we took formal steps toward legitimizing our band by signing ourselves up.

"If you're both dead set on playing music next year, this is a great way to prove it," she said to us on the drive home.

"We could use the new recordings from Broadcasting. They're better than the Plunk ones," Tegan suggested.

"I guess," I said.

"Why are you acting so weird?"

"We're just not really a band," I said. "We don't even call ourselves Plunk anymore."

"Just put your names on the tape," Mom said. "They're your songs."

"That sounds kind of boring," Tegan said.

At home that night we slipped a cassette tape of our recent songs inside a yellow envelope and scrawled "Sara and Tegan" on the outside. As suggested on the flier, we included in the package a handwritten note from our mom.

"Go," Mom said to us in the parking lot outside the campus radio station on the final day they were accepting applications. Tegan walked ahead of me, swinging the envelope confidently as I dragged behind. The door to the radio station, plastered with band stickers, was locked, so we slipped the package through the mail slot.

"Done!" Tegan said as we climbed back into the Jeep.

A month later we received a phone call from someone at Mount Royal College.

"Is this Sara and/or Tegan?"

Tegan's eyes widened as the news sunk in: we were in.

In the week leading up to the competition, Mom offered to take us to get something pierced. She had offered to do this annually since we were twelve, but we'd never been brave enough.

"Um, yes!" Tegan roared, leaping up and tossing the guitar back down onto the mattress. We loaded into the Jeep and drove to a popular tattoo and piercing shop in Kensington.

I wanted my eyebrow pierced, and I selected a small silver barbell from the tray placed atop the glass by a woman working behind the counter. Her tattoos snaked up her arms and across her chest and neck. Her lips, eyebrows, and cheeks were jammed with studs and metal. I was fascinated and terrified.

I eagerly sat with my face turned toward the piercer, whose black latex gloves held both my chin and a needle.

"Pretty cool of your mom to let you do this," he said, stabbing clean through my right eyebrow. There was never any doubt that Mom was cooler than both of us. Perhaps we were finally ready to let her prove it. Slipping the barbell in, he spun me toward the mirror. I loved it. Mom stood next to Tegan, who was having the skin below her lip pierced.

"What about you, Mom?" the piercer asked when he'd finished with Tegan.

"Oh, pfft," she said. "They're the rock stars."

We left the shop with grins across our new faces.

As Mom looped through the large campus grounds of Mount Royal College on the night of the semifinal, Tegan and I were still arguing about the set list.

"You can't have two slow ones right next to each other!" Tegan yelled, drawing black lines across the page. "Plus, I don't even sing that one."

Mom parked the car in a spot reserved for students, a fact she ignored when Tegan pointed to the sign. "I was a student here once," she said, slamming the car door closed.

We were all on edge. We set off across the lot, hurrying behind her like children afraid to be separated in the mall. Inside the bar, daylight splashed through the windows onto the black, beer-sticky tabletops. Rock music droned out of speakers that hung in every corner. We crossed between the tables checkered with patrons, some of whom were lifting pints of beer to their mouths while turning pages of their textbooks. I wanted to grab one of the glasses and chug down every drop. We lurked behind Mom, too shy to address the young man who was crouched on the stage twisting guitar cords into stacks of perfect circles.

"My daughters are competing in Garage Warz!" Mom screamed over the music.

"Okay," he replied. I died a thousand deaths.

"So where do they go?" she shouted into his ear.

Shuffling off the stage, he disappeared through a door and returned with an older man, who stretched out his hand and said, "They're not really allowed in the bar."

Because we were underage, our performing in the competition had required a slight bending of the rules, he explained to us. There was no age restriction on the application, but they'd never had high school students submit. We were instructed to follow him to the dressing room behind the stage, where we were to remain before and after our performance.

"If you're caught taking one sip of alcohol, we'll be fined," he warned us.

"Can our friends be allowed in if they're not eighteen?"

"Of course not," he said, shaking his head.

"I'll get them in," Mom whispered in my ear, when his back was turned.

As the backstage filled with musicians, it became apparent that we were the youngest competitors. No one said a word to us, and we nervously tuned and retuned our acoustic guitars.

"It's like we aren't supposed to be here," I said to Tegan. "Even the bartender gave me a dirty look."

There was a natural flow of introductions between

the other bands. One musician moved confidently through the room. His ears were pierced with hoops and his jeans and shirt were preppy. Another guy was twirling a drumstick between the long fingers of his left hand, a toothpick dangling from his bottom lip.

"Are you sure about our opening song?" I asked.

Tegan rolled her eyes. "Sara. Relax."

"Can we have chairs?" we asked when we were told to make our way to the stage.

We'd never done a sound check, and we were both flustered. We stared grimly at the mic stands towering above our heads. The sound guy twisted the stands sharply, and each of the mics dropped to our height.

"What do you want in the monitor?" he asked, pointing to large, filthy speakers on the floor.

"Each other," Tegan suggested as he walked to the sound desk. We pulled two wooden chairs from the bar and set them on the stage.

"These chairs have arms," I whispered to Tegan.

We sat perched on the edge of each seat so we could hold our guitars. We blushed as the grumpy sound guy pounded the stands until they folded in half like upside-down L's. With the mics pointed to our mouths, an even broader scowl stretched across his face. "Guitars need to be mic'd, too," he grumbled, and walked offstage to dig around in a row of milk crates overflowing with snarled cords and clips.

When all the equipment was finally set, he told us there was no time for a sound check. Stunned, we carried our guitars backstage, where we cowered in silence. Tegan could no longer hide her anxiety and copied out our set list on a fresh strip of paper that she pulled from her backpack. We were up first. A trickle of students filed in and ordered drinks at the bar as we readied ourselves onstage. I worked up the courage to search the dark room and watched as the judges took their spots at a long table draped with advertising for the campus radio station and local entertainment magazines. My eyes found our mom, who was now joined by our dad and Bruce, our grandparents, and Tracy. None of our friends were visible.

"They're still in high school, so let's give a big round of applause to our first act tonight, Sara and Tegan!"

I heard a roar in the main foyer outside the bar. Beyond the glass, our friends peered in. A bouncer stood nearby with his arms crossed over his chest.

"Yes, we are the underage teenagers," Tegan said into the microphone. That got a laugh, and she began to sing a melody over the opening chords of our first song. Under the hot lights I felt exposed, blinded. There was a disorienting awareness that the audience was free to stare, and to scrutinize Tegan and me, as never before. I steadied my eyes on her face. Her songs were always a different length. She added and subtracted lines of the chorus, building and emphasizing the intensity of each section by bending the tempo faster and then slower. By the end of the song, she was tearing her hand across the strings and yelping in full voice: "*Remember my name!*"

And then together in unison, we repeated the line again and again. "*I really think I like you, I really do, I do.*"

When we finished, there was a polite smattering of applause from the room—and a crashing cheer from outside where our friends hooted and hollered.

"Thank you! If we don't win tonight, our mom is going to make us go to college," Tegan said. I saw smiles stretch across the judges' faces.

Backstage after our set, I could feel my heart beating in my chest. I looked to Tegan, and she appeared as shaky as I did. "I was so nervous up there; I can't remember anything I said!" I whispered to her as we packed our guitars into their cases. We were then escorted by security out of the venue and back into the foyer to our waiting friends.

"From out here it sounded fucking awesome!" Christina shouted as everyone crowded around us. We loitered outside the bar, talking loudly and drawing the attention of older students, who watched us suspiciously. The music of our competitors spilled out through the open door. When the judges were ready to declare the winner, my head felt like it was underwater. There was a spike of noise and then Mom ran out the door of the bar shouting, "You won!"

Our friends began pogoing and we all screeched loudly.

Tegan swung her arm around my neck. "I knew we would win!"

We broke apart and received Mom's crushing hug. "I'm so fucking proud of you guys!"

I could tell for the first time in a long time that she really was.

After the buzz of our victory wore off, Mom slipped back into parental mode, nagging us to keep studying for finals, and yelling up the stairwell when she got home from work for us to empty the dishwasher. We entered a pattern: school, work, tutor, study, practice. From the time I woke up in the morning until I climbed back into bed, my body threatened to collapse. After I shut off the light, adrenaline rocketed through my skull, keeping my eyes wide open until 3:00 a.m. I was overwhelmed. I wanted to win Garage Warz, to get good grades, to make Mom proud. It was as if winning the semifinal had startled me awake after years of unconsciousness. What had I been doing all this time? How would I ever catch up?

For the Garage Warz final, Mom arranged for our friends to be allowed inside the bar in a roped-off section near the back. At the entrance to the bar, we were read the riot act about underage drinking while the security staff drew large X's on the tops of our friends' hands. There were six bands in the final, and we were slated to perform third. A man with an acoustic guitar started the night off but was quickly drowned out by the crowd. During the second band's raucous set, Mom whispered in my ear, "You're going to win. You're just so different from all of this." She swept her hand across the room.

When it was time for our set, Tegan and I carried our guitars to the side of the stage and stood silently as the final pieces of the drum kit were carried off. The host introduced herself, beaming down at us in chunky platform shoes. "You're all anyone is talking about," she said. The sound guy in a Black Flag T-shirt helped carry our guitars to the stage and shuttled the empty cases under his arms behind the monitor booth. Everyone was being so helpful, friendly. It was dizzying. When we sat on the chairs behind the microphones, a cheer erupted from the bar. There was still music blasting from the speakers, and my head whipped to the right, searching for Tegan's eyes. She shook her head subtly, warning me it wasn't quite time to start. Neither of us could stop smiling.

Finally, the host stepped up to a microphone and the music was stopped abruptly. "Let's give a very big hand to these lovely young ladies, Sara and Tegan." Mom let off a bright whistle between her fingers and our friends hammered their hands together and cheered. From the stage I could see Dad struggling with the video camera, and Bruce beside him, peering over his shoulder into the viewfinder. I thought I might throw up.

"This is called 'Here I Am,'" Tegan told the crowd before strumming the opening riff. When Tegan started to sing, I heard Stephanie let out a long screech in the crowd, and then a few of our other friends joined in. It was as if their voices were now part of the song. I felt goosebumps on my skin. When it was my turn to sing the countermelody that we'd practiced a thousand times, I felt my mouth stretch into a smile. I loved to balance Tegan's growl with something soft and unexpected. We broke down into a quiet section that we slowly built into a deafening crescendo. Tegan's strumming accelerated into the final moments of the song and I struggled to match her pace, our words and downstrokes jerking apart and then overlapping as a perfect double. Landing on the final lyric, she muted the strings, and in full unison, we belted out, *"Here I am, I said. Here. I. Am."* It felt euphoric.

"This is called 'Collide,'" I said into the microphone.

"I just sit here," Tegan said, smirking. She rested her chin on top of her guitar, cranking her head toward me. She'd convinced me to do the song alone and as I started to sing, I worried it was a mistake. The noise in the room grew louder around me. I felt a growing anguish that I wasn't able to keep their focus. I tried to push my voice the way Tegan sometimes did, right to the edge of my throat. With my jaw jutted forward until it felt like my ears were plugged, I mimicked her rasp as best I could. *"But I'm so tired of pretending that I am so strong! When I don't even know yet, what it is that makes you seem so wrong!"*

By the time I hit the chorus I sensed a shift of attention

back to the stage, to me. It was like regaining balance after a near fall. There was a surge of adrenaline and heat. Then relief.

"Did it go okay?" I asked Tegan side stage when our short set was finished.

Her face was flushed. "It was fucking amazing!"

We crossed to the bar and joined our friends and family.

"They fucking loved you!" Mom squealed.

"Proud of you, babe!" Dad said, hugging me.

"You're really good!" a judge said as she passed on her way to the bar. Even strangers began to approach us with compliments.

I turned in circles looking for Tegan. She was beaming. I felt drawn to her. When she saw me, she dug a few business cards out of her back pocket. "People keep giving me these."

They were from music journalists and a radio station programmer. I stared down at them, not sure what to think.

When the final band stepped onstage, the lead singer introduced herself to the crowd. "Sara and Tegan should win," she said into the microphone before launching into a song. Our friends once again broke into a cheer. I kept my gaze fixed on the stage, head spinning from the recognition. After their performance the host of Garage Warz climbed onstage and thanked the event sponsors and judges. Then she said, "I've looked over all the scores, and without a doubt, our first-place winner is Sara and Tegan!"

Our friends exploded. Arms wrapped around us from every direction, crushing us in a chaos of hugs and body slams. It felt like we'd all won something. Tegan and I broke off to thank the judges and shake their hands.

"A few of us are still relatively sober," one of the judges reassured us.

Most of the bar started to clear out after that, so Tegan and I gathered our guitars and backpacks. Near the exit, one of the judges who wrote for a local magazine was chatting with Mom and Bruce.

"He wants to interview you," Mom told us later in the car.

Tegan and I couldn't stop grinning.

The next week two local television stations were set to interview us. The first sent a camera crew and a host to our high school and filmed us after class in the empty theater.

"You had the highest marks in the history of Garage Warz! What does that feel like?"

"We're so happy!"

"You were bedroom artists before winning this competition! What's next?"

"Finals and graduation!"

"Can you two read each other's thoughts or feel each other's pain?"

I flinched. This type of twin-mind-reading nonsense always bothered me. "Um, no!"

It was a rapid-fire interview, and we punctuated each answer with laughs and quick glances at each other for reassurance.

"That went badly," I said to Tegan when we emerged from the school into the parking lot. Walking home, we brainstormed better answers to future questions.

Later that evening a second television crew was led up the stairs to my bedroom, where Tegan and I played a song while the cameraman stood on top of the mattress on my floor and filmed us from multiple angles. As he swept his lens past the books on my shelves and the CDs stacked below the stereo, our parents and the producer of the segment crowded into the doorway.

"Here we are in the bedroom where they wrote the songs that made them 1998's Garage Warz champions!" the host said into the camera before turning to us.

"Well, one of the bedrooms," I said.

"We don't share a room; I write my songs in *my* bedroom," Tegan added.

"So, you don't write the songs together?"

"No."

"How does that work?"

"Well, when I'm done writing the song, Tegan comes into my room, and I play it for her, and she just adds stuff to make it cool."

"What are your songs about?"

"They're a reflection of how we feel, of what's going on around us, of anything that's happening in our lives."

When the segment aired the following night, nausea passed through my body as we materialized on-screen, slouched over our guitars on the couch in my bedroom. The posters on the wall seemed staged and sunbursts of glare from the camera obscured the faces of my heroes. I cringed when the camera panned to my cat Taya, who was asleep on the patchwork quilt of my bed. We looked dewy and plastic. Our face piercings looked like blemishes. We were familiar, and yet I didn't recognize us.

"My hair looks horrible," I said.

"Stop. You both look adorable!" Mom said. In the interview, our words were cut up and our answers turned into a string of giggles and eye rolls. "That was so cute!" Mom blurted out, hitting mute on the television.

That was the problem. They'd made us cute.

I was lying in bed still half asleep when Mom knocked on the door on Saturday morning. I turned over and opened my eyes. There was a peculiar look on her face, and she was holding a folded newspaper page in her hand. She placed it next to me and sat down stiffly on the edge of the mattress.

"Everything has been so positive," she said, then trailed off. I could see a small photo of me onstage at the Garage Warz final. The university newspaper had run a full-page review of the competition. There were images of six bands fanned out across the page. Each band was displayed like a trading card, as if each were an athlete, with statistics and a review of the performance. Next to each card, the words "KEEP IT" or "TRADE IT" were stamped in bold capital letters:

> If you have faith the local music scene will redeem its declining reputation, twins Sarah [sic] and Tegan will shatter it. Incomprehensibly, this acoustic duo of 16-year-old Ani DiFranco wannabees won Garage Warz. What the judges saw in this uninspired lesson in power cords [sic] we may never know. Without question, these two did not deserve to win. The judges' mental faculties must have collapsed when Sarah [sic] and Tegan's high school class unleashed wails of Beatlemaniacal proportions. No explanation of their victory is forthcoming. It must have been their oh-so-hip piercings.

Next to our trading card, and my face, were the words "TRADE IT."

"It's bullshit, Sara. She doesn't know what she's talking about." Mom clasped her hands together as if to stop herself from tearing the page in half.

"It's okay, Mom," I managed. "I don't care."

She turned and left my room, softly closing the door behind her. I pushed the paper onto the floor, pulled my knees to my chest, and sobbed into the mattress.

When Calgary's *VOX* magazine came out the following week, our faces filled the entire cover. We dangled from above, our two heads floating in a swatch of surreal blue sky. We looked cool. We looked very cool. Copies were stacked at the entrance of Crescent Heights. I snatched one up, reeling between excitement and panic. Inside, the journalist gushed about our Garage Warz set, calling us "the future of folk." The sting of our bad review from the previous week was diminished. I let myself feel as good as this writer said we were. I rolled it up and stuffed it into my backpack.

At our table in the student center our friends cheered for us when we walked up.

"Signature, please!" Christina said, pushing a copy of *VOX* toward me.

"Stop, please," I said, blushing.

Zoe side hugged me when I sat down next to her, letting out a squeal into my ear.

"You're *so* famous now!" she said, winking at me.

It felt perfect and embarrassing—the way I sometimes felt on our birthday, or after I'd broken my arm. I wanted to bask in the glow of their attention, and also disappear.

The first sign that something had changed drastically in my life came in my second-period biology class. A student who had never spoken to me before asked if it was true that I was one of the twins on the cover of *VOX*.

"Yes, it's me."

"What high school did you go to last year?"

"This one."

She and her friends laughed.

For two and a half years, they'd never noticed me. But now they did.

38. TEGAN THE FIRST CUT IS THE DEEPEST

Winning Garage Warz set a number of things in motion. After we won, it felt like all the local press wanted to talk to us. Our phone rang off the hook; our voicemail was always full. We got offered opening slots for bands coming through Calgary and were invited to host an open mic night at a club on Seventeenth Avenue, and the local news visited our school to do a big piece on us. People started to recognize us, and not just at school. When we were on the bus people would stare, and during a shift at the coffee shop where I worked a guy dropped a newspaper down while I made change and said, "That you?" It felt like we were everywhere, and I loved the feeling. It was overwhelming in the best way, and I floated through the first weeks of it with the confidence and audacity of someone who has had their first taste of success and thinks they've already "made it."

I loved the interviews in particular. Talking felt instinctive, as if navigating questions and filling time on the radio were genetic traits, like our eye color or the shape of our faces. I thrived under the shower of compliments and positive reinforcement we got from the adults who leaned in around us, dissecting our "process" and "relationship" and "future." Until Garage Warz, my "future" had been a giant black hole that kept me up at night, dragged me down as I studied, and created tension when anyone pressed me about it. All of a sudden, I'd gone from invisible to notable. Sara and I had a future. And everyone wanted to hear about it.

While I let myself drift higher and higher, Sara remained firmly planted in reality. I'd gone into overdrive dreaming and scheming, but Sara was running on empty, swiping out of the air everything I conjured for us. She was skeptical about all the attention, unsure of herself, and questioned if we were any good at all. When our mom gave her blessing for us to take a year off after we graduated, something we'd been desperate for her to consent to, I was elated.

Sara just shrugged and said, "I still might go to university, I don't know."

University had been a source of so much turmoil and tears all year that it felt deliberately contentious to not be excited by Mom's change of heart. But she wasn't.

"Who cares?" I said to her when she came to me upset about the one bad review we got after we won Garage Warz. "So, some random girl thinks we should be traded. What the fuck does that even mean? Who cares?"

Sara had taken the paper I'd tossed off the bed and left my room without a word. *She* cared.

But what eclipsed Sara and her feelings completely was me: what I wanted, what I felt, what I saw. A lifetime of calibrating myself alongside her ended abruptly. I couldn't empathize, I couldn't relate, and I didn't want to try. The things she might have been struggling with and why were obscured by an overgrowth of ignorance and lack of compassion on my part.

In all the excitement of Garage Warz and pervasive conflict with Sara, another relationship of mine became sick. A melancholy spread like a virus between Alex and me as I focused more and more on myself.

"Your music is a gateway to you, to your heart," she said after the win. "I've always known that. And I'm proud. No one could be prouder that you won. But I'm afraid now that everyone can see it, it will take you away from me."

"How is it going to take me away from you?"

"The world is going to find out how amazing you are, and it's going to change things. Change us."

"*How* is it going to change us?"

"Soon you'll be gone."

"*I'll* be gone? You're the one leaving for England in three months. Where am *I* going?"

I felt angry with her sudden hesitancy and fear. Her claim that my success would lead to the eventual end of us felt unfair: *She* had driven me to take music seriously. *She* had counseled that Sara and I were destined to make a career with our music even when our songs were still in complete chaos. She had tracked my progress as I learned to write and construct songs and, in doing so, built myself up in the lyrics and the melodies I wrote. She was the first to see that I had learned how to put to music the things I could never say out loud to anyone, even her. Alex had unraveled the fear and the guilt I had about not wanting to go to university from the desire and need to pursue a career in music after we graduated.

It was Alex who reassured me when I worried I might never get out of Calgary. "You're not trapped here," she told me while lying next to me in the dark. "Believe that. I do." She had pushed me to apply for Garage Warz after our mom's cousin Tracy told us about the competition at the university. Alex made sense of everything—music *and* me. What didn't make sense to me was how she felt after we won. Perhaps I was naive, too in love, and too excited by the win to ever see or understand her fear. Maybe I was too young and caught up in the dream to consider it might actually be one. But to me winning Garage Warz was a sign we were on the right path. I was sure of it.

The only thing I wasn't sure of after Garage Warz was how I looked in the press. Watching the video footage my dad had taken of us performing, I couldn't reconcile the person I saw singing onstage with myself. For years I'd hidden my hair, tying it back, unsure what to do with it. For years I'd hidden my body behind baggy clothes and under layers of sweaters and jackets. But now Alex had taught me to love my body. And the last time I'd loved my hair was when I'd had it cut short as a kid. I'd been in hiding for a long time. But now I wanted to be seen.

Alex was devastated when I told her I was going to get my hair cut.

"But I love your hair." The haircut was another example of how I was changing, growing away from her, she said.

Sara seemed nervous when I told her. "Do you think I need to cut mine?"

"No," I answered honestly. "This is about me."

In the mirror at the salon, I watched as the hairdresser cut away inches of my long brown hair in severe snips.

"Shorter," I said, again and again. As she cut, the me I had imagined finally materialized when my hair came close to chin length. "There. That's perfect."

No haircut would reassure Alex that distance wouldn't change us, that music wouldn't take me away from her. But I felt intent on proving it didn't have to. No haircut was going to convince Sara to let go of her fear, to trust me or what I felt sure that we were on the cusp of. But I left the salon with one obstacle out of the way.

My 6:00 a.m. shift at Robin's Donuts on Saturday morning felt particularly brutal with a hangover. Standing with the donut manifest, I kept my eyes on the video monitor hanging precariously over the prep table in the back of the restaurant, watching for customers. My older coworker smoked the last of her cigarette and threw the butt into the garbage can next to where I was working. She grabbed a tray of donuts, leaving me in the kitchen alone. Underneath my uniform—a thick brown shirt, stiff as cardboard and scratchy as sandpaper where it rubbed on my neck and biceps—I could feel sweat pooling under my arms. My stomach lurched dangerously up to my throat. I lowered the racks of freshly baked donuts into vats of glaze, letting the excess pour off like paint. When I was finished, I stacked them in the display case next to the counter in the restaurant. In the smoking section I dumped the ashtrays overflowing with butts and black ash into the garbage. I avoided cleaning the bathrooms.

By 9:00 a.m. the restaurant was crowded with old men reading the paper and smoking cigarettes. Talking loudly to one another across the tables, they snapped at me when they wanted a refill of their coffee. A long line of regulars snaked out the door to the strip mall parking lot, impatiently calling out their orders and rolling their eyes when I didn't remember how much cream and sugar went into each of their cups.

"I'm just part-time," I warned each customer as they approached me.

My mouth was chalky. I wanted a Coke or just a hunk of ice to suck on. In between transactions I pressed my thumbs into my eye sockets and crouched down behind the counter to pray for the earth to spin faster.

"Time?" I asked my coworker.

"Nine thirty-two," she said, looking at the clock above my head.

My shift ended at one.

"I hate the smell of coffee," I said.

"I can't live without it."

"Is that why you work here?"

She looked at me like I'd said something incredibly stupid.

Every hour I took Windex and paper towels to the outside display and cleared away the sticky handprints and long pieces of hair collected on the glass. My boss loved it when I did things like this unprompted. He told me he liked that I took initiative. He liked me so much that when Mom made me ask him if Tegan could get a job there, too, he agreed to give her shifts at another Robin's Donuts location. Though I worked only a few blocks from our house, I envied that Tegan's job was at a kiosk, located in a Canadian Tire store. It had low foot traffic, and there were only a few regulars to disappoint.

At the end of my shift, I dragged the heavy, gray mop across the floor, collecting piles of ingredients in its tangles. The clean, soapy bucket turned putrid and black after a few dunks.

"Where did you learn to do that?" my boss asked me across the counter.

"Um, I learned it by using . . . a mop?" I said. Was he

kidding? I went back to the kitchen, pulling my apron over my head. This was the only moment I enjoyed having a job: when my shift was over.

"Sara, you are just fantastic!" my boss said when he found me in the back.

"Oh, thanks," I said.

"Listen, can I ask you a favor?"

"Yeah, I . . . guess."

He gestured silently for me to follow him into his office. I crowded in next to him and shut the door. "Sara, I know that you're still in high school . . ." he said, pausing. "Would you consider coming on Wednesday after school to swap out the registers between shifts?"

"Swap out the registers?"

"I just trust you. You know?" He showed me the combination for the safe and walked me through the steps.

"I think I've got it," I said to him before I left.

"Put 'er here," he said, extending his hand, beaming.

When I got home, I stripped off my uniform and shoved it straight into the washing machine. My skin stank of smoke and sugar.

"Did you grab your check from work?" Mom asked me, unpacking groceries into the cupboards.

"Yes. It's a joke." I threw the envelope down on the kitchen counter.

"Well, it's good inspiration. You don't want to sell donuts for the rest of your life."

"I'd be better off selling drugs at school. Or my body, for that matter!"

"I keep telling you and your sister this is why you need to go to university. That's your future you're looking at right there if you don't get your math mark up."

"That's not helping!" I said.

"What do you need all this money for anyway?"

"Stuff! Food!"

She popped her eyebrows at this, her hands deep in bags filled with groceries. "Oh, I see. Food. Because there's nothing to eat in the house."

"Or clothes or CDs or whatever!"

"It's only two shifts a week, Sara. That isn't very many hours."

"Well, what do you expect me to do? Quit school so I can take more shifts?"

"I worked *and* went to school. Not to mention that I raised you and your sister full-time. So don't complain to me."

"It's not the same thing!"

"And I grocery shop and empty the litter boxes that are overflowing with cat shit and drive you and your sister around to raves and parties and pick you up again in the middle of the night!"

"I volunteer, I go to school, I take piano lessons!"

"You also find plenty of time to talk on the phone."

"Mom!"

"And play guitar—"

"I thought that's what you wanted! We're supposed to be practicing—"

"Sounds mostly like you're just screaming at each other."

"Instead I'm cleaning toilets and ashtrays!"

"If you don't like your job, quit. But I am not going to start giving you an allowance again."

"Can you at least drive me to the bank, so I can put this in my account?"

"Oh! And drive you to the bank!"

"Jesus, never mind!" I stormed from the kitchen and upstairs to my bedroom.

Winning Garage Warz hadn't exactly changed Mom's mind
about us going to university, but it did give her a sense that
we were interested in something other than our friends and
talking on the telephone. When she gave Tegan and me
permission to quit working at Robin's Donuts so we could
focus on studying for finals and performing shows, we were
ecstatic. After school the next day I pulled my uniform from
the dryer, still warm, and folded it neatly into my backpack.
I rushed up the street toward the donut shop as fast as my
legs would carry me. I found my boss in his little office,
working on a stack of invoices.

"Hey! What's up?" he asked.

"Um, can I talk to you about my job?"

His face went slack. I wasn't his first quitter. "Let's grab
a coffee," he said, standing up.

It was disorienting to be on this side of the counter, to be
seated where I'd watched customers sit for months. I didn't
have the heart to tell him that the smell and taste of coffee
made me ill. I fidgeted with the handle on the mug at a table
near the window.

"I'm going to have to quit," I said. "I'm really busy with
school and music and—"

"I have to be honest, I'm extremely disappointed," he
said. "You have real management potential."

I struggled with how to respond. I didn't want to hurt his
feelings. "I'm just too busy," I said. "I'm really sorry." I pulled
the uniform from my backpack and placed it between us on
the table.

"Good luck," he said, and shook my hand.

In the vestibule between the restaurant and the exterior doors was a stack of *VOX* magazines with our faces on the cover. I grabbed one. I wasn't a quitter, I just finally knew who I wanted to be.

Sara and I unraveled pretty quickly in a *real* recording studio. After two years of Broadcasting and Communications classes and countless hours cross-legged in Sara's bedroom recording ourselves, we didn't have a clue what we were doing when we went to make our first professional recording, our prize for winning Garage Warz. We'd prepared for the four-hour block of free studio time by arranging for a drummer to rehearse with us. Brian, the husband of a woman Mom worked with, was ten years older than us but had a goofy way about him that made him seem younger. His sideswept bangs covered a set of wide eyes that shined with kindness at Sara and me as we taught him the songs in our living room at our first rehearsal. The three of us shared a similar sense of humor, and we spent a lot of that afternoon crafting jokes to make one another laugh between songs. Some of our friends had come over to watch, and even though it was just a rehearsal, it felt like a show.

The day of the actual recording Mom drove us to the studio. We met Brian outside, where he was jumping from foot to foot, his conga drum in his hand, his face full of confidence and excitement. Inside, the recording engineer directed Sara and me to individual booths to set up. As we shuffled across the wooden floor with our guitars, I gaped at the high ceilings, wobbling around the mic stands and the drum kit already set up toward the small room he'd said would be mine, next to the one he'd pointed out as Sara's. I felt overwhelmed by the reality of where we were as I slipped on the headphones in the booth, teetering on the stool with my guitar balanced on my knee. It felt surreal to be there. Though only thick glass separated Sara and me once we were set up, it felt like cement. We'd always recorded right next to each other, where we were able to follow each other's subtle movements and gestures. But the engineer had insisted we be isolated so he could get a clean recording. I hadn't had a clue what that meant but felt like we shouldn't argue. As we prepared to start, I glanced back through the glass toward the booth where we'd left Mom and Brian. They were both there peering out from behind the engineer toward us. Seeing them, I felt a jolt of stage fright fill my chest.

Sara started "Here I Am" but kept losing her place, stopping and starting again and again. She said, "Sorry, sorry," every time.

When we messed up at home, we would laugh, keep the recording going, and use the comedy or our arguments as fodder. But in the studio, it felt like every fuck-up was another wasted minute, a lost opportunity. It wasn't just Sara fucking up. I couldn't follow her; I kept anticipating the wrong part at which to jump in. "Here I Am" was complicated, long, and probably not the best song to start with that day. I was perched on the stool like a bird. Sara's feet were obscured by wood paneling, so I tried to feel the subtle movements in her body to keep time with her. It felt nearly impossible.

"Our songs are like duets. We go back and forth the whole time. It would be easier if I could be in there with her," I tried to explain to the engineer when, after twenty minutes, we hadn't managed a full take of the song.

"You'll be bleeding into each other's mics if I put you in

there with her," he huffed back. I shrugged, feeling frustrated and embarrassed. He might as well have been speaking a foreign language. In this context, I had no idea what "bleed" or "isolation" meant.

Every foreign term the engineer threw at us and every failed attempt at getting to record what we'd worked so hard on for two years, tugged on the precarious thread holding Sara and me together that first hour. But coming undone wasn't an option; we needed to leave with a professional demo. We had our hearts set on it.

"It's *their* demo," Mom said. She was sitting on the worn leather couch behind the engineer, mostly obscured from my sight, and her voice sounded small and far away.

I squinted. "What?" I called out, but they were still talking, and my mic wasn't reaching them.

"Maybe they need to just do it the way they're used to," Mom said.

The sound from the booth in our headphones cut out. The engineer dragged a second mic and stand into the little room Sara was in.

"Let's try it with you both in the same room," he said, popping his head into my booth.

I hauled my guitar after him; the cord, still plugged in, dragged behind me.

"This will be easier," I reassured Sara, taking a seat on the stool across from her. She looked pained, flushed, and near tears. I'm sure I looked the same. "It'll be fine."

After a few passes, we watched anxiously as the engineer walked across the room toward our booth. "Now what?" I asked.

"It's all over the place, what you're doing. It would sound better if you guys played to a click track."

"What's that?" Sara asked.

"You don't know what a click track is?"

"Like a metronome?"

"Yeah, exactly."

"We've never played our songs to a metronome before," I said, annoyed. "Won't that just make it harder?"

"I don't know what to tell you. You two are pushing and pulling all over the place. It's a mess. Your drummer is going to have a tough time adding his congas to this. That's all I want you to understand. I just want this to sound good, so that's what I'm suggesting you do. But if you want to get him in here, all three of you playing together, that's fine, too. More of a live thing, that's fine. It's your demo."

"Yeah," I said. "That's what we want. More of a live thing."

"Alright, you're the bosses."

Brian came sauntering across the room, his drum in his hands.

"Tight fit," he said, and laughed. His goofy smile immediately settled my nerves, filling the tiny space with a sense that everything was going to work out just fine. He grinned at us and said, "You guys sound amazing. *Relax*. That guy's mind is about to be blown."

We both burst out laughing.

"Let's try it again," the engineer said, popping into our headphones as he sat back down in the booth.

"Alright," Sara said.

The second the three of us started, the passion, intensity, and joy returned. We recorded five songs after that, playing through each song twice. When we were done, there was an hour to spare. We stuffed in behind the engineer to listen to each take, deciding which of the two was strongest.

Adjusting the guitars, we asked for our voices to be perfectly matched. "They should be equal," Sara said.

"I'm going to add a little reverb," the engineer offered. "It'll help distinguish your voices, make them sound bigger, more powerful, too."

"Cool," Sara agreed happily.

"Alright, here we go," he said, spinning the volume knob up.

"We sound like a real band," I yelled as "Here I Am" blasted through the massive speakers in front of us.

"You *are* a real band," Brian said, shoving me playfully. "Believe it."

"Not bad," Sara said.

"Yeah, not bad at all," the engineer said, smiling. "Turned out pretty good actually."

"You guys sound fantastic. I can't believe it." Mom looked proud, and on the way home we played the copy of the recording as loud as it would go in her Jeep.

The next afternoon we took the tape to a warehouse where they dubbed cassettes. I placed the tape down on the counter gingerly. "We need fifty copies of this," I said. Filling out the order form, we chose a yellow label and wrote out the names of the songs as they appeared on the tape. We decided half would have our phone number on them and would go into our press kit to give away to industry people. The other half we could sell at shows.

"Band name?" the guy asked as he checked the details one final time.

"Sara and Tegan," I said proudly. It was official.

41. SARA WHAT DO YOU KNOW ABOUT LOVE?

Tegan played *The Yellow Tape* in Mom's Jeep over and over again. Bruce nearly wore his copy out in the truck and Dad had us sign a stack to sell at work. Everyone was happy with it except me. (And Uncle Henry, who told Mom the squeaks of our guitars' strings were distracting.) I latched on to this criticism, unable to hear anything but these mistakes on future listens. I spent hours in vain trying to figure out how to move my fingers from chord to chord without creating those squeals of imperfection.

"I'm worried it's not good enough," I told Tegan finally.

She groaned and rolled her eyes. This was oddly comforting. Like pushing on a bruise.

Our first official support gig was opening for Hayden at the Multicultural Centre. It was another bonus prize of winning Garage Warz, and that we were opening for an artist whom we loved only added to our excitement. On the way to sound check we listened to our favorite Hayden song, "Bad as They Seem," over and over. Singing loudly in the back seat I couldn't stop smiling at myself in the rearview mirror. We were about to play our music in front of an audience that was there to see a *real* artist perform. A professional musician with a record deal and a merch table full of T-shirts. We were about to experience firsthand the life that we wanted for ourselves.

We'd only ever been inside the Multicultural Centre on Sunday afternoons for all-ages punk shows, and when we arrived for sound check, half the room was drenched in fluorescent light. The other half, nearest the stage, was all shadows.

"Look," Tegan whispered.

She was pointing in the direction of a man taking small steps in a circle, strumming an acoustic guitar near the stage. It was Hayden. His neck wrapped in a white scarf, his face all stubble.

"I can't believe he's just walking around!" I gasped.

We'd never met anyone famous, and we nervously approached him and introduced ourselves. He smiled and shook our hands. When he turned back to the stage, picking the strings of his guitar and singing softly, Tegan and I looked at each other in disbelief, then clutched at each other's arms.

Because the venue was all-ages, our friends were allowed to come. And after the doors opened, they noisily filed in and dropped their backpacks and coats near the front of the room. They sat in a straight line as if at assembly, calling out our names as we tuned our guitars and prepared to go onstage. There weren't many people there when it was our turn to perform, but my heart beat faster nonetheless. The room was silent, a welcome reprieve from the loud clubs we'd been performing at. There was no alcohol being ordered, no clinking of glasses or shouting voices. Just our music bouncing off the wall back at us. We'd become brazen about trying out new songs any chance we got, preferring to play them over the ones that our friends called out for again and again.

"Play 'Here I Am'!"

"'Just Me'!"

I smiled, shaking my head. I felt a strange pleasure in

disappointing them, as if it were a test of their devotion. Tegan settled into a song that I'd heard only twice before, but in the chorus I sang along off the microphone, like a fan in the front row.

"Keep them close 'cause they will fuck you too, I will keep you close! I got nothing better to do."

I cut Tegan's meaning away from the bone and heard the words as if they were my own. I'd missed the rapturous applause of our friends and family and the way it suggested to anyone who didn't know who we were that we were worth paying attention to. I searched the small crowd, hoping and fearing that I'd see Hayden watching us.

After we performed our set we sat with our friends on the floor. More people gathered near the microphone onstage, standing in the halo of lights. I sometimes felt more nervous after our set than before we performed. It was as if we'd survived something dangerous and I had only just realized it. There was also a bittersweet comedown after what we'd looked forward to was over. When would we play our next set? Were we still good? While we watched Hayden's show, I kept staring at his feet and the black stage where we'd just been standing, searching for any reminder that we'd been up there, too.

After the show was over, half a dozen adults crowded around us near the merchandise table, telling us what we did well, and what we could do better. Occasionally, they turned and gave Mom feedback right in front of us, as if we weren't even there. Tegan passed our demo tape to the ones who seemed interested. Beaming, flipping her new short hair, fidgeting with her lip piercing, she was completely comfortable, in her element.

As we filed out of the venue with our guitars, a man

yelled into my ear, "I hate that kind of music, but I like the way you and your sister do it." His next statement seemed to suggest something was not quite right about our songs. Smirking at me, he asked, "What do you know about love?"

On the drive home Mom shared suggestions through the rearview mirror for future performances. Someone had said we should talk more, while another warned we should talk less. The consensus was that we spoke too quickly. The chairs we sat on were too low and we should consider ditching them altogether, since it was difficult to see us from the back of the room. These details fired into my head like punches.

"I can't wait for our next show," Tegan said, grinning to herself. She was immune to Mom's buzzkill. But she wasn't immune to mine.

"You only hear the negative," Tegan said during one of our fights that week.

"You only hear the positive!" I shouted back.

"I'd rather spend my time focused on the good things, and not fucking obsessed with the one bad thing some random person said about us."

It was as if each of us were only capable of hearing what the other wasn't.

It was Christina's reassurance that we were just as good as we were before the adults discovered us that finally cut through the feedback loop. In front of Bruce's wall of stereo equipment, ominously black, we played her *The Yellow Tape*. The imperfections didn't seem to bother her one bit.

"You don't think it sounds out of time?" I asked.

"Out of what? It sounds fucking amazing."

"Right? I keep telling her that!" Tegan said.

"Do the guitars sound lame?" I asked.

"Lame? No. They sound . . . sparkly?"

"But are they girlie-sounding?"

She shook her head, baffled. "I don't think they sound girlie. They sound fucking perfect."

"See?" Tegan said, dragging the word out.

"This one sounds so good," Christina said, rolling over onto her knees, leaning in to the speaker. Sitting close to her, I could almost feel the high of performing under my skin. The muscles in my face pulled into a smile, a tic I couldn't control when I sensed something important was happening between the music and our voices. There was a brief reprieve from self-doubt. As if Christina's ears were suddenly my own, I heard a song I loved playing back from the speakers.

"I want to hear it again," Christina said, turning the tape over in the deck, hitting Play. And then, so did I.

We left for Vancouver with Mom before the sun came up. Bruce helped us load our suitcases, guitars, and merchandise into the teal Jeep in the dark and then stood back on the front lawn with his arms crossed against his black T-shirt.

"Bye!" Sara and I screamed out the windows as we pulled away.

As a family we'd driven the twelve hours to Vancouver through the Rocky Mountains to visit Bruce's family every summer since we were seven, but things between Mom and him had felt increasingly strained, and she suggested he stay home to take care of the cats and he didn't put up a fight. We had been accepted into an industry festival called New Music West last minute. Mike Bell, one of the judges from Garage Warz, had arranged it. Sara and I had begged Mom to be allowed to go after Mike called and told us we had been given a showcase. Mike had come over one night to reassure her it was worth it to go. "They could get a record deal," he told her. "Or meet someone who might eventually offer one." After that she had agreed to let us skip school to go.

I slept the first three hours until we hit Golden, just over the border into British Columbia. Mom woke me up after she parked in front of a McDonald's for breakfast.

"What if someone offers us a record deal after our showcase?" I asked between bites.

Sara smiled back at me. Mom just said, "I sure hope so. This is a long drive."

I ground together our futures as I daydreamed through the mountain passes, dozing off again until we reached Hope, a town an hour from Vancouver. After that, I watched anxiously as Vancouver appeared in front of us, and a thousand butterflies came to life in my stomach. Our showcase was at a small club on Granville Island, a busy market near downtown. The market was teeming with tourists, but the club we were playing was quiet when we arrived. As we loaded our stuff through the front door I almost turned around, thinking we were in the wrong place. I fidgeted with the strings, tuned and retuned, next to the stage, and tried not to look at the empty tabletops. Each time the front door would open, I lifted my head, thinking this was the moment a flood of sunglasses-wearing, contract-wielding agents and record execs might spill in from the outside. But most of the people glancing in were just tourists, and when they saw it was a club, they'd back out.

"How long?" Sara asked.

"Forty minutes," I said, eyeing the clock above the bar.

When the sound guy came over and told us, "I'm going to put you two on a little early," we were naturally confused.

"We're not supposed to start until six thirty, and it's only after six," I stammered.

"Yeah, well, she"—he pointed toward another artist lingering nearby—"has some people coming right at seven, so I want to get you on and offstage in time so that she can be up there for the people coming to check her set out."

"People are coming to check out our set, too," Sara asserted defensively.

"We came all the way from Calgary," I interjected. "We told people six thirty."

He shrugged and walked off. "You've got five minutes."

I tuned my guitar slowly and watched Sara do the same. I willed myself not to cry. Onstage, I reached for the cable to plug in my guitar as I sat down. Sitting up, I took a breath and shouted "Hi!" as enthusiastically as I could to the dozen or so people there. "We're Sara and Tegan." A few people clapped, including Mom.

"And we're from Calgary," Sara added. "And we skipped school to be here."

"Woohoo!" someone yelled.

"This is called 'Just Me,'" I said into the mic.

"And it's on our tape," Sara quickly added. "For sale by our mom." She pointed.

A guy up front chuckled.

As I started to pick the opening of the song I tried to relax. I closed my eyes and began to sing.

> *Talked myself into being you, it seemed easier than*
> *finding something new.*
> *And I broke them down did it all for you, no need, no*
> *need for thank yous.*

I backed off the microphone to let Sara sing the next lines.

> *Go ahead and change, go ahead and change, go ahead*
> *and change.*

Weaving our voices in and out, I retook the lead.

> *Talked myself into being strange, to take your very*
> *breath away.*

*And I asked myself why love won't change, if I could take
  your very breath away.
Someone brave the waters for me, and for you, I will do
  the same.*

Sara leaned in and finished the verse.

No one's very real today, no one's very real today.

The two of us returned the lyrics of the pre-chorus back
and forth after that.

*All I have to give this world is me, and that's it.
And all I have to show this world is me, and that's it.
And all I have to face this world is me, and that's it.
Just me just me just me,
Just me just me just me,
Just me just me just me.
And that's it.*

Sara barely let the cheering die out before she launched
into "Kissing Spiders." Halfway through our third song,
I saw another cluster of people arriving through the Press
Club's front door. Mike, who'd arranged the gig, was with
them. I let out a sigh. The people with him weren't wearing
sunglasses and suits, but I was so relieved I didn't care. *It's all
happening*, I thought. Sara told a simple story between songs
and I teased her about a tiny detail, something small and
inconsequential. She stopped the story and teased me back.
"Why does it matter?" she asked, feigning annoyance.

"All these people traveled a long way to hear the truth," I
said, deadpan. "Don't you think?"

The crowd laughed.

I could feel each joke, each moment of conversation between songs slicing away the tension in the room. As people took seats up front, Sara asked them where they were coming from, making small talk as they settled in. I felt us take possession of the stage, of the room, of the set. The fear and disappointment I'd felt twenty minutes earlier was a distant memory. But as I started to introduce our next song, the bartender gave me the "wrap it up" motion.

"This is our last song," Sara interrupted.

I thanked the crowd, disappointed our showcase was already over, as Sara strummed out the first notes of "Hello." After we finished, Sara and I went to the side of the stage to pack up our guitars.

"I think it went well."

"Yeah, I think so, too. I think those were industry people out there, right?"

"I think so. Mike was with them, so probably?"

"Can I ask you two a few questions?" I heard from behind me. I turned. "I'm from the local news. I'd love to talk to you about this incredible thing you two have. Those harmonies are something only family is capable of. Do you mind?" He motioned toward a guy near the front with a camera on a tripod. "There's more light there in the window."

"Sure!" we shouted, leaving our guitars and following him to the front.

After the interview, a dark-haired man with black glasses and a leather jacket approached. "I'm Bryan Potvin. I work for PolyGram. I already talked to your mom, and I don't want to bug you but, is this really your phone number?" He held up *The Yellow Tape*. "Like, to your home?"

"Yes," Sara said.

A crooked smile spread across his face. "Okay then," he responded. "I'll be calling you first thing on Monday."

When we got back to the hotel, we jumped between the two beds in the room as Mom told us about each person she'd talked to after we played, handing us their business cards as she did. Cheering with Sara, I forgot the disappointment of being put on early, the anxiety I'd felt imagining we'd missed our shot. I kept thinking about Bryan while Mom listened to the messages on the phone.

"Get me a pen, get me a pen—quick," she said, flinging her hand around. I raced to grab one and gave it to her. She scribbled out a long line of numbers and hung up. "They've offered you a chance to go up and play a song on another show tomorrow, to make up for your early start tonight. And there's press who want to interview you beforehand."

"Oh my god!"

"It's a real show, with other artists, at a theater or something. I have to call him back. Yes, right? Yes?"

"Yes!" we screamed.

Sprawled in varying positions on the floor backstage, Veda Hille, Kinnie Starr, and Oh Susanna were midstretch when Sara and I were led into the green room and introduced quickly before the show the following night. I felt immeasurable shyness as we left. These were professional musicians. Good ones. This was a theater, not a bar. I felt underwater, out of our depth, on the verge of a total meltdown. Between Mom and Sara in the theater, I watched the women perform while holding my breath.

"And now," Veda announced after an hour, "we have a special surprise for you all here tonight."

My stomach dropped.

"Go," Mom whispered, pushing me out of my seat,

toward Sara and the aisle. "Good luck." As we dodged across the stage, I heard Veda say, "Sara and Tegan are going to come up here—here they come—and play us a song. They're from Calgary, and they are in . . . high school." As I sat down with my guitar, she leaned back from the mic. "Is that right? You're in high school?"

"Yes," I said, startling myself; my mic was on, and my voice blasted into the theater. A chuckle rippled through the audience. "Yes," I said more softly. "We skipped school to come here. We're in grade twelve."

"Well, then we're even more happy to have you. Let's give them a big cheer, you guys. Sara and Tegan."

We leapt into "Here I Am" like runners off the line. We had chosen the song because it was five minutes long. Though far from our favorite, we had agreed beforehand that if we had only one song to make an impression, we should choose the longest and the most emotional. I forgot about the other artists onstage and the audience as we started to sing. Weaving our way through the different sections, I listened intently to the reverberation of our voices and instruments off the back walls. I had dreamed of record deals, but not of this. It felt immensely satisfying to play in such a big and beautiful space. In the final minute of the song, as Sara screamed, *"Louder and louder it will build and fade, and soon your love will turn to hate,"* again and again, I layered my final line, *"I'm underqualified, I'm undersatisfied, and I lie,"* into the beats between her own words. Smacking the strings for the final refrain, Sara yelled, *"I will take you to the end of tomorrow, I will take you to the end of my world,"* and when I joined her, the two of us singing loudly in unison, our bodies nearly lifted off our seats. I felt a collective intake of breath from every person in the room, including the women on the stage with us, as we abruptly stopped. The ending of the song was intentionally ragged and sharp, to leave listeners feeling uncomfortably unresolved. There was a pause that felt minutes long, and then the crowd erupted. As it subsided, Veda leaned over to Suzie next to her. Suzie did the same to Kinnie.

Then Veda said into the microphone, "We think we should hear another one, what do you think?"

The crowd went wild.

"It couldn't have gone better," Mom assured us in the Jeep afterward. "You sold every tape!"

"All of them?" I shouted.

"All of them! The girl selling them was practically throwing them at people."

As I fell asleep that night, my face hurt from smiling.

The drive back to Calgary felt impossibly long; our first day back at school, excruciating. All I could think about was getting home and checking our voicemail. We nearly ran home after school. Rushing inside, we fought to be the first to the phone as we clambered up the stairs to our rooms. Tossing my bag onto my couch, I fell onto my mattress and grabbed the receiver.

"Pick up!" Sara yelled from her room.

"What?"

"Listen!"

"Hey, this is Bryan from PolyGram, we met at the Press Club, I promised I'd call. Now I'm calling. Give me a ring back. I'd like to come to visit you guys, hear some more music, maybe take you to a few studios . . ."

"There's more," Sara said as the machine beeped again.

"Hey this is Don from EMI, saw your showcase in Vancouver, it was memorable and powerful. We'd love to talk about what you guys are going to do next year after you graduate."

I hung up the phone and ran into Sara's room.

"There's more." She laughed, still holding the phone to her head. "There's so many."

"What do we do?" I yelled.

"I don't know!" she yelled back.

"Well, who should we call?"

"I don't know!"

"Let's call Mom," I suggested. "She's gonna freak."

Sara nodded thoughtfully. "She'll know what we should do."

Mom called it a *separation*, but I had my doubts.

"I need space," she said. "I'm tired of trying."

It didn't come as a shock, but maybe only the first divorce does. Bruce and Mom had been fighting constantly, and Mom had been sleeping on the living room couch for six months. It seemed like the only time we saw them together was when we performed shows or after the drives they sometimes took alone at night when they didn't want us to hear them arguing. When Mom offered to drive us to Vancouver alone for New Music West, it should have warned us that something was up. Vancouver was Bruce's city, and he'd always told us that he would be moving back to Vancouver Island, where he'd grown up, after he retired. It felt strange without him, as if Bruce had died, or had never existed at all.

"Is it about us?" I asked.

"No, of course not. We're different people than when we first met. I changed," she said. "He didn't."

She had changed. When she met Bruce, she was a single parent, attending college, and struggling to make ends meet. Now she was thirty-nine, with a master's degree and a career. But Bruce had changed, too. That tough kid with a sports car who'd shown up at our house to woo Mom ten years earlier had grown into a dad Tegan and I could count on. I'd always assumed that Tegan and I were the ones responsible for the tension between them. It had never occurred to me that while we were locking our doors to keep each other out, they'd been doing the same thing to each other.

She and Bruce had a plan. They'd sell our house in the summer; Bruce would move back to the suburbs in the fall. She'd found a home in Crescent Heights with a basement suite for Tegan and me. We drove by in the Jeep, just the three of us, idling out front as the sun went down. The house was on a corner lot, with a wide porch and a big yard.

"It's what I've always wanted," she said. "There's a separate entrance, so you can come and go as you please."

With her hands clasped together, it was as if she were begging for permission. We nodded our approval.

Moving was an addiction in our family; a new home was the perfect bandage to quickly wrap around any wound. But I couldn't shake the feeling that this new house was her way of breaking up with us, too. We were almost eighteen, about to graduate high school. Finally moving toward a future all our own. She wasn't going to let herself be left behind.

After school the next day, Bruce took Tegan and me out for dinner.

"I know that your mother told you what's going on with us," Bruce said when we were seated in the booth at Denny's. He looked tired; the bags under his eyes were dark as bruises. Through the restaurant's dirty window, I set my eyes on Bruce's Camaro in the parking lot. Tegan fidgeted with the paper torn from her straw.

"It's not what I want, but once your mom's decided something—"

"Nothing's going to change with us," Tegan said, looking to me for support.

"It doesn't matter where you live because you're still going to be our dad," I added.

"I tell people that all the time: 'Doesn't matter if they're not biologically mine, they're my daughters, and they always will be.'" His face was flushed, his eyes wet.

Almost as far back as my memory went, Bruce had been a constant. He'd brought an entire world into our house. We loved our dad, but with Bruce we'd become a family.

"When you're eighty we're going to push your wheelchair out into the sun, so you can look at the ocean," I said.

"But if you're grumpy, we'll push you straight in the water," Tegan added.

He laughed. "Sounds about right."

We were outside my house in her parents' car when I told Alex that Mom and Bruce were planning on splitting up after we graduated.

"How come you don't seem that upset?"

"I don't know. I am." I felt defensive. As if I owed her a performance of sadness, even though I didn't have one in me. I pressed my finger into the leather, picked at the stitching of the seat under me. "It's just . . . I mean, who knows what will happen? They said 'separating,' so maybe it's just temporary. Anyway, they don't seem happy."

"Right, but do you think they'll go to counseling? Or try to work it out? I mean, have they?"

"No. I don't think they will. They've been processing this for months. All they do is talk, and this is where that got them. My mom said they're selling the house this summer. She wants to buy something near here—an old house. We're going to move in the fall when our house sells. She's already found a place, apparently. She told Sara and me she wants to live somewhere without a gym in the basement. Without a man stomping around. And Bruce wants to build another McMansion in the suburbs. And she's tired of moving. They just want different things."

"Does it make you sad? Do you want them to stay together?"

I groaned.

"What?"

"People should stay together only if they make each other happy. And they don't seem happy. So it's not that I'm not sad, I'm just like, not selfish enough to want them to be unhappy together, for my sake. You know? I'd rather they both be happy, apart, than arguing in the Jeep in front of the house every night."

I started to feel like we were talking about us instead of them. Often Bruce and Mom left with the intention of seeing a movie, and then spent the night out front "talking," and lately Alex and I were spending more time "talking" up the street in her car, too.

"But they should try, right? To fix it, to save it?"

"They did try. They're just done trying. Or at least my mom is. It isn't savable, or fixable, I guess. Some love doesn't last forever, you know? That's just how it goes."

"That makes *me* sad."

"Not me."

"What if we're like them?"

"Together for ten years?"

She laughed. "No, what if we break up?"

"Alex, we're not like them. We're *us*."

In the shadows between the streetlamps, we talked ourselves a great distance that night, first in circles, then in long, rambling lines, winding ourselves around each other until we had convinced ourselves we'd survive anything life threw at us, as long as we had each other.

It was one of the last Fridays of the school year, and Spencer offered to throw a party at his house.

"There's so many crazy things happening to you guys, huh?" Zoe was drunk, one of her eyes half closed. She rested her bare feet in her hands as she spoke.

I smiled, letting my knee rest against hers.

"Our mom says we can't sign the record contract until September. She wants us to be eighteen."

"I'm jealous. You'll probably get out of Calgary before I do," she said.

"What do you want to do next year?"

"I'm going to go to Los Angeles and be a backup dancer for Janet Jackson."

I wanted to tell her how everything I knew about L.A. made me think of her—vast, permanent things, like the sun. How I'd imagined myself a thousand times living with her in the shabby apartment from the photograph she'd taped to her bedroom wall—surrounded by the pyramid of beautiful girls she'd lived and danced with the previous summer.

"I'd trade all of it for you," I blurted out.

She laughed.

"I mean it. You're the only thing I think about."

And then she wasn't smiling anymore.

She turned to the door as if her boyfriend might be waiting right outside. "Dustin," she said. "I should go."

I sat on the floor with my head in my hands after she'd shut the door behind her. Panic and curiosity gnawed at my guts. I rejoined my friends in the living room, pulling my toque a little lower over my eyes. A few minutes later I watched Zoe taking wobbly steps over everyone's legs and the backpacks littering the carpet. Her boyfriend, Dustin, was doing the same, their hands interlocked. They found a spot near the wall and sat down together. In his tracksuit, he looked like the coach of a sports team, or a youth minister. He was a born-again Christian and didn't swear or drink alcohol. He'd started showing up at raves with Diego the previous summer. When he and Zoe started dating, I took solace in the fact that his religious beliefs prevented him from having sex with her. Over the summer we'd gone to see *All Over Me* in the theater. It had a gay story line, and during the scenes where the two leads were having sex, Dustin kept his head bowed, refusing to watch. Afterward we'd laughed behind his back. But it made me furious.

When Spencer finally cleared us out of his parents' house after midnight, I watched Zoe climb into Dustin's yellow sports car, her face streaked with tears.

On Sunday morning I woke with a fireball in my guts worse than any hangover. I was acidic with regret. I called Dad and asked if it would be okay for me to stay with him that night. When I couldn't stand to be at home or I was feeling guilty about something I'd done, the sterility of our bedroom at his house—the bunk beds we'd had since we were five years old, the comforters from before that—was a place to reset, to disappear.

After dinner I worked a little on my homework, but my thoughts raced back to my confession to Zoe again and again. At bedtime I was crawling out of my skin. It was unbearable to imagine showing up to school without talking to her first. There was a single phone in the house, and it sat next to Dad's bed. I asked his permission to use it, then snooped in his closet, holding his clothes up to myself in the mirror while I worked up the courage to call her. Finally, I lifted the phone and dialed, pacing in time with the ringing.

I felt so startled when she answered that I almost hung up.

We made small talk. I could hear her mother's voice and the television in the background. When she moved to the bedroom and the line grew quiet, I gritted my teeth and said what I'd spent all day rehearsing.

"I thought we should talk about last night." I buried my face in my shirt. Years of drunken hookups and flashes of undefined moments between us clouded my vision. Why had I waited so long to talk about it with her?

"Dustin asked if there was something going on between us."

"What did you say?"

"I told him that we were just talking, and that you told me . . ." She stopped.

I pressed my face to the metallic screen of the open window. I shifted the phone from one ear to the other. "That I like you," I said. My jaw was as tight as a fist. I waited for her to respond, a hundred steps ahead, imagining with her a future that I'd never quite allowed myself to see before with a girl.

"I don't feel that way about you," she said softly. "I don't like girls."

It was as if I were sucked into a void alone, the finality of her words as permanent as death.

After we'd hung up, I sat for a long time in the bathroom, crying into one of Dad's threadbare towels.

Shutting off the lights later, I lay down on the bottom

bunk. I slept in fits. My mind touched down on her words again and again. *I don't feel that way about you.* In the morning, my body felt numb.

I arrived late for first period, and quickly walked between classes, avoiding the student center and hallways. Steeling myself at lunchtime, I met Tegan outside the school and we walked to the lawn where our friends were sitting together on the grass. Zoe was there, of course, distressingly cute in striped overalls.

Stephanie bounded toward me, her cheeks pink. "Hi!" She rested a consoling hand on my shoulder. "You okay?"

I was afraid I might cry.

"I gotta meet Diego." She hugged me goodbye.

Zoe's face softened as I joined her at the outer edge of the group. Here was the cause of my suffering, but also the cure. Was it possible I felt *more* in love now that I knew she didn't like me? Or was it the intimacy of my confession that bound her closer?

"How was your sleep?" she asked.

"Fine," I said, grabbing fistfuls of grass between my fingers. "Did you tell Stephanie?"

She went pale.

"It's okay," I said. "I could tell that she knew."

"I only told her because, well, I guess I just tell her everything."

I changed the subject, and at the afternoon bell, we went our separate ways back to school. For the rest of the day I thought of all the boys who'd asked me out, who I'd laughed about with friends, or had broken up with and never spoken to again. Had I hurt any of them like this? It was impossible to imagine ever having that kind of power.

I went home that day with pages of new lyrics furiously

etched with thick pencil in my notebook. Words that screamed back at me from the page. In my bedroom I sat cross-legged on the carpet with my guitar and began to work on a new song. It was the only thing I knew how to do to make myself feel better.

"*This is the last song that I'll write for you. This is the last song that I'll sing for you. This is your last song.*" Singing those words, I felt tears roll off my chin.

That night I woke up anguished, replaying the conversation with Zoe again in my head until I thought I might be sick. I crept to the bathroom and once again sat sobbing into a towel. When I'd exhausted myself, I stood looking out the window at the moon. *I'm gay.* It was the very first time I had allowed myself to say the words I had been desperately afraid of. From that night forward, I carried the words in my mouth, tempted to tell everyone and no one.

On my last official day at Crescent Heights, I had one exam. My Math 30 final. I spent the hours before it cramming with Alex—she trying to keep me focused, me desperately trying to distract her. I had been preparing for it for months and I felt ready.

Math 30 had been my sole academic focus second semester. Although I imagined a future for myself without university in it, I would need that credit if I ever decided to go. I didn't have the prerequisite to take the class so to get in I had to agree to get a tutor, to keep a grade of sixty-five or higher, and to never miss a class, or the teacher would kick me out. When I got strep throat and missed a whole week of school in the winter, Mom still woke me up and drove me so the teacher wouldn't fail me. I wanted to prove him wrong. And prove that all the dumb stuff I'd done in high school didn't mean I was dumb. At times it also felt like I was proving something to Mom. That I'd heard all those pleas and lectures she'd given us the last three years about her life and how hard it had been for her to raise us and to go back to school as an adult. Those mornings she drove me when I was sick it felt like she and I were on the same team, for the first time in a long time. And it felt good.

A few days before our final exams, I tried to enjoy watching our graduating class walk the stage at the Jubilee Auditorium to collect their diplomas, but I felt so preoccupied.

Swiveling my head to take in the massive three-story performing arts center, I couldn't help but imagine the day when Sara and I would come back there—to perform, not just collect a meaningless diploma. That's what I wanted. Onstage, taking the rolled-up paper from the principal, I was sure he wouldn't have been able to tell me my name had I asked him. He never even met my eyes. I stopped briefly at the front of the stage, looked out at the theater, and smiled. Below me, Bruce snapped a photo. Behind him, my friends cheered.

At the graduation dinner I watched impatiently as my classmates hugged one another and said tearful goodbyes around me. I nodded and made promises to stay in touch with kids I would never talk to again. "Who are all those people?" I asked Christina. "I barely recognize *any* of the kids getting awards. Did we go to a different school?"

"We did do a lot of drugs at the start of high school. Maybe we met them in grade ten?"

We howled at that.

At the after-party, I felt the divide between our friends more than ever. Stephanie and Zoe had rented a limo, and I'd gone with Spencer in his dad's beat-up Nissan.

"You're not taking this seriously," I quipped to him the third time I asked him to dance and he said no, or just laughed.

"You are?"

"I guess not."

Graduation was nothing like the movies. Somehow it was even more disappointing.

At home, I tried to feel something about the news that Bruce and Mom were splitting up. As they divided their things and made jokes about it, I mostly just felt numb.

Their separation, like those final moments at school with my friends and other classmates, all aired on mute.

All I wanted was to finish my exams, to pack up my room, to wait out the months before our eighteenth birthday, and then sign the contract from PolyGram sitting on the desk in the kitchen. After that, everything was going to be about getting out of Calgary, getting on with the rest of my life.

While I crammed for my exams those final days of June, I tried to see Alex every second I could. She was leaving when she finished her exams for one last summer at camp, a choice she made that further injured the already hurt love between us. I'd wept when she told me. She had her reasons—none of which I could understand.

"But I thought we were spending the summer together before you left for France."

"We'll see each other before I leave, then at Christmas, maybe even for my birthday. Then I'll come back next summer, and we can spend that one together."

But I had my sights set on a different kind of future than the one Alex had ordained for herself. Or us. I wanted to move to Vancouver after we signed our record deal in the fall. Mom was going to move into her own house, and I didn't want to get stuck in a basement suite with Sara forever. At night, instead of crowding my head with formulas for my math final, I constructed equations to get myself to Vancouver, where everything I imagined was waiting for me.

The afternoon of my math final, Alex filled eight pages in our journal about the love we'd shared that year, the friendship we'd built the two before, and the life she imagined might be waiting for us both if we stuck it out. Though painfully beautiful, like Mom and Bruce's split, or graduation, or final exams, or the last days of my education, it failed to capture my full attention. I dropped it on the bed after I read it, and left for school without giving it another thought.

I had no possible way of knowing at that moment how devastating her departure would be that fall. How difficult I'd find it to fill the space in my life she'd left empty. How insurmountable coming out and making our relationship official would feel when she returned from France a year later, and the secret between us, once ripe, had gone rotten. Just like how it was impossible for me then to imagine how long it would actually take to get a *real* record deal, or how intoxicating and all-encompassing building a career with Sara would actually be. How much harm we'd inflict on each other, and how much damage the industry would cause as we made a career for ourselves. The volume on the life I had lived before that moment was turned all the way down; the questions or the concerns I might have had were silent. As I walked the twelve blocks to Crescent Heights for the final time, all I heard was music.

epilogue

SARA EXPELLED

We signed a demo deal with PolyGram Records on our eighteenth birthday. Tegan and I celebrated by shaving our heads. When the stylist chopped my hair off at my neck, it felt as if a terrible mass had been severed from my skull. The act was violent, and the relief, immediate. She held up the ponytail in her hand like a limb, waving it at me in the mirror. She took the clippers to my head next. I closed my eyes.

"You look exactly like yourself," my aunt told us later when Tegan and I arrived at our birthday party.

I knew exactly what she meant. It was as if I could finally pull my shoulders back after years of paralysis. Before bed I stood in the bathroom mirror marveling at the transformation. I was convinced that Zoe would reconsider her rejection if she saw me looking so much like myself. I felt like someone new, someone with a second chance.

A few weeks later Tegan and I moved with Mom to the new house in Crescent Heights. Zoe showed up to our housewarming party, tanned from her latest trip to Los Angeles. I could hardly hide my joy when she admitted that she and Dustin had called it quits. We made plans to hang out the following night, and she arrived at the house flushed, her skin radiating warmth. I played her some of the demos Tegan and I had recorded, songs I'd written for her, shyly staring at the floor as she sat cross-legged in front of the speaker.

Just when I thought she was preparing to leave, she leaned over and kissed me.

It didn't take long for us to get caught.

It was early in the morning a few weeks later, the first time I'd slept over at her house since we'd started dating. The phone rang, and we both startled awake in her single bed. Zoe jumped from under the covers, leaving the receiver off the hook, on the carpet. After she disappeared up the stairs, I lifted the telephone to my ear, holding my breath.

It was her mother, calling from work.

"I saw you two in bed together."

Zoe's mother's voice was like a hand around my throat. "Get her out of the house, *right now*."

I dropped the phone as if I'd been stung. Her mother was furious. She wanted me *expelled*. I dressed quickly, and sat numbly on the unmade bed. When Zoe returned to her bedroom, she was white as chalk.

"My mom knows about us," she said, biting at her lip. I was doing the same. I tasted blood in my mouth. There was a soft knock at the door.

"Are you two . . . *decent*?" Her father's deep voice raised new goosebumps on my skin.

"Yes, we're decent." Zoe sat next to me.

He opened the door and took a seat on the chair across from us. His skin carried the scent of aftershave and alcohol. He looked tired; there were bags under his eyes.

"I want you both to know that I don't care if you're—" He stopped short and looked at Zoe. "Sara's a lot cuter than Dustin," he said.

I let out a punch of air from my lungs, but Zoe's brow remained furrowed.

"Your mom will get over it," her dad said.

After he'd gone back upstairs, Zoe and I finished dressing in silence. Making the bed, I realized now how careless we'd been to think we could share the single mattress without raising suspicions. We weren't in high school anymore.

"I'll drive you to work," Zoe said, passing her hand across the back of my head, a gesture so tender I nearly collapsed.

"I'm sorry," I said.

"There's nothing to be sorry about."

That night, I waited at home for hours, too afraid to call Zoe's house in case her mom picked up. At midnight, through the bars in my basement window, I saw a pair of legs and rushed to the back door to let her in. In my room we cried together on my bed, clutching at each other's faces. She promised that everything with her mom was settled, but we both knew that wasn't true. To protect us, she'd been forced to define us, and that was a step into the unknown. My heart swelled dangerously in my chest. I wanted to be that brave, but I wasn't. Not then.

The following week, Zoe and I went to reggae night at the Night Gallery. We drank half a dozen screwdrivers and danced until after midnight. We took an expensive taxi back to my house, singing Bob Marley songs out the window. In the morning, she insisted I stay in bed when the alarm went off at seven. Upstairs in the kitchen, I heard her talking with my mom, the kettle whistling, and then the door closing behind her. When I woke up at ten, I called her at work to see how she was feeling.

"Oh my god, you gave me a hickey!" she whispered.

"No!"

"Yes!" She laughed. "A coworker spotted it the second I walked in."

"I'm so trashy!" I covered my eyes. "I'm sorry."

All day long at work I felt spun out by desire recounting our night in my head, even the sloppy parts I couldn't quite remember. I was Zoe's girlfriend and I had given her a hickey. I was the luckiest person on earth.

After my shift, Mom picked me up at work. Just over the hump of my hangover, I rested my head on the window, nodding off a bit. When we pulled up to the house, she turned the car off but didn't undo her seat belt.

"What?" I asked.

"Zoe is sure over a lot." Her voice was curt. It wasn't a question.

"Yeah."

"Is she still dating Dustin?"

"No, they broke up."

"Is she seeing someone new?"

"I don't know."

"Does she go out to bars a lot? Hook up with random guys? Or—"

"I don't know! Why are you asking such weird questions?"

"I'm just wondering how it is that she ended up with a *hickey* on her neck if you're the only person she's spending time with. Did you give it to her?"

My heart boomed in my ears. "Yes."

"So, you're a *lesbian*."

Out of her mouth, the word sounded grotesque.

"*No*, I'm not."

"I don't know any girls who *aren't* lesbians that give other girls hickeys."

"I'm not a lesbian! I guess—I don't know. Maybe I'm bi." It felt like half the truth.

Her knuckles went white and then red as she opened and closed her fists on the steering wheel. "So, you've been lying to me for how long?"

"What do you mean 'lying'?"

"You and Naomi?" She spun her head to look at me, slamming her hand on the steering wheel. "The entire time you've been lying to me!"

"What does this have to do with Naomi?"

"Zoe isn't allowed to stay overnight at the house anymore."

"That's not fair!"

"Your sister isn't allowed to have her boyfriend sleep over, and you . . ."

My face broke into a smirk. "I'm eighteen! I pay rent! I can have whoever I want sleep over," I said. We pulled into the driveway. I reached for the handle of the car door.

"It's *my* house," she hissed.

"Then I'll move out."

I leapt from the car and across the front lawn. Flipping the latch on the fence to the backyard, I slammed it closed behind me. At the door, I fumbled with the keys in the lock, dropping them on the cement. I heard Mom's steps on the front porch; she wasn't following me. Inside the house, the interior door to her suite was closed. In my bedroom, I shut and locked the door. Although I had been hiding it in plain sight all those years, my sexuality was a secret no more.

For three days, I crept in and out of the house, my guts knotted with cramps. I told an unsparing account of our conversation to Zoe over the telephone, warning her to stay away until things blew over. I promised that I wouldn't accept anything less than an apology. "I'm eighteen," I repeated again and again. "It's *my* life."

On the fourth day, I collected my stuff to take over to Zoe's house. Tegan was watching a movie on the small television in the living room. I didn't know how much she knew about what was going on with Mom or Zoe, and though I knew she had her own secrets to protect, I read her silence as betrayal.

"Mom left you something in the bathroom," Tegan said, snickering.

"What?"

She opened her eyes wide, a warning that it wasn't a gift I'd want.

Flicking the light of the bathroom on, I saw on the counter a small wicker basket spilling over with dental dams and a brochure about safe sex for lesbians. Picking it up, I carried it like garbage to the kitchen, where I threw it in a black trash bag.

Upstairs at Mom's bedroom door, my shame hardened into anger. In the darkness I could see that she was lying in bed under the covers. "Mom."

"What."

"You're just going to ignore me?"

"You lied to me."

"Why did you leave that stuff in the bathroom?"

"If you're going to have lesbian sex, you should be having *safe* lesbian sex."

"Why are you being like this?"

"You lied to me," she repeated.

"I wasn't ready to talk about it."

"I asked you if you liked girls more than once, and you lied to my face."

"It wasn't your business."

"You slept with Naomi *right under our noses* for years."

"Well, look how you're acting."

"I'm your mother! I deserved to know!"

"Well, now you know that I'm dating Zoe!"

"Which you weren't planning on telling me about."

"That's not true! I would have told you."

"I had to figure it out from a hickey on her neck."

"It just happened!"

"Like a slut, parading through the kitchen, showing off."

"What are you fucking talking about?"

"I don't even know how I can trust anything you say."

"You're being horrible! And rude!"

"I wanted you to have a great life, to get married, to have a family—"

"I can still do those things!"

"Do you know how worried I am for you?"

"You don't have to worry about me! I'm going to be fine."

She was silent.

"Mom!"

"Do whatever you want."

After the holidays, Zoe was preparing to leave for a six-month dance trip to Toronto, so I occupied myself with the weekly shows Tegan and I were performing at coffee shops around the city. We were as divided as we'd ever been, and disagreements about our music career became increasingly acrimonious. We'd replaced our fights over the telephone with wrestling matches over the computer upstairs in Mom's suite, screaming at each other as the dial-up modem sputtered to life.

Mom didn't intervene anymore. Instead, she'd push us back toward the thick wooden door at the top of the stairs. "Get out of my house if you're going to treat each other like that."

After these confrontations, we'd treat each other to days of silence. We passed each other in the hallway of our suite without so much as a nod. The only remedy was a performance, the salve of an audience. The thick callouses that built up between us wore away as we laughed and told stories into the microphones.

The week Zoe left for Toronto, it was bitterly cold and the entire city was white with snow. We traveled between each other's houses, frostbitten and desperate to spend every waking moment with each other. On our final night, we were dancing to Janet Jackson in the kitchen when I caught Mom watching us from the dining room. A rush of fear, so familiar it was instinctive, made me pull away from Zoe. I busied myself with the stove.

"Sonia, come dance with us!" Zoe grabbed for Mom's hand, but Mom laughed, shrugging her off.

Years later, Mom told me that was the moment she realized I would be okay. Watching Zoe and I dance together, she could see for the first time that I was truly happy.

"Maybe," she admitted, "happier than I've ever been in my own life."

Alex left at the start of September, and I missed her down to my marrow the second the wheels of her plane left the tarmac. As I watched the aircraft disappear into the clouds, I cried so hard I thought I might throw up. Back at home I sobbed the entire day, only getting out of bed once to pee. That night Sara slept in my bed with me. Relating how hard, how painful it had been for her when Naomi left for Montreal, she reassured me it would get easier, that I would survive. When Zoe left for Toronto, I tried to return the favor by reminding Sara of the things she'd said to me that first night after Alex left for school. For a while, in mourning, both of us alone, Sara and I were brought closer together those first few months after we graduated.

Bridgette, one of the Frenchies, got me a job at the same coffee shop she worked at downtown. I saved every tip and paycheck so that I could quit at Christmas. "No way am I getting stuck here," I told Bridgette one shift as the two of us scrubbed the coffeepots together. "Making cappuccinos for stockbrokers and grumpy shoppers is too soul sucking for me. I can't do it."

The record deal from PolyGram sat in the kitchen until Sara and I signed it on September 19, 1998, the morning of our eighteenth birthday. Mom faxed it when she got to work that morning, and that afternoon Sara and I went to a hair salon and shaved our heads.

After we signed the deal, Bryan Potvin, the A&R from PolyGram whom we'd met at New Music West, suggested we visit Toronto to play some showcases for the other label executives. Sara and I went alone; it was our first time flying without our parents. We didn't have a credit card or a cell phone, so when we landed at midnight, we called home collect from a pay phone at the airport to tell Mom we were safe. I felt scared but tried to hide it from Sara, who seemed miserable.

We were staying with Bruce's aunt, a woman we'd met once, who had offered to put us up for the week. When we woke up that first morning, from the thirty-sixth floor, I was surprised to see the ocean outside her windows. At breakfast, she explained it was Lake Ontario. Toronto was massive, overwhelming, steaming, and stinky. Its brick buildings and streetcars seemed foreign. Sara and I hungrily accepted money from our aunt when she left for work; we'd brought almost no money with us. We silently wandered the mall near our aunt's house and saw dollar movies to fill the afternoons before our showcases that week.

Sara and I played three shows while we were there, inviting a few industry people we knew who'd stayed in touch since New Music West. We did well, but somehow I left Toronto feeling less sure about things. "Don't get stuck here," one A&R urged us after the final gig. "Sign a deal in America if you can. Even a small label would have a vested interest in letting you develop. You need time, time a major label won't give you." It was the absolute best advice we ever got. But how do you get a deal in America when you live in Calgary? I worried as we headed home. I returned to my coffee shop job with Bridgette that fall, and felt a growing hopelessness take root in me with every coffee I made.

We recorded the two remaining demos PolyGram had contracted us to make. But the six songs didn't induce much excitement at the label. When Bryan left PolyGram shortly after, no one offered to sign us. We were officially on our own. The engineer who recorded those demos was named Jared Kuemper. He was young, finding his footing like we were, and said that for eleven thousand dollars we could rent a Pro Tools rig and make a whole record in our mom's house, without the need for a studio, a tape machine, or a massive soundboard. We'd own the recording, just like our songs, and we could sell the record, or license it to a label, and keep control over ourselves, our image, our sound—all things we'd have to forfeit if we signed a record deal. Sara and I agreed that *this* was what we wanted. We convinced Grampa to lend us the money to make the record, after we passionately explained, while Mom and Gramma looked on, we weren't just going to be artists; we were going to be business owners.

"We'll play shows every night and sell the CD and pay you back," we vowed.

I felt invigorated again, and with my bank account fat with the money to pay Mom my half of the rent she charged Sara and me every month to live in the basement, I convinced Bridgette to quit Grabbajabba with me. On Christmas Eve we tossed our oversize work shirts at the owner and I never looked back *or* got another job again.

Alex came home at Christmas and told me she was miserable in France without me. The depth of her depression reassured me she wasn't moving on. The next three weeks we were together I felt drunk in love. Everything felt right again. But when she left in January, it was easier—the first red flag that things were starting to change between us.

That winter Sara and I wrote and rehearsed every night in the basement suite of Mom's house when we weren't out hosting open mic nights or playing our weekly coffee shop gig. Fighting viciously as we tried to prepare for the recording, I spent the afternoons while she was at work stuffing manila envelopes and mailing them to folk festivals and clubs across Canada to try to get us more gigs. A friend designed us our first website, and I created an email account for us where I diligently responded to every fan letter and inquiry that came into its mailbox from Mom's impossibly slow PC in her office upstairs.

In the spring we recorded our first album with Jared with the loan from Grampa. We took over the first floor of Mom's house for a month to make it. Every morning I crackled out of bed like lightning and raced upstairs to eat breakfast and wait impatiently for Jared to arrive and Sara to get up.

When it was done, we called the record *Under Feet Like Ours*. Newly obsessed with carving our own path, we felt the name embodied the spirit of our desire to go it alone, without a label. The record starts with a clip from a cassette tape from when we were four years old. "It's my tape recorder," Sara says.

"Yeah, talk like that so when you're eighteen you can hear what a brat you were," my mom quips. Then the first notes of "Divided" start, a song I'd written about the friction growing between Sara and me about our future: *"There's something so divided. Don't worry about me, I'll be fine. Don't live your life for me or for anyone. You live your life as if you're one."*

When the first box of fifty CDs arrived on Mom's front porch, I cut it open outside as Sara and Zoe watched over my shoulder from the doorway. I pulled out a CD, placed it in my hand, and stared at it in awe. Sara and I had managed to accomplish something that I knew some bands never would. I felt proud as I examined it that warm May day as the girls watched from behind me. It would take us a long time to find success, to sell records, to win awards, to be acknowledged by our peers, the industry, and the world. But at that moment, years from any of that, I felt my first taste of success.

SARA ACKNOWLEDGMENTS

To my dearest friends: No one is thrilled to learn that their most difficult years are being mined for a memoir. And yet, so many of you generously allowed for your private experiences to be written about in these pages. Without your support, there would be no words, no music, no book.

To Mom, Dad, and Bruce: I won't apologize for the LSD, but without your love and guidance, I would never have found my way through any of it.

To Sean, Nita, Naomi, and Sarah: Thank you for believing in the story we were trying to tell.

To Marc, who told me ten years ago we'd *know* when it was time to write a book: Thank you for that wisdom.

Piers, Nick, and Kim: With your management, we had the confidence to make space to try something new.

Stacy, my best listener, and Emy, my first reader: I love you both.

Tegan: Thank you for always carrying half the weight of the world.

To every brave person I've met over the last twenty years who has shared a story about coming out: This book is for you.

TEGAN ACKNOWLEDGMENTS

It is with incredible gratitude that I thank my friends from high school. The laughs you delivered this past year, as well as the photos, journals, notes, and memories you unearthed, were the seeds I used to grow my part of the book. Thank you for trusting me with them and for finding me in our youth and sticking with me in adulthood.

To Mom, Dad, and Bruce, though you never signed up for the exposure that comes with being the parents of public people, you have handled it with so much grace. My greatest hope is that anyone who reads this book will come to the conclusion I have—nothing in my life would have been possible without each of you clearing the path for me to achieve all that I have.

To Sofia, thank you for letting me read you every verbose and bloated chapter I wrote. Even though you were clear that you preferred to read the stories yourself, I love that you let me disregard what you wanted to get what I needed.

To Nita and Naomi, thank you for the patience you showed as you carved out what Sara and I set out to tell, even as we threatened to bury ourselves in unnecessary details and an excess of characters and stories.

To Sean, thank you for believing we had a story worth telling from those first half-dozen chapters we let you read. And thank you for fighting to have our names come alphabetically and for the guidance and wit you produced along the way.

To Sarah, thank you for your encouragement and enthusiasm through each draft.

To Piers, Nick, and Kim, thank you for letting us abandon music to write a book only to find our passion for music again. And thank you for protecting the perimeters of our lives to ensure we have the time and space to do what we do.

To Marc, thank you for your early belief in us. And for the light trickery you used to get us to write the proposal in the first place.

To Sara, thank you for elevating, enriching, and improving everything I set out to accomplish in my life. I endeavor to always do the same for you.

ILLUSTRATIONS

A NOTE ABOUT THE AUTHORS

During the course of their twenty-year career, Tegan and Sara have sold well over one million records and released nine studio albums. The duo has received three Juno Awards, a Grammy nomination, and a Governor General's Performing Arts Award, and was honored by the New York Civil Liberties Union. They have performed on some of the world's biggest stages, from Coachella to the Academy Awards. In 2016 the outspoken advocates for equality created the Tegan and Sara Foundation, which fights for better health, economic justice, and political and social representation for LGBTQ girls and women. The sisters reside in Vancouver, British Columbia.